Tirekicking
USED CAR
BUYER'S GUIDE

James M. Flammang

TK Press
A division of Tirekicking Today (est. 1993)
Des Plaines, IL 60018

**Tirekicking
Used Car Buyer's Guide**

Copyright © 2014 by James M. Flammang
Cover art for the electronic edition Copyright © 2014 by James M. Flammang
Cover image supplied by National Independent Automobile Dealers Association

All rights reserved. No part of this book may be used or reproduced in any manner whatsoever without written permission, except in the case of brief quotations embodied in critical articles and reviews.

Published by TK Press (a division of Tirekicking Today), Des Plaines, IL 60018

Library of Congress Control Number: 2014914696

ISBN: 978-0-9911263-5-4

Contents

Acknowledgments vi
Introduction vii

Part I: New vs. Used
1. Why buy a used car? 3
2. Where to buy 18
3. How to choose a good dealer 27
4. Go CPO: Certified pre-owned vehicles 32

Part II: Homework Comes First
5. Don't rush on research 43
6. Which vehicle to buy 46
7. Looking for luxury 58
8. Condition is critical 60
9. Fuel economy 66
10. Safety 72

Part III: Test Drive
11. Questions to ask about the car 79
12. Visual inspection 83
13. Out on the Road 89

Part IV: Dollars and Sense
14. Down to dollars 96
15. Used car valuations 99
16. Guidebooks: how to use them most effectively 106
17. Factors that affect used-car prices 109
18. Equipment and options 112
19. Negotiating the final price 119
20. Warranties and service contracts 123
21. Financing 129
22. Insurance 141
23. Concluding the car purchase 145

Part V: Resources
A. How to read the ads 150
B. Test Drive Checklist 155

C. Manufacturer-Backed CPO Programs 157
D. For more information... 165
E. Used Car Buyer's Worksheet 168
F. Sample Bill of Sale 170

Part VI: Popular Used Cars (including valuations)
Best-selling popular-priced models 173
Subcompact cars 177
Compact cars 186
Midsize cars 201
Full-size cars 213
Minivans 222
Compact crossovers/SUVs 229
Midsize crossovers/SUVs 240
Full-size crossovers/SUVs 253
Pickup trucks 256
Sporty cars 262
Hybrid cars 275
Electric cars 280

Addendum: A closer look at today's used-car market 285

Acknowledgments

Without the cooperation of several individuals and organizations involved in used car marketing, covering that business as an automotive journalist would be impossible. Each has been helpful and cordial at every turn, providing information that serves as a foundation for the *transparency* that has recently become a byword in the used car business.

Special thanks go to:
Bill Zadeits, publisher of *Auto Remarketing* and related trade magazines for Cherokee Publishing, and organizer of the annual group of trade conferences that comprise Used Car Week
Ron Smith, publisher emeritus of *Auto Remarketing*
Ricky Beggs, senior vice-president and editorial director at *Black Book*
Tom Kontos, executive vice-president of analytical services at ADESA (a major wholesale auction chain)
Scott Lilja, senior vice-president of member services for the National Independent Automobile Dealers Association
Tom Webb, chief economist for Manheim (a major wholesale auction chain)

Introduction

Just about anyone who's purchased a used car in the past has some preconceived notions of how the process works. Chances are, it's not something you look forward to experiencing again.

Traditionally, used-car buying was like a jousting match between customer and salesperson, with each party thrusting and parrying until a deal could be reached.

This book emphasizes a less adversarial, non-confrontational approach. From initial research to interacting at the dealership to signing on the dotted line, the used-car purchase need not be an ordeal, an altercation, a setting for subsequent regrets. Buying secondhand might never quite qualify as fun, but it doesn't have to be painful.

That might sound like an impossible dream. Those of us who learned early on that buying a used car was going to be a battle aren't likely to forget that lesson easily. Yet, it's the modern way, and increasingly is becoming the norm for progressive dealerships. In the end, this non-confrontational method can be valuable to both buyer and seller.

Plenty of dealerships nowadays encourage their employees to engage customers on a cordial, non-aggressive level. Not phony friendship, but customers aren't viewed simply as "marks" to be sheared and fleeced. Even the most progressive salesperson doesn't have to be your friend; he or she simply has to sell you a vehicle with minimal fuss, at a fair price.

Besides, if you happen to find yourself in one of the old-style, "hard-sell" dealerships, you always have an easy option: Just walk away, as soon as the aggressive tactics become evident. Another, more ethical dealer down the street might be waiting to give you better treatment.

You simply don't need to put yourself through those assaultive ordeals anymore. The used-car trade has changed, as has the world itself, even if some old-style dealers and their employees don't see it, or refuse to acknowledge what's happening. They're dinosaurs, mired in a pattern of denial. Well-informed, ready-to-buy customers should feel perfectly free to scorn them, or even to laugh at them and their con-man antics, as relics out of the past.

Really, if a few potential customers *do* walk away, ignoring the salesman's pushy pleas, maybe the offenders will finally get the message.

Despite the move toward progressive selling, though, buying a used car from a dealership – any kind of dealership – isn't a simple matter. Figures must be bandied about and agreed to. Papers must be examined, initialed, signed, and filed. Sales managers still have to be consulted at some point, before the final sale is concluded. Matters of licensing and insurance may have to be discussed.

For countless shoppers who've gone through the process, the F&I (finance and insurance) person is more threatening than the salesperson, the sales manager, or the dealership owner. Watching a flurry of documents slip in front of you, one after another, can make even the most figure-friendly buyer suddenly want to jump up and dash out the door.

Admittedly, for some dealers and salespeople, expecting them to adopt the new ways is a tough sell. They're hogtied to the past: to the old days, when the rule was, "anything goes" to make a sale.

For much of the past century, used-car salespeople have scored near the bottom in opinion polls. In recent times, that spot has become occupied by Congresspersons and other political figures, with journalists ranking not much higher. But bad images tend to last a long time, so the used-car folks are still down at the lower portion of that favorability scale.

To some consumers, they always will be, regardless of all the progressive business methods and practices that come along. Poor impressions die hard, especially when they involve mistrust and disrespect. And money, of course.

New-car salespeople haven't fared much better through the years, in the public mind. A vivid example can be found in a seldom-seen movie: *No Down Payment*, a film about suburban American life, released in 1957. Tony Randall portrays a car salesman who, in dire need of quick cash due to a sudden family issue, pulls out all the stops to sell an elderly farmer a fully-loaded automobile that he couldn't possibly afford without manipulation of legitimate financing procedures. In doing so, Randall pushes forcefully against, if not quite actually violating, the law. In the film, he's found out and gets his comeuppance, including a demand to give that hapless farmer a full refund.

In real life, plenty of nefarious car salesmen have gone uncriticized and uncaught, year after year.

What if you're a salesperson in a traditional, hard-sell dealership, where every walk-in is perceived as a veritable victim to be fleeced? You, too, can walk away. Even in this era when jobs are hard to find, plenty of other dealerships – progressive ones – would (or should) be happy to hire a person who places ethics and honesty above quick profits. Responsible, ethical dealers don't demand big sales totals if they're acquired by underhanded methods.

Of course, any customer who's been victimized by a nefarious dealership in the past, or known someone who has been "taken" by one, is likely to scoff at the notion that automobile dealers might *ever* be worthy of admiration. Plenty of automotive journalists, for that matter, have an automatic aversion to car dealers and their sales forces. All we can say is, spend some time with progressive dealers at one of their trade events – something that few media people ever do.

Transparency is today's big buzzword. Market-based pricing, too. That means not necessarily pushing for the highest possible figure that can be squeezed out of a customer, even if trickery and deceit are the only ways to make that happen.

Profit is still paramount, of course, as in any other business. But progressive dealers are finally realizing that treating the customer fairly is ultimately more important than pushing that profit level to extract every possible penny from the hapless buyer.

One huge reason for the change is the rapidly-growing emphasis on, and availability of, vehicle history reports, which put customers on a more equal footing. Now, customers can easily find out a host of valuable details about a specific car they're considering. Shoppers also have ready access to *pricing* information, plus helpful details on market trends.

Another factor is that vehicles on the road – and on sale – are getting older. That means their owners are more likely to be in the market soon. Or, conversely, because cars do last longer than they used to, many will choose to simply hang onto the old bus a little longer, until it finally gives out.

What many of us fail to realize, too, is that car dealers, in the course of their business, act as both sellers and buyers of used vehicles. When wearing one hat, selling to a retail customer, they're seeking to get a *high* price for that vehicle. The same is true when they choose to sell a used car to another dealer, for a wholesale sum. But when they purchased that used car at wholesale, either at an auction or by other means, they sought the *lowest* possible price.

The same is true if they accepted the car as a trade-in; the dealer sought to obtain it for the *lowest* amount that could be accepted. That's how the capitalist market system works, and how companies of every sort make a profit on sales of any commodity.

Consumers, too, are likely to be sellers at some point: when it's time to dispose of the existing vehicle, as part of the process of buying a new one – or a "new" used model. The only difference is that consumers do so only occasionally, whereas dealers are doing it every day.

So, don't underestimate those dealers. Both the progressive ones and the "bad apples" are far more experienced with used cars than any customer. If a battle is going to take place, they'll win. Be open-minded, but be prepared. Remember, too, that it's better for everyone if that battle can simply be avoided, or at least toned down, in the interest of fair dealing.

This book contains four basic sections and 23 chapters, followed by a Resources section that covers six additional topics. Part VI contains brief rundowns of selected, popular used cars, including a description, history, technical details, and current average valuations. At the end, an Addendum section provides further details on the used car market, today and for the near future.

No need to read the 23 chapters from start to finish. Pick out what's most helpful to you, knowing you can always go back later for more details, if necessary.

1. **New vs. Used:** How to decide which is best for you, and where to buy. Also included is a summary of the used car market, emphasizing the likely impact of current trends on consumers.

2. **Homework Comes First:** What to look for in your pre-buying research, what's most important to know, and where to find the most helpful additional information.

3. **Test Drive:** What to watch for when inspecting and test-driving a vehicle you're seriously considering.

4. **Dollars and Sense:** Everything you need to know about the monetary aspects, from asking and transaction prices to fees and financing.

5. **Resources:** Details on manufacturer certified pre-owned vehicle (CPO) programs, a sample Bill of Sale, a Buyer's Worksheet, and more.

6. **Popular Used Cars:** Facts and figures, including brief test-drive reports and average valuations, of selected models in each major vehicle category.

Addendum. **A Closer Look at Today's Used Car Market:** Not every car-shopper is interested in additional details, beyond what's needed to make wise buying decisions. But for those who are, and for readers who are involved in the used-car business, this supplementary chapter provides plenty of facts and figures that convey a valuable picture of changing practices, trends, and prospects for the near future.

While breezing through these pages, you might even determine that a used car isn't the solution to your transportation needs at all. Perhaps a new one makes more sense, in cases where a similar late-model costs almost as much. Maybe leasing is a better choice.

For that matter, you might not need a car at all. It's become increasingly evident that young people, in particular, aren't quite so fond of car ownership as their parents and grandparents were. All the more so for those who live in urban areas, where they can take advantage of the growing number of car-share services, as well as public transportation.

Whatever your research leads to, we hope some of our explanations and recommendations help a bit with your decision.

James M. Flammang
TK Press / Tirekicking Today
Des Plaines, IL 60018

Part I

New vs. Used

The Used Car Market Today

1

Why Buy a Used Car?

Buying a used car is a time-honored tradition. Though often ignored by academics, journalists and other observers of society, it's a meaningful part of American (and Canadian) culture. In some parts of the world, for that matter, the used-car culture is even *more* vigorous than in North America.

Even the least-costly used car, after all, is a major purchase for most folks. For many, even that $100 jalopy of the past or $1,000 "beater" today instills more lasting memories that can be called up later, than a six-figure sports car does to a more affluent customer. Used cars are big business, too, with some 42 million of them sold to a new owner in 2013.

Not long after the first motorcars were sold in the U.S., in the 1890s, some of their initial owners were ready to "trade up." By the 1930s, industry analysts worried about a "used car glut" that could threaten the market for new models.

Nowadays, the "typical used-vehicle buyer is representative of mainstream America," said Tom Webb, chief economist for Manheim Auctions, speaking at the National Remarketing Conference in 2010. Finally, after decades of being viewed as "buying someone else's troubles," typically sold aggressively by mistrusted dealers and their hard-driving salespeople, used cars have been getting a much-needed image adjustment.

Risk is reduced, but not gone

Significant changes have been occurring in the consumer buying process. Far more facts are available to shoppers about each model, and also about an individual vehicle that's offered for sale.

Transparency, as we shall see, is the keyword today. Serious-minded dealers and their employees have shunned the misleading, tricky gimmicks of the past, preferring to offer a square deal to well-informed customers. And make an acceptable profit at the same time.

As a result, secondhand cars aren't nearly as risky as they used to be, courtesy of increased professionalism among dealers as well as more available information on a secondhand car's history.

Still, *every* used car, regardless of its make, model and history, is a gamble, at least to some extent. Even the most meticulously maintained automobile, after all – driven by an always-careful owner who bought it new and loved it – could break down a moment after you drive it away from the dealer's lot or the previous owner's driveway.

All of the nefarious dealers haven't disappeared, either. Some have simply modified their devious methods and illicit behavior to suit the digital age. Then there are the diehards, who haven't even made that minuscule jump, operating their businesses as if it were still 1954, when rules and laws had no place in the used-car jungle. They'll probably never change, but you certainly don't have to deal with them, or pay any attention to their frenzied ads and claims.

Some folks *like* the risk-taking aspect of buying used cars, of course, and might not view the kinder, gentler, well-informed form of salesmanship so favorably. Many others prefer greater assurance that trouble isn't lying in wait. For the latter, *certification* might be the answer (as outlined in Chapter 5, covering CPO, or Certified Pre-Owned, cars).

Changing times

When the American economy fell upon hard times in 2008-09, both new-car and used-car sales took a dramatic plunge. As new-car sales gradually regained strength in subsequent years, the used-car supply began to grow correspondingly. However, it takes several years for changes in new-car sales to be reflected significantly in the used-car market. That shortage of used cars, especially late-models in prime condition, has eased somewhat, softening (reducing) prices at least moderately.

Availability is not yet back to pre-2008 levels, but it's getting close, on both the new-car and used-car side of the equation. New-vehicle sales topped 15.5 million in 2013, while franchised new-car dealers sold about 16.5 million secondhand vehicles. Total used-car sales, including those by independent dealers and private sellers, approached the 42 million mark, according to CNW Research.

Ricky Beggs, editorial director of *Black Book*, estimates that the ratio of used car sales to sales of new cars is about 3:1. That ratio has persisted for quite a few years, though in the difficult period of 2009-10, Beggs believes it might have been higher.

Don't discount the oldies

Meanwhile, if a tempting late-model cannot be found, older and middle-aged used vehicles may be the best value choices. Partly because of the economic turmoil that led to recession, owners began hanging onto their cars longer. The average age of vehicles on the road is now a whopping 11.4 years, while the average odometer reading of used cars in general is around 53,000 miles.

As the economy improves, owners of older cars who held back on buying a new one have been edging into the market. That means more trade-ins, which translates to more choices for shoppers.

Economic issues aside, used cars have gained stature and lost most of their stigma in recent years. After all, even well-off folks buy secondhand – though most likely, they drive home higher-end used models.

Used-vehicle buyers generally have less flexibility about the timing of a replacement. Some purchases become necessary after an accident, or due to mechanical failure of the old car. Other owners suspect that the old bus won't keep going much longer, without trouble brewing beneath the hood.

Still, most shoppers are simply trading up, seeking a "better" car – which can mean a newer one, another make or model, a different body style or vehicle size. Often, as we'll see, those revised preferences are tied to lifestyle changes, such as older parents facing an "empty nest" after the children have left home.

Whatever the reason, used-car shoppers are in a better position to acquire a dependable vehicle, at a fair price, than ever before. Even so, the risk isn't gone; but the facts and suggestions in this book can help you make a wiser, more satisfying choice.

Benefits of buying used

Traditional benefits and drawbacks of buying secondhand aren't quite so clear-cut as they used to be. For obvious reasons, used cars have long been the choice of budget-minded shoppers, simply because they're *cheaper* than new ones.

That's a simple matter of depreciation. As soon as a new car is driven away from the dealership, it begins to depreciate (lose value). That process continues for most of the car's operating life, so it's worth less with each passing year. With few exceptions, a three-year-old car is less expensive than a two-year-old of the same model; and the four-year-old version is cheaper yet.

During periods of low supply, however, used car prices aren't quite as enticing. In fact, they can rise to forbidding levels when good used cars are scarce. It's a simple matter of supply and demand: when a product is in short supply, prices for those examples that do exist tend to rise – sometimes by a lot.

That's what happened in the wake of the 2008-09 recession, whose impact on the economy has lingered for years after its official end. Rapidly-shrinking sales of new cars meant fewer trade-ins and, a couple of years later, fewer cars returned at the end of their lease terms. As the supply of clean, late-model used cars dwindled, their prices began to increase.

According to the National Automobile Dealers Association, the average new vehicle sold for $29,650 in 2010, versus $16,474 for the average used model offered at a franchised new-car dealership. However, that used-vehicle figure had risen from $14,976 a year earlier (a 9.5 percent hike). By 2013, the franchised-dealership average reached $31,762 for a new vehicle, versus $18,111 for a used one.

CNW Research reports that used-car transaction prices rose by a whopping 16.7 percent between mid-2013 and mid-2014. Prices at independent dealers, which sell only used cars, are nearly always lower, partly because they tend to offer more *older* vehicles.

Shopping online, we have many more choices than in the old days, when newspaper classified ads were the rule. With a few clicks of a mouse or taps on a smartphone screen, we can see details on dozens of potential purchases, available at a nearby dealership or from a local private owner. Potential choices can be arranged by price, by model, by vehicle type – whatever works best for you. Dealers and analysts keep pushing the need to make the buying process quicker; but the real benefit of online shopping is convenience, not saving a couple of hours of hunting.

When buying used, you can either spend less than a new one would cost, or get "more car" for a given number of dollars. Instead of settling for a bottom-end, basic version of a brand-new model, you can step up to a more abundantly equipped example, with more amenities, which just happens to be a year or two (or more) older than the new one.

Saving money is only one advantage to buying used. For one thing, you have less reason to worry about minor damage while you own the vehicle. With a new car, there's a tendency to agonize over every little nick and scrape. Used cars are – almost by definition – less than perfect from the start. So, a few more dents, scratches and dings aren't worth fretting about.

There used to be a fear that first-year examples of a redesigned model likely had deficiencies that would be addressed in subsequent model years. So, car-shoppers often were urged to wait until the "bugs" were worked out. When those supposedly flawed cars hit the used-car market, they were presumed to be worth a little less than usual.

That first-year phenomenon was never as universal as people suspected, and it's largely a thing of the past now. Certainly, problems may be found and recalls may be issued a year or more after any model goes on sale. But because the quality of cars in general has risen appreciably in recent years, first-year models no longer warrant automatic shunning.

Buying a used car invariably involves some risk, but not as much as in the past. Why? As we'll see, not only is so much information available nowadays, even for a specific vehicle, but cars on the whole are far better in quality than they used to be. Since 2005, said Larry Dixon, senior automotive analyst for NADA Used Car Guides, the number of issues reported in the J.D. Power Vehicle Quality survey each year has shrunk by 50 percent.

Whenever you hear someone proclaim that cars aren't as good as they used to be, remember that those uninformed folks are just plain wrong. Despite the tales of old cars that delivered hundreds of thousands of trouble-free miles, recent-model vehicles on the whole are *far* better built, more reliable, and longer-lasting. That's good news for used-car shoppers.

Drawbacks of buying used

Certainly, the Number One drawback is uncertainty about condition and reliability. Unfortunately, that's the toughest aspect of a vehicle to assess, much less quantify. Definitive information that could lead to a helpful prediction about dependability of a given model isn't easy for analysts to derive, or for shoppers to obtain.

Consumer Reports has long issued summaries of information received from its readers about their experiences with a specific vehicle model. Details of those problems can indeed be helpful, though it's important to remember that one person's bad experience doesn't automatically translate to trouble.

Besides, even the comprehensive Reliability Ratings from *Consumer Reports* summarize experiences with particular models, but can provide nothing about a specific example of that model. Still, if a large number of people report a particular problem, it's definitely worth noting when deciding on a purchase of that vehicle.

Online forums are far less organized than the charts in a publication like Consumer Reports, but it's sometimes possible to unearth useful details of potential troubles for a certain vehicle model. Whenever current owners report on trouble spots, though, likely bias has to be considered. Nearly always, people who've experienced problems are far more likely to report them to a magazine, an organization, or an online forum. Those who are content with their purchases tend to keep quiet about it.

Entering a query about problems on specific vehicles into Google or some other search engine also can bring some helpful results. It can also result in confusion, because so many of the non-expert respondents who post opinions or reports on their experiences with a certain car can speak only for themselves. Yet, there's an inclination to make their personal observations sound like definitive facts about that model. All the more so, when opinions are submitted to web sites that encourage snarky, harshly critical commentary, whether it's justified or not.

As we all know – or should realize – not everything on the Internet is true, or accurate. Far from it. Bias rules, and uninformed opinions typically are given the same weight as expert analyses. Without question, more vehicle information is available nowadays, with little effort – although not all of it is truly useful, and much of it is misleading.

We tend to forget that information sources didn't suddenly appear as the digital age emerged. Plenty of sources were available decades ago, even if using them meant purchasing a magazine or buying guide, or picking one out at the local library. In those days, too, test-drives were reported on by expert journalists who were familiar with every car on the market. Today, the experts are rapidly disappearing, shoved aside by the countless amateurs who issue customer reviews on automobiles and just about every other product or service. Since customer reviews are inherently biased, their opinions are by no means more helpful than expert, professional commentary.

Online information and car-selling services, on the other hand – Edmunds, cars.com, AutoTrader, Kelley Blue Book – do provide more reliable information on owner experiences with specific car models. Still, there are no definitive, comprehensive lists of what's typically gone wrong with, say, a 2008 Malibu or 2010 Grand Cherokee, much less what is likely to happen to the one that you're considering.

Details on a specific car are limited to what's available through Carfax and other vehicle history reports. Though invaluable in terms of ruling out questionable choices, that information isn't enough to make a valid prediction about the likely fate of any individual vehicle. Therefore, risk and uncertainty remain an inevitable part of the used-car buying process.

Thorough inspection by a third-party expert – a proficient mechanic, or an inspection service – might allay those fears. Despite warnings to consult a mechanic that have been publicized for years and years, not many of us bother with such inspections, or even think about the possibility.

Unfortunately, too, not so many local and independent mechanics – the ones with regular long-term customers, and whose opinions can be counted on – are active anymore. Far fewer of us than in the past have a trusted mechanic who gets all our business. In the absence of a reliable local technician, national organizations such as AiM (Alliance Inspection Management) or carchex.com can evaluate a car for a fee. Local inspection services also can be found. Still, the vast majority of shoppers never take that step, but take a chance instead.

Besides, even their impressions are no guarantee. A car that handily passes inspection today could falter badly tomorrow. Anything can happen, once you've made the purchase.

Warranties are a partial, less-than-perfect, solution. As we'll see in Chapter 20, used-car warranties (actually extended service contracts, which are a form of insurance) are expensive, have various limitations, and may even be riddled with loopholes that make reimbursement for repair expenses difficult or impossible to obtain. You could be in for a nasty surprise, if big trouble happens and you suddenly discover that it's not covered by the service contract.

Shoppers who tend to worry incessantly might be better off with a new car; or, as we'll see in Chapter 4, a certified pre-owned (CPO) example that's undergone more extensive inspection than other used cars on sale at a particular dealership.

To get your research started, remember that a history report is available for most vehicles offered for sale, providing details on its accident history, recalls, ownership history, and more. (See Chapter 8 for further details on history reports.) Today's dealers, too, rely on Carfax, not only as a selling point for their retail inventory, but when considering the purchase of a vehicle for resale, at an auction or from a private seller.

Safety data needs to be considered carefully. Crash tests also provide some helpful insights into a vehicle's safety potential. Recalls, also discussed in Chapter 10 (Safety), are often overlooked, but vital. Even though they're repaired without charge, a startling number of cars on the road have not had their recalls dealt with. Some are supremely serious; many are not. But it's important to see the full list in order to make a judgment. A dealer for the make you're considering can find out if recalls were corrected on a specific car.

Transparency changes everything ... almost

The "industry is quickly shifting toward more transparent pricing," said Alec Gutierrez, senior market analyst for Kelley Blue Book, echoing the comments of many experts at Used Car Week in 2013.

Transparency comes about because of access to information. "Documentation is really the new negotiation," added Cary Donovan, of the Sam Swope Auto Group. The dealership world is changing fast, and the old methods simply don't work anymore, said Donovan, also speaking during Used Car Week. Customers have alternatives during their shopping process. They're able to acquire information from many sources before dealing with a dealer in any way.

Back around 2007, Donovan noted, the average potential customer shopped at 4.7 dealerships before making a decision. Now, the number of dealerships shopped has shrunk to a mere 1.2. Furthermore, when that customer finally arrives at the chosen dealership, you can bet that he or she is well prepared for the transaction, armed with a stack of facts and figures.

Despite the move toward more progressive sales practices, fraudsters definitely haven't disappeared from the used-car trade. Throughout the buying process, be on guard for false statements, exaggeration, pretending to know too much, and so forth.

Fraudulent behavior has a way of fading away, then slipping back again. Odometer rollbacks are a good example. After the Truth in Mileage Act was passed in the mid-1980s, analysts thought the era of tinkering with odometers to lower their mileage reading was gone. All the more so as electronic odometers edged aside the old mechanical units. Lately, though, odometer rollbacks have been reappearing, giving used-car shoppers another factor that has to be considered when evaluating a vehicle. Yet here, too, history reports can provide at least a clue to whether the reading you see on the dashboard is a correct one.

Older cars vs. late-models

Late-model cars are generally the best bets, but that's not always the case at present. Because of sluggish new-car sales beginning in 2008, coupled with shrinkage of leasing, the supply of high-quality, low-mileage late models began to sink appreciably. Therefore, prices remained relatively high. That's inevitable when low supply butts against high demand.

Because vehicles continue to depreciate through their entire working lives, older models are clearly cheaper than late-models. At the same time, overall quality is way better than it used to be, so the risk of trouble isn't as great as it was in the past.

Still, the older a car gets, and the more miles it's been driven, the more likely it is to develop mechanical and electrical problems. Plenty of cars go through their entire lives with few difficulties; but as a general rule, older models are more likely to fail.

Of course, older cars may be the only choice for buyers with imperfect credit. As we shall see in Chapter 21, on Financing, if a credit-challenged person can get a loan at all, it's almost certain to carry a high interest rate, and be for the purchase of an older model.

With a late-model, you get *almost* the latest technology, without paying a hefty premium for those extras – some of it valuable in terms of safety and convenience, some aimed simply at providing pleasure while motoring.

Late models, logically enough, tend to be the most reliable. They also may have more safety features, including electronic stability control, lane-departure warnings, and many other high-tech helpers.

Older cars are simpler, which is both a benefit and a detriment. They may be solidly made, but their technology dates from closer to the turn of the 21st century, a time when complexity and digitization were beginning to escalate rapidly.

Dealers know consumers want those clean late-models. Therefore, they're willing to pay more for them at wholesale or when acquired as trade-ins. Sensible dealers make their buying decisions based strictly on how much they can expect to get at retail for a given vehicle, and whether it's likely to sell quickly.

Whether late-model or older, it's important to know if a car was maintained properly, including having its oil changed regularly, mechanical and electrical problems dealt with promptly, etc. Take care to draw distinctions between minor and major flaws. Safety-related problems, for instance, are far more important than a mildly malfunctioning entertainment system.

In decades past, certain components – specific automatic transmissions, for example – were known to have a high risk of failure after a certain number of miles, or years. That's not so likely anymore. And if a high failure rate does occur, it's more likely to be publicized by owners and observers, whether through forums, Twitter, or other contemporary means of instant communication.

Not many jalopies and clunkers are roaming the streets anymore, or appearing on used-car lots. The back rows of rundown wrecks have been eradicated from many dealer lots, though those who cater to credit-challenged customers are still likely to have a batch of rough vehicles at hand. Far fewer people nowadays than in the past, unless they're seriously strapped financially, willingly agree to purchase, and drive, an unsafe, unsound car.

Nearly-new cars vs. brand-new models

Cars that are only a year or two old may be equipped with more comfort/convenience features – whether they originally came as standard equipment or were purchased by the initial owner as an extra-cost option.

Deciding between a nearly-new car and a brand-new model used to be easy, because the used one was almost always significantly cheaper. Not anymore. Certain late-model used cars can cost nearly as much as new ones. Occasionally, a used-car price may even *exceed* that of an equivalent new model.

Certain cars are well known to have especially high resale values when only a year or two old. For instance, a 2013 Mini Cooper with no extras sold new for $19,700 (plus the inevitable $795 destination charge). Incentives and discounts were likely to have been minimal, so the initial buyer probably paid close to that figure. At one year of age, that Cooper was likely to sell at retail for more than $18,000. That's only a $1,700 difference, with depreciation over that year amounting to less than 9 percent. So, which is the wiser purchase: a brand-new Mini Cooper, or a year-old one?

It's much easier to make a decision about, say, a 2013 Dodge Avenger R/T, which tends to depreciate substantially quicker. That one sold new for a Manufacturers Suggested Retail Price of $25,495, though incentives and discounts likely dropped the figure considerably. Secondhand, at one year of age, that Avenger is likely to go for about $19,000. Big difference, there: $6,495. That's how much you might save by accepting a year-old car over a brand-new one of the same model, if it's a model known to depreciate relatively steeply.

Before buying a late model, it pays to find out what it cost when new, as a comparison. Unless the selling price secondhand is appreciably lower, why take the risk? In those cases, turning to the new-car department – or perhaps to CPO – may be the wiser course.

Look for new-car selling prices in the NADA or KBB used-car price guides (in print or online), and use the same guidebook to compare used-car valuations.

Incentives keep some new-car prices down

New-car incentives make a considerable difference in a person's choice between buying new or purchasing a secondhand vehicle. In pre-recession times, actual "cash back" to the new-car buyer was the rule: Maybe $2,000 "on the hood," as they used to say. Now, when deciding on incentives, manufacturers focus on certain models: notably, those that haven't been selling well. They also consider how far along the vehicle is in its life cycle. If a redesign is expected soon, for instance, incentives may be needed to stimulate sales of the existing version.

At the National Remarketing Conference in 2010, Tom Kontos, executive vice-president of customer strategies and analytics for ADESA (a major auction chain), noted that the average new-vehicle incentive was more than $2,500. In many cases, taking advantage of that incentive could make the new car a better value than an equivalent year-old one.

More recently, incentives on new cars have been easing downward. Subaru, according to the National Automobile Dealers Association, has been the lowest of the low, with an average incentive of $921 per vehicle.

New-car incentives "have had a muted impact on used-car values the last couple of years," Kontos said in early 2014. Though the average amount is still near $2,500, their impact is "fairly benign."

Still, more than 95 percent of new vehicles have some sort of incentive, according to CNW Research. Prior to the recession that began in 2007-08, the proportion of vehicles with incentives was below 70 percent.

When they're employed, incentives are far more likely to consist of special finance rates and subvention (reduced prices) of leases than "customer cash," meaning actual dollars given as a rebate.

When to buy

Any of several factors can cause a person to start searching for a "new" used car, with varying degrees of urgency. Jack Simmons, dealer training manager for cars.com, pointed out five of them during his presentation at Used Car Week in November 2013:

> 1. **Lifestage change:** Children leaving home, transitioning into retirement, getting married, first child born, moving to a new job or location, etc.
> 2. **Car milestone:** You've had the previous car for a certain number of years, and feel it's time for a change.
> 3. **Need for more than one car:** You're keeping the existing vehicle, but now have need for a second one (or perhaps a third), likely due to changes in family or work situation.
> 4. **Routine upgrade:** It simply seems like time to start shopping once again.
> 5. **Pure desire:** You're ready for a change, or find yourself gazing longingly at certain newer models on the street or at dealership lots.

Quite often, said Rick Wainschel of AutoTrader at the same conference, "there's a trigger event" for initial consideration. It could be a chance viewing of a TV commercial, realization that a new driver will soon be in the family, an accident has damaged your existing vehicle, and so on. Wainschel also noted that some shoppers fall into a "loyalty loop," simply buying what they had before. However, the Brand Loyalty of the past has been fading rapidly. Not so many of us can say "I'm a Ford man all my life," or "I'll only buy a Toyota." Not anymore, when we're all aware of so many tempting choices on the market.

How important is the season when you're buying? For decades, the rule of thumb has been that prices for new vehicles fall late in the model year, before the next season's models are out. That's still true, though not quite as much as in the past.

Secondhand cars have their own seasonal differences. Logically enough, winter tends to be the low point, while prices ordinarily escalate as spring emerges. Dealers pay close attention to these up-and-down trends, but the saving achieved by a retail buyer is less dramatic.

How about leasing instead?

Watch the TV commercials and newspaper ads prepared by auto manufacturers and by dealers, and you're sure to hear about some truly tempting lease offers. The monthly payments quoted for a brand-new, leased vehicle are often lower than you might have to pay for a used car that's a couple of years old.

So, why isn't every prospective used-car buyer turning instead to leasing?

There's one good reason: many of them *can't obtain* a lease. Only shoppers with a high credit score are likely to be issued a lease. The commercials state this fact quite clearly: leases are available to "well-qualified" customers. Those with nonprime credit need not apply.

That might be changing, though. Some smaller dealerships that specialize in lower-priced cars for the credit-challenged have been dipping their toes into the concept of Buy Here-Pay Here leasing. BHPH dealers, which sell and finance cars at the same location, have been around for decades. But until recently, the notion of making leases available to the less creditworthy would have produced fearful reactions from most of those in the business. So, those dealers catering to financially-troubled customers, who couldn't possibly qualify for a new-car lease due to their subprime credit history, just might have another way to make them motorists. But you can be sure they'll pay a hefty price for that privilege, as they do for the high-interest loans they wind up with when buying the traditional way.

Overall, credit approvals for lease applicants have been growing. In December 2013, according to Swapalease.com, 73.3 percent of auto lease applications were approved, versus 70 percent in the previous month. The approval rate for all of 2013 hit 72.7 percent, up from only 65.3 percent in 2012.

According to CNW Research, the number of leases written has been growing every year since 2009, following a downturn that lasted for three years. Lease penetration (how many leases are written, as a percentage of total new-vehicle sales) reached 27.8 percent in 2013, versus 25.6 percent in 2010. Furthermore, nearly 20 percent of households that lease a vehicle have two or more leases in effect.

Getting a "better" car, in a higher trim level and/or with more equipment, for a lower monthly payment is among the big advantages of leasing. Up-front costs can be considerable, however, especially if the car you're leasing is not the beneficiary of subvented (subsidized) lease terms by a manufacturer.

Leasing definitely isn't for everyone, whether for a new or used car. In addition to the tighter restrictions regarding acceptance, some people simply don't like the idea of never owning the vehicle. (Of course, the question of whether you ever really own a car on which you've been making monthly payments over a long term is debatable.)

Whatever you wind up buying, remember that "everybody drives a used car," says Ricky Beggs, editorial director of the *Black Book* price guides consulted by dealers.

2

Where to Buy a Used Car

Shoppers have three basic choices: the used-car department of a franchised new-car dealership, an independent used car dealer (who does not sell new models), or a private seller. Each source has advantages and disadvantages.

In 2010, according to the Manheim Used Car Market Report, franchised dealers sold 12.8 million used vehicles. Independent dealers sold 13 million (up from 11.7 million in the previous year). Private transactions accounted for 11.1 million sales.

By 2013, franchised dealers accounted for nearly 15.6 million used-vehicle sales, while the independents moved 14.5 million. Purchases from private parties, once a big part of the used-car picture, have been declining lately: below 12 million in 2013, according to CNW Research.

One easy possibility: Shop where you bought a used car before – provided you were satisfied with the experience and the vehicle. Also, ask friends and neighbors where they've bought cars recently, and whether they were pleased by their treatment at the dealership. Ask about their experience during the sale, and also how the dealer handled any problems that came up afterward. Most people are willing – even eager – to give details about a dealer who treated them properly. They're also eager to warn you about one who failed to do so.

Let's look at the benefits and drawbacks of each source.

Franchised new-car dealers

Traditionally, the used-car departments of franchised dealerships have been considered the most reliable, with the best-quality merchandise on hand. Though more likely to have a wide stock of well-kept late-models, they're also traditionally the most expensive.

Most franchised stores belong to the National Automobile Dealers Association, and they're directly connected to automakers. Many dealerships have franchises for a number of makes; the era of the single-make dealership has been ebbing for years. Franchised dealers, therefore, are the source of manufacturer-certified vehicles (see CPO, Chapter 4). They're also far more likely than independent used-car lots to have trade-ins for sale, many of them one-owner or lease returns – though not as many as in the past. Those are generally the most desirable vehicles to search for; but again, the most costly.

Best Bet may be a dealership that handles the make of the used car that interests you. Such a dealership has a service department and an ample stock of parts for that make, and is more likely to offer a warranty (at extra cost, of course). Service technicians are mostly factory-trained, which means they have specific knowledge and expertise about that make of car or light truck. How do you know a technician at a dealership for a different make can do a comparable job?

An even better bet might be a vehicle sold by, and maintained at, the dealership that's selling it now as a used car. Most reputable dealers keep only the top trade-ins. Others are sold at wholesale, taken to the auction – or nowadays, sold to other dealers through online wholesale auctions.

Franchised dealers have been increasing their commitment to used vehicles, according to the Manheim Used Car Market Report. Of course, that's partly because profit margins have remained consistently higher than those for new vehicles. As new-car profits sag, dealers rely more on their used-car and service departments to soothe the bottom line.

Regardless, many have broadened their inventories to include more makes, models, vehicle ages, and price categories. Dealers also are more likely to retail unwanted trade-ins than to wholesale them at auctions or directly to independent dealers, which used to be the standard practice.

Some new-car dealerships have established standalone used-vehicle stores. Members of the AutoNation group, for instance, have Vehicle Value Centers for budget-minded shoppers (with vehicles priced in the $7,000 neighborhood). Those auxiliary used-car lots might adjoin the regular new-car dealership, or be situated at a completely different location. Either way, they're likely to have an entirely different set of salespeople and other employees, operating separately from the new-car business.

Independent used-car dealers

Sales at independent dealerships, which handle only used vehicles, rose 11 percent in 2010, to 35.3 percent of the total, according to CNW Research. Since then, the independent share of the used-vehicle market has shrunk a bit, down to 34 percent in 2013. Franchised dealerships (which also sell new cars) accounted for 37.4 percent of used-vehicle sales, while casual/private sales amounted to 28.6 percent. Still, just over 37,000 members of the National Independent Automobile Dealers Association were active during 2013, selling an average of about 378 cars per year.

Independent dealers are the ones who have most often been mocked and derided in the past, for alleged shady dealings. Comedians have made them the brunt of jokes for decades. They even played a role in presidential politics, when opponents of Richard Nixon asked voters: "Would you buy a used car from this man?"

Many of those allegations were valid. Some of *today's* independents, for that matter, could use some lessons in ethical customer treatment. Old-style dealers, often dubbed "used car dogs" in the trade, are still around. Some are up to their usual tricks, if less flagrantly than in the past. Others have simply adapted their hard-sell gimmicks to the digital world.

Don't make rash judgments, though: reliability and professionalism of independents is markedly higher than in the past. Most independent dealers have turned a corner, at least in part. Trade groups like the National Independent Automobile Dealers Association (NIADA) have actively tried to weed out the disreputable practitioners.

Cars at an independent dealership are typically older and less spiffy. They're also more likely to have come from wholesale auctions. Even the best independents acquire most of their vehicles from auctions, or buy them at wholesale from new-car dealers.

In decades past, learning that a car came from an auction was a sure warning to "Beware." But auctioned vehicles aren't necessarily poor choices anymore, a result of today's comprehensive condition reports and vehicle history data. Until fairly recently, independent dealers often knew little about each car on sale. Nowadays, a lot more information is available to the dealer; and by extension, to the retail shopper and ultimate buyer.

Inspection of cars that are placed on sale may be more cursory than at a franchised dealership. Not too many independent dealers have a sizable service facility (if any at all). So, if you elect to pay for a service contract, be sure to find out where any repair work must be done. That might not be an issue, since independents are less likely to include a warranty of any consequence.

New third-party certification services are gradually changing that situation. But as a rule, warranties, if offered, might be effective for only a short period of time, or be burdened by loopholes. Or, they could cover only a portion of the actual repair cost, leaving you to put up the lion's share.

"Independent dealers have modified the age and condition guidelines to reflect what their customers can afford," declared former NIADA president Anthony Underwood. Those "dealers are doing more reconditioning to get vehicles front-line ready" for sale to retail customers

An independent with a reputation for fairness may be a reasonably good bet, provided you're careful in making a selection and don't let yourself be swayed into buying something you don't really want – or that's absurdly overpriced. For customers seeking basic transportation, or who are unwilling or unable to pay the price for a prime-quality automobile, independents make sense.

Buy Here–Pay Here dealers

A specific subgroup of independents caters to high-risk shoppers with poor or marginal credit. That category of independent, operating Buy Here-Pay Here car lots, is the one most likely to flaunt claims that "We Finance Everyone" and "No Credit, No Problem!"

Even if such statements are true, credit-challenged shoppers had better be prepared to make a substantial down payment and/or accept a finance rate far above the average. BHPH dealers generally specialize in low-budget cars, and therefore are the only feasible source for the financially desperate. But they're best avoided if you can afford something a bit higher up the quality line.

According to the National Independent Automobile Dealers Association (NIADA), the average person buying from a BHPH dealer finances a bit over $10,000, for an average term of 40 months. The down payment averages $887. How much are the monthly payments? To help alleviate the possibility of substantial loss by the dealer, seriously credit-challenged folks typically are compelled to make payments *weekly*, not monthly: an average of $87 per week.

More and more credit-challenged buyers are required to have a starter-interrupt device installed in the car, which prevents it from starting if the driver falls behind in those payments and the dealer/lender activates the system. Some dealers also installed a GPS tracking device, so they know where the vehicle is located at all times. Attempting to ward off default and the need for repossession, these dealer/lenders employing such "payment assurance" techniques obviously want to make the seriousness of the delinquency perfectly clear. Privacy advocates and other critics take exception to the growing use of such devices, which tend to treat customers with marginal credit histories as potential deadbeats.

BHPH dealers have their own trade association, and have been taking steps to enhance their reputation as a desirable place to shop for lower-end automobiles. Many take the position that they're providing a valuable service to financially-strapped shoppers; and in a sense, they're quite correct. Without them, millions of families with credit ratings in the Nonprime, Subprime, or Deep Subprime category wouldn't be able to possess automobiles at all.

If you're in one of those categories, just be careful and take your time. Sign nothing unless you're certain you know exactly what you're agreeing to. Credit-challenged customers often wind up with "balloon notes," which offer low monthly payments. But they demand a huge final payment, which is nearly always impossible to obtain and, therefore, has to be refinanced: again, at interest rates well beyond those paid by less credit-troubled customers.

Best choice for the credit-challenged: wherever you choose to buy, steer clear of late-model, fully-equipped cars that are far beyond your means. Signing up for such a purchase, at any level of dealership, is simply begging for trouble later on.

Private sale: friends and relatives

Since the dawn of the automobile age, buying from a friend, relative, or neighbor has been the least costly option for securing a secondhand car. Ask yourself first, though: Do you totally trust that relative or neighbor? When it comes to selling cars, not everyone is quite as trustworthy – or knowledgeable – as we'd like them to be. Sad, but too-often true.

Naturally, the warnings are more stringent yet when it comes to strangers. Frauds and cheats exist among private sellers, just as they do among some licensed dealers.

What were once called "curbstoners," who function as virtual dealers but have no lot, business license, or official location, have a long and dubious history. Watch out for these unscrupulous bandits, posing as private sellers. Some go so far as to claim a car had only one owner, or was driven only on Sundays, when in reality it's been the property of several people, suffered accidents, and racked up a ton of hard miles along the way.

Today, legal requirements in most states have placed greater limits on their operations; but these low-end con men still turn up, typically offering dubious merchandise at appealing – but actually outlandish – prices.

Private parties can sell more cheaply than any dealership simply because they have no overhead, no expenses, no salespeople to pay. They may be the least likely to use high-pressure sales tactics – but subtle measures can be just as dangerous to the buyer, if not more so.

Private transactions may be exempt from sales tax, or subject to different rules (depending on the state and city in which they're located). On the other hand, you can't normally get credit from a private stranger. Not unless you do your shopping for financing in dark alleys, at least, seeking lenders who employ thugs to enforce non-payment.

Remember, too, that even basically honest people don't always disclose every flaw in a vehicle they're selling. Not all cars have been cared for properly, either, no matter how honest the person is. A seller may truly believe his or her worn-out relic is in fine shape and worth plenty.

Always be skeptical of oral statements, unless they can be backed up by documentation. Few private parties will have a history report to show you, but they might have maintenance information. Ask to see repair/maintenance records or receipts.

If you're buying from the original owner, or someone who's owned the car for several years, he or she might have kept a comprehensive service history. Or at least, tossed receipts into a box. Then again, some people just don't bother keeping records.

One basic question must always be asked: Does the car really belong to this person? Is it properly titled and legal in every way, and does this person have the authority to sell it? If there's even a shred of doubt, or the title's date or state of issue raises concerns, walk away. Buying a vehicle with a questionable title is asking for *serious* trouble. Even if an explanation sounds reasonable, and the price is ever-so tempting, is it worth taking a chance?

Online shopping

In this digital world of the 21st century, you may ask, doesn't buying cars online have an impact on the used-car business? For dealers, definitely so. Instead of taking the time to attend physical wholesale auctions, buyers from many dealerships are staying in the office, consulting computers or smartphones to participate in auctions that are conducted far away, but viewable online.

Buying cars through online wholesale auctions "has mitigated some of those regional differences in price," said Tom Kontos, executive director of analytical services for the ADESA auction group. Some dealers send employees only once a month to a physical auction; otherwise, all their car-buying is done via computer, bidding on cars that they see only on a video screen.

In addition to time-saving convenience, going online lets a dealer "attend" auctions all over the country, thus providing a far broader selection of vehicles to choose from. Yes, those vehicles then have to be shipped to the winning bidders; but transporting cars nationwide is a big business, and the costs are readily absorbed into the ultimate selling price.

As we'll see in our chapters on Research, retail shoppers – especially those in the younger age groups – are doing most of their information-gathering online. Under-30 shoppers consult 28.6 sources of information, said Jack Simmons, dealer training manager for cars.com, during his presentation at Used Car Week in 2013. Over-30s look into fewer, but all age groups are relying more on the computer and less on personal contact for the buying information they need. Currently, the average used-car shopper spends nearly 11.8 hours online before visiting a dealership, and some devote a lot more hours than that to their investigation of availability and price.

That doesn't mean the buying process is concluded online, however. Not yet, anyway. For most shoppers, a dealership visit is still part of the procedure, even if it happens later in the sequence of steps toward a purchase. Still, a growing number of shoppers are expressing willingness to buy "sight unseen," without even a test drive, according to Heather MacKinnon, vice-president of national accounts for DealerRater. With so much information available in vehicle history reports, buying a late-model without physically experiencing it isn't as risky as it used to be.

Not every car is a suitable candidate for the online buying world, though, such as older models and those with higher mileage. A lot of bidders "just wouldn't be comfortable buying [them] online," said Jerry Heinecke, wholesale director for Morries Automotive Group.

Unless you're one of those early adopters of online car-buying, you'll have to proceed the old-fashioned way, even though a hefty part of the process will probably involve shopping online.

Off-lease and fleet vehicles

Millions of vehicles for sale secondhand were never owned by an individual person. Plenty of them were leased to an individual. But others came out of rental fleets, or were part of a fleet operated by a business of some sort.

Unless you're financially challenged and must pick the cheapest vehicle around, it's definitely wise to steer clear of former rental cars. They're doubtless in better shape and more reliable than in the past, and likely to have been better maintained. Even so, a car driven by dozens – or hundreds – of different people is inevitably a bigger question mark.

Business-fleet vehicles probably had fewer drivers, and may have been driven relatively mildly. But it's difficult to find out that information. If you're willing to take the risk, and the price is particularly appealing, at least they're more suitable than former rentals.

Off-lease cars, on the other hand, are considered prime candidates for resale, partly because they've normally been driven by one person or one family. Furthermore, lease agreements require that specific maintenance tasks be done on a regular schedule. For privately-owned cars, maintenance is up to the individual. Some folks are meticulous about following the maintenance schedule issued by the manufacturer; others are more lax, which adds to the probability of trouble later on.

Most used-car shoppers are willing to consider a formerly-leased vehicle, partly because of the helpful information provided on history reports. Though some drivers are more careless with a car that's leased than one that's owned, most lessees try to avoid harm to their vehicles. If for no other reason, any damage beyond ordinary wear-and-tear has to be paid for at the end of a lease term.

Were it not for the large number of off-lease automobiles, the whole used-car business would likely collapse. A shortage of lease returns after the 2008-09 financial crisis was the foremost reason for trouble in the used-car market, which is only now (in 2014) getting back to normal.

3

How to Choose a Good Dealer

Long ago, the battle lines were drawn. Dealer versus customer. Salesperson against shopper. Rampant mistrust of the other party, resulting in a tense, adversarial relationship. That's how the used-car business has been perceived ever since, by folks on either side of the equation and by the general public.

Despite all the negative portrayals in the media and elsewhere, it doesn't have to be that way. Contrary to popular belief, that purchasing encounter need not turn into a jousting match, with each side determined to "win." Instead, we can – and should – be striving for transactions that are friendly exchanges, and for dollars-and-cents discussions that amount to congenial negotiation.

Sound impossible? Not anymore. Sure, every dealer wants to get the most dollars for a given car. At the same time, the retail customer wants to pay as little as possible. That's an indisputable "given." Those twin facts are never going to change. After all, that's how a market-based economic system works.

Yet, sticking rigidly to that theme, perceiving the other fellow as an opponent, even an enemy, does no one any good. Just because the process has long been dominated by those opposing forces doesn't mean we have to be slaves to such an outmoded practice and principle.

As we've already observed, modern, progressive dealers and salespeople have been moving away from those sales methods of the past. If anything, it's the customers who are a little slower to move into the present. Many of us remain certain that whenever a car purchase looms, a battle will be fought at the dealership. In fact, some of us actually relish that battle, enjoying the back-and-forth dickering and the struggle to emerge victorious.

Resistance to change isn't surprising. Salespeople have been told for years, directly or implicitly, that the goal of every sales transaction isn't merely to make a sale. No, the underlying objective is to win: to beat the other party. That's been done by selling each car for the highest possible price, even if hard-sell tactics and dubious methods had to be employed.

Retail shoppers, meanwhile, have heard and read a comparable line. Nearly all buying guides written for consumers have insisted that it's essential to beat down the price to the lowest possible figure, leaving the dealer as paltry a profit as possible.

Customers need to accept that it's not the end of the world if you pay a little more for a car you really like. Neither is it a tragedy to sell a vehicle for a bit less than intended, if it results in a truly satisfied customer.

Old habits die hard, clinging to our psyches like barnacles. But we'll all be better off if we accept that a friendly, more equitable and modern used-car marketplace already exists, and is growing.

Starting your search

Before starting out, consider what type of vehicle you want (see Part II, Research); how much time you care to spend on shopping; and how much you're willing to pay. But be prepared to flex a little, if the situation warrants.

Good dealerships aren't always easy to spot, but it's important to realize that many car dealers have been trying to distance themselves from the old image of less-than-scrupulous traders. Then again, others have not made that adjustment. A businesslike attitude and willingness to cooperate at every step are good signs. An attractive lot and buildings may be a favorable sign, but not necessarily a reliable indicator.

Some undesirable choices can be eliminated at the earliest stages of research. Web sites and ads that seek to inform are worth considering. Those that shriek and scream, frenetically assaulting readers with vague promises in bold type and loud voices, are the ones to omit from your search.

We've already noted that *transparency* is the big buzzword in the used-car business. Web sites that display useful information rather than pushy promotional verbiage are the ones that are worth consulting. That includes posting prices of all the used cars on sale.

Why should a dealership show pricing transparency on its website? Making that information readily available builds confidence and trust, said Kraig Quisenberry, director of sales and variable operations for the DCH Automotive Group.

Remember, of course, that any posted figures are asking prices. Even at the most progressive dealerships (except for those that embrace one-price selling), negotiation to some degree is still expected. Or at least, accepted as part of the procedure of finishing a "deal."

Look for salespeople who appear to know the products, and convey a helpful attitude. Avoid those who gush and fawn, or who keep harping on the "good deal" that you can get here. Helpful behavior of employees isn't always easy to assess until you get well into the transaction.

Even more important, pick the kind of dealership that promotes the quality of its merchandise, rather than low selling prices and "easy" monthly payments. Beware of ads and signs that proclaim "No Money Down," "No Down Payment," "Everybody Drives," or "Instant Credit." Those dealers may as well be in the credit-issuing business rather than the car business, and their vehicle stock might be filled with repos and dogs.

Your local Better Business Bureau can provide information – positive or negative – on a specific dealership, but they're not as prominent a factor as they used to be. Being realistic, most shoppers never consult the BBB at all, and probably never will. Fortunately, there are other ways to assess a dealer's likely behavior.

Customer reviews

All over the Internet are customer reviews, for virtually every product or service. They aren't necessarily helpful when choosing a vehicle, but they can provide useful tidbits of information about a dealership. Consult them with caution, though. Too many customer reviews, of every kind of business, have turned out to be fraudulent in one way or another. Then too, some people are too inclined to be generous in their appraisal of services they received, while others are eager to find fault with even the most trivial imperfection.

How about paying customers, or dealership employees, for submitting or encouraging reviews? Should a dealer pay for reviews? Bribe the customer? With free oil changes, for instance?

Heather MacKinnon, vice-president of national accounts for DealerRater, advised during her presentation at the CPO Forum in 2013 that Mazda dealers had been handing out postcards telling customers how to submit reviews on such web sites as DealerRater, Yelp, and Google. Is that ethical? Maybe so, and lots of businesses engage in similarly mild intimidation. But such efforts do make the opinions that are stated more suspect.

Some companies have gotten some nasty publicity for doing so. But MacKinnon brought up one business that makes a small contribution to a customer's favored charitable organization if they write and submit a slogan – one that's supplied by the company. Where do we draw the line, ethically speaking?

MacKinnon also noted that while 90 percent of customers *read* online reviews, only 6 percent write them. A "positive online review is a compliment," MacKinnon added.

Dealer groups

Membership in an appropriate association, such as the National Automobile Dealers Association or National Independent Automobile Dealers Association, is a plus, but not an assurance. Members of both groups still vary considerably in their attitudes. Both groups conduct advanced training of dealership employees, awarding certificates to those who have gone through specific programs. Of course, completing a training program in modern methods is no guarantee that what's been learned will be put into practice; but it's a helpful fact to consider.

Training also is provided by a slew of third-party business services, many of which (but not all) have adopted modern, progressive principles – at least in part. Viewed realistically, some sales trainers never got the message, and educate their "students" with frantic recommendations that sound more appropriate for car salesmen in 1954 than in 2014.

"There are no secrets in today's automotive climate," says Brian Benstock of Paragon Honda in Queens, New York – first named CPO

Dealer of the Year at the 2010 CPO Forum. Transparency is the answer today. In recent years, there's "been a cultural change in the way we do business."

Rather than tackling an ordinary dealership, some shoppers are more at ease in a huge selling environment. Used-car superstores have been around since 1993, when CarMax came into existence, though many have faded out of existence. Rather than a couple of dozen cars, a superstore will have hundreds to choose from. Many have non-negotiable prices posted on the vehicle, and emphasize low-pressure, customer-friendly practices.

Making those customers feel welcome is crucial, said Jonathan Banks, executive automotive analyst at NADA Used Car Guide, if dealers are going to cope with near-future change. Progressive dealers, he said, give $15,000 used-car buyers the same experience as new-car buyers.

Truly progressive dealers will go the extra miles to earn a fully satisfied customer. Says David Andreuss, of City Auto in Memphis: To make them happy, "we'll give them their money back" if they aren't satisfied.

Crucial rule

When you observe irksome high-pressure sales tactics at any dealership (or even from a private party), prepare to walk away. The same response is suggested if paperwork looks questionable, or anything doesn't feel right. There are a lot more dealers and salespeople these days who operate in a more civilized manner. Sticking with a dealership that's not treating you courteously and appropriately need not be an option. Not anymore.

4

Go CPO: Certified Pre-Owned Vehicles

"Factory-certified" or "manufacturer-certified" vehicles emerged during the early 1990s, starting with the luxury automakers. Mercedes-Benz, Audi, and Porsche led the way toward the CPO phenomenon. By 1997 or so, well over a dozen manufacturers were backing certified used vehicles, including mainstream models as well as luxury-level vehicles.

Most car-shoppers have probably heard of certification, but not everyone is familiar with how it works. Mainly, the certification process is intended to give "peace of mind" to the used-vehicle buyer.

As new cars dipped in sales, used cars tended to follow along, said Arianne Walker, director of automotive marketing and media research at J.D. Power. "We saw these fleet sales go down dramatically," Walker recalled at a CPO Forum in 2010. Leasing also declined. As a result, there were fewer candidates for certification, because there were a "lot fewer two-year-old vehicles in the marketplace."

Certification may not get as much publicity lately, but it's still a big factor in used-car popularity. "CPO is absolutely on fire," said Joe Derkos, director of the J.D. Power Used Car Market Report, during the CPO Forum in November 2013. CPO sales reached a record 2.1 million in 2013, up 15 percent from the 1.8 million sold during the previous year. Manheim, a major wholesale auction group, foresees a potential doubling of CPO sales in the next three or four years.

Average transaction price for a certified pre-owned car in 2013 was $23,900, according to a J.D. Power analysis.

Why buy CPO?

J.D. Power research has found that 79 percent of customers planned at the outset to buy a certified vehicle. Half said the salesperson at the dealership influenced them to consider CPO.

CPO shoppers typically cite three reasons for going CPO. Near-new condition was the top factor for 71 percent of survey respondents. Low mileage induced 65 percent of those surveyed, closely followed by extended warranty coverage.

"People expect to get that warranty coverage," Arianne Walker said. More than one-third cited getting more features for less money, as well as the detailed inspection process. Price has invariably provided the least satisfaction – doubtless because certified cars cost more. One interesting tidbit: 15 percent of those surveyed said the most influential reason was the simple fact that the "vehicle they wanted just happened to be certified."

Customers "get that it's going to cost more," said Matt McKenna of AutoTrader, once they understand it. Unlike McDonald's supersizing of its sandwiches, "the car or truck doesn't get bigger" just because it's been certified.

"To a certain extent, you burden the vehicle" with extra costs by certifying it, added Dale Pollak of vAuto, addressing dealers at the 2010 CPO Forum. But "in the end, you'll get a lot happier customer."

Manufacturer-backed CPO sales rose by 7 percent in 2010, to 1.6 million, according to the Manheim Used Car Market Report. By 2013, customers were buying more than 2.2 million certified vehicles per year.

Luxury brands have always remained high in CPO sales. More recently, franchised dealers for mass-market brands have focused on certification, as part of increased emphasis on used vehicles. Chrysler and GM are among the automakers that have offered special financing terms to CPO buyers.

The near future looks promising for availability of CPO vehicles, after several years of shrunken totals. At the end of 2013, Art Spinella, president of CNW Research, predicted that 3.1 million leased vehicles would be returned to the dealership during 2014. As reported in *Auto Remarketing*, more than 44 percent of those would be ideal for CPO programs.

To be specific, CNW forecasts that 1.3 million lease-return vehicles would be "prime" choices for the certified pre-owned market. "With leasing hitting the 30-percent share in December [2013]," Spinella concluded, "the next five years will see 14 million off-lease cars and trucks returning" to dealerships, even if no additional leases were written during that period. "Of those, 6 million would be CPO candidates."

What does certification mean?

Essentially, certification consists of reconditioning and beyond; plus an inspection covering specific areas, and a warranty. Certification is limited to vehicles that are no more than a few years old, with no more than a stated number of miles on their odometers. For manufacturer-backed programs, factory-trained technicians are assigned to inspect potential CPO vehicles, following a specific checklist of point-by-point items.

A warranty also is part of the CPO process. The warranty that's included may start with the sale date of the used car. Or, it might begin from the original sale date, as a new car. Every manufacturer's CPO program is different in details, and certification by third-party organizations – a growing phenomenon – has its own set of standards.

Some critics scoff at certification, or at least question its value, suggesting that a thorough inspection should be given to every used car that's sold at a dealership. Or at least, to every late-model that commands a relatively high price. A reasonable-length warranty should be part of each sale too, some contend. Why, they ask, should consumers have to pay a substantial premium for what should be provided without extra charge?

Naturally, dealers who provide the service paint a more positive picture, asserting that the assurance that comes with a certified pre-owned vehicle is well worth the additional cost.

Who does the certifying?

Mainly, it's the manufacturer that built the car in the first place. Many customers appear to believe it's the selling dealer that does the certifying and backs up the result. Dealership employees typically conduct the inspection of a vehicle that's going to be certified, but it's the manufacturer of that car that stands behind the CPO procedure.

Alternatively, some dealers have set up their own certification programs, but they're not backed by an automaker. More recently, several third-party organizations have joined the CPO parade, including POADA and NIADA.

Operated by the group that publishes *Auto Remarketing* magazine, the Pre-Owned Automobile Dealers Alliance (POADA) has a program for middle-aged vehicles only. Specifically, it's limited to vehicles that are five years old or newer, with less than 100,000 miles on the odometer. Administered by EasyCare, the CarMark certification program was launched in September 2010. No bumper-to-bumper warranty is included, but customers can upgrade to a full service contract.

Many participating POADA dealers are independents, but others have new-car franchises. The CarMark program lets them offer certification for makes other than the ones they're franchised to sell as new cars.

Another later addition to the certification race is the National Independent Automobile Dealers Association (NIADA), which launched its program in June 2010. This program includes a 125-point inspection and 72-month/100,000-mile powertrain coverage dating from the car's original sale date (or 12-month/12,000-mile from the purchase date as a CPO model). A 3-month/300-mile or 12-month/12,000-mile warranty (with $100 deductible) covers most major powertrain components, but buyers can upgrade to any of four extended-coverage options.

Neither the POADA nor NIADA program is backed by a vehicle manufacturer.

Publications and other organizations also have been offering CPO programs to independent dealerships. *Motor Trend* magazine, for one, has been promoting a CPO program known as Motor Trend Certified. Enterprise Car Sales has a CPO program; so does Payless Assurance.

IntelliChoice notes that third-party certification programs don't necessarily include a warranty beyond what's left of the original new-car coverage. Some do include extended coverage, so it's vital to check exactly what that warranty entails, for how long, and where any needed repair work would have to be done.

A number of organizations that aren't well known for being auto-related also have begun CPO vehicle programs. Costco Auto, for example, expects to be expanding its certified pre-owned vehicle program during 2014, adding an offshoot called Select Pre-Owned. As reported in *Auto Remarketing*, Gina Paolino, president of the Costco program, described those offerings as "higher-end pre-owned vehicles," which might not be eligible for certification under an automaker's own CPO program. Yet, they still have part of their original new-car warranty remaining. Among the benefits stated by Paolino, "repairs can be made at any franchised dealer, under the terms of the manufacturer-backed warranty."

How do manufacturer-backed programs compare?

As the CPO Program chart in our References sections indicates, every automaker has a different standard for vehicles covered, in terms of maximum age and mileage. Each inspection covers a specified number of points, but a larger number doesn't necessarily prove to be a more vigorous or comprehensive examination. Duration and details of the extended warranty also vary, and may differ depending on the vehicle's age.

Let's look at some typical CPO program details:
- Acura (near-luxury) dealers can certify cars up to six years old, with no more than 80,000 miles on the odometer. A 150-point inspection is made. If bought while the new-car warranty remains in effect, comprehensive coverage runs to 60 months or 62,000 miles. Otherwise, comprehensive warranty coverage is for 12 months or 30,000 miles, plus 84-month/100,000-mile powertrain coverage (from original sale date).
- Mercedes-Benz (luxury) dealers may certify models up to six years old, with 75,000 miles. The inspection covers more than 155 points. Comprehensive warranty coverage lasts 12 months after expiration of the new-car warranty, or 50,000 miles (up to 100,000 total vehicle miles).
- Chevrolet's CPO program covers cars and light trucks up to six years old (the current model year, plus five previous model years), with as many as 75,000 miles. Chevrolet dealers undertake a 172-point inspection. Comprehensive warranty coverage is for 12 months or 12,000 miles beyond the new-car warranty, with 60-month/100,000-mile total powertrain coverage.

- Nissan dealers offer certification of vehicles up to five years old, whose odometers have not yet reached 60,000 miles. Nissan's inspection covers 156 points, and the powertrain warranty coverage is for 24 months or 40,000 miles (beyond the new-car warranty).
- Toyota dealerships provide certified pre-owned vehicles from the current model year and six previous years, with fewer than 85,000 miles on the odometer. Toyota does a 160-point inspection. Comprehensive coverage is 12-month/12,000-mile, and the 84-month/100,000-mile powertrain warranty begins with the original in-service date.
- Honda can certify vehicles up to nine model years old, with fewer than 80,000 miles, giving a 150-point inspection. A 10-year/100,000-mile powertrain warranty starts with the car's original in-service date.
- Ford dealers can certify cars up to six years old, with under 80,000 miles on the odometer. A 172-point inspection is made. In addition to a 12-month/12,000-mile comprehensive warranty, Ford's 72-month/100,000-mile powertrain coverage starts with the original in-service date.

For further details on these manufacturer-backed certification programs, and those offered for other car models, check our comprehensive CPO chart in the Resources section.

For all programs, it's worth noting that the number of "points" to be inspected is not a reliable indicator of the thoroughness of the work. Each manufacturer's list of points to be inspected is compiled differently, so a 172-point inspection isn't necessarily better than one that only delves into 150 points.

Deeper into CPO

Now that we've seen some basic facts about several manufacturer programs, let's take a closer look at one of them: say, Volkswagen. VW Certified Pre-Owned accepts vehicles up to six model years old, with fewer than 75,000 miles on the odometer. Of the 625 Volkswagen dealerships, more than 98 percent participate in the CPO program.

Certified Volkswagen vehicles get a 24-month/24,000-mile bumper-to-bumper warranty, beyond the existing new-car warranty's expiration date. That bumper-to-bumper coverage can be as high as 56 months or 56,000 miles (whichever comes first). Powertrain coverage totals a minimum of 5 years or 60,000 miles from the original in-service date. Warranties have a $50 deductible, and are transferable to a next owner. Volkswagen's inspection covers 112 points, and a vehicle history report is supplied. Special financing and lease terms are available. CPO buyers also get three months of free SiriusXM radio service.

Best factory CPO programs

Each year, IntelliChoice gives awards for the top CPO programs. At the CPO Forum in San Diego, in November 2013, Eric Anderson, the ownership database supervisor for IntelliChoice, announced the awards. Anderson cited a variety of factors that are considered each year, including:

1. Warranty
2. Inspection criteria
3. Title verification
4. Roadside Assistance
5. Special financing
6. Return/exchange policies
7. Dealer compliance
8. Cost of ownership (IntelliChoice's specialty)

Among popular brands, Hyundai took the prize for best program. Best CPO program for premium brands went to Volvo. Our thanks go to IntelliChoice for making up-to-date details of all the factory-certification programs available to everyone – journalists and customers alike – at their website (IntelliChoice.com).

Benefits and drawbacks of certification

"Peace of mind" is the benefit that's heard about the most. Customers get a level of assurance that might be impossible to acquire with a conventional used-car purchase. Many shoppers also feel easier knowing that significant additional warranty coverage is being provided – though the details should always be scrutinized, so you know what you're paying for. Not all warranties are equal, by any means.

And pay you will, because CPO vehicles cost significantly more than their regular counterparts. How much more? Estimates vary among the experts, but the acceptable "premium" is well into the thousands of dollars.

Looking at a typical group of certified vehicles in 2011, CNW Research found that the additional amount that people were willing to pay for a CPO vehicle reached an average of $1,384, compared to $1,202 a year earlier. Two years later, used-car shoppers who expressed willingness to pay more for CPO said $2,163 was acceptable. New-car shoppers who'd indicated in 2011 that they were willing to pay $1,245, stated in a later survey that an additional $2,940 would be appropriate. In mid-2014, CNW Research estimated that the average premium paid for CPO was $2,800, and had been for more than a year.

That may sound like a lot, but peace of mind is clearly something that warrants paying a hefty bounty. Said one happy customer on AutoTrader video: "That warranty is going to pay for itself."

Citing an NADA report, on the other hand, AutoTrader.com reported that the number of used-car shoppers willing to pay a premium price for a CPO vehicle had dropped, from 51 percent in 2011 to just 34 percent in 2013.

Larry Dixon, of NADA Used Car Guides, suggested during Used Car Week in November 2013 that the premium amounts paid for certification have "maybe grown a little bit." He estimated the typical add-on for a three-year-old vehicle to be $1,400 to $1,500. That premium rises for more costly and newer models. For a BMW or Mercedes-Benz, you're likely to pay *at least* $2,000 for a certified example, compared to a non-certified vehicle. *Automotive News* magazine advises that three-fourths of certified transactions involve a premium ranging from $500 to $2,000.

Kelley Blue Book (kbb.com) includes suggested add-on figures for certification in its valuations of used cars. So does the NADA Used Car Guide. Most other valuation guides do not; at least, not yet.

Alec Gutierrez, lead valuation analyst for KBB, has noted that a year-old BMW 3 Series or Mercedes C-Class may cost 85 to 90 percent of its original price. If an add-on for certification is applied, the used-car price could approach its original new-car figure. Like IntelliChoice, KBB also provides information about each manufacturer's program.

According to Rick Wainschel, vice-president of automotive insights at AutoTrader.com, CPO consideration on the part of new-vehicle shoppers is approaching levels previously seen only for used-car shoppers. In 2013, some 55 percent of new-car shoppers were considering a certified pre-owned model instead (up from 43 percent in 2012). Sixty percent of used-vehicle shoppers expressed willingness to consider CPO. "There are more used shoppers than new shoppers," Wainschel reminded the audience for his presentation at the CPO Forum in November 2013.

On the down side, fewer people seem to know about CPO. Wainschel noted a "decrease in familiarity with the program," at least for new-vehicle shoppers. Only 65 percent of new-car shoppers knew that CPO vehicles were fully inspected (down from 73 percent). The number who expressed familiarity with the CPO extended warranty fell from 68, down to 55 percent for new-car shoppers.

In fact, Alec Gutierrez of Kelley Blue Book reported that 11 percent of *CPO considerers* don't know what CPO means.

Echoing the misinformation several analysts had observed, 66 percent of new-car shoppers believed it was the dealership that certified the vehicle, while 70 percent of used-car shoppers got that one wrong. (Remember, it's the *manufacturer* that backs up a factory certification program.)

Reasons for CPO consideration haven't shifted much, according to AutoTrader: 67 percent of respondents cited "peace of mind," while 37 percent said they simply couldn't afford a new car.

Because of weak car sales after the 2008-09 financial crisis, availability of cars that were candidates for certification has suffered. Nowadays, a lot of trade-ins are 8 to 11 years old, said Ricky Beggs of *Black Book*; not the 2- and 3-year-olds that meet certification criteria. The supply of 2- to 4-year-olds is growing, though, due largely to increased leasing in the past few years.

In the opinion of David Nelson, director of pre-owned vehicle operations at Hendrick Automotive Group, 2014 is "going to be a big year for certified, with all the lease returns." Nelson also noted that buyers do express some "angst" because CPO vehicles cost more.

Which vehicle categories do best in CPO? It's still "luxury, of course," said NADA's Larry Dixon. Luxury models are heavily-leased (40 to 50 percent), which typically makes them prime candidates for certification after the lease term is up. Compact cars also are "heavily leased right now," Dixon added. In fact, Experian Automotive states that the most-leased model has been the Honda Civic, followed by the Ford Escape, Honda Accord and CR-V, and Ford Fusion. AJ Schoonover, vehicle valuation manager at Kelley Blue Book (kbb.com), noted that there are "some growing segments" in CPO, including crossover wagons and midsize cars.

As stated earlier, a case can be made that *all* cars – or at least, late-model examples – should get similar treatment as a matter of course, without the ample extra charge tacked on. Until that day arrives, CPO programs divide the used-car market into two distinct camps, with distinctly different prices and degrees of customer confidence.

Part II

Homework Comes First

Researching and evaluating a used-car purchase

5

Don't Rush on Research

Research is just as necessary when shopping for a used car as it is when selecting a new one. Probably more so, though the breadth of useful information is somewhat skimpier – or at least, harder to locate – when you're buying secondhand.

Today's shoppers face a bewildering, perhaps overwhelming choice of vehicles, whether new or used. Narrowing down the search by planning ahead, focusing on factors that matter most to *you,* is sure to save time, effort, stress – and yes, money, too.

At least you have access to a lot more information nowadays. Jonathan Banks, executive automotive analyst for NADA Used Car Guide, has noted that such independent web sites as AutoTrader.com and cars.com provide "pricing, content and condition information [that] creates an environment with complete transparency." As we shall see, many more helpful web sites and publications are out there, to make the decision-making process even less worrisome.

At the National Remarketing Conference in 2010, Len Crichter of eCarList accurately advised dealers that "your customer is more educated than the dealer, in most cases." That shopper has been researching a single model, or small group of models, and has likely studied several web sites devoted to used cars.

Dealership employees are generally limited to one, or a few, makes, and may or may not be fully conversant with all of the competition in a given category. Because used cars – even at a franchised new-car dealership – might be of *any* make, it's unrealistic to expect salespeople to know all the details about each vehicle on the lot. In fact, if a salesperson at any type of used-car lot seems to know way too much about a car he or she is pushing, we have to wonder if some of those statements are exaggerated. Or, simply made up on the spot.

Surfing for facts

More than three-fourths of both new- and used-vehicle shoppers research first on the Internet. They also spend about 75 percent of their shopping *time* online, says Heather MacKinnon, vice-president of national accounts for DealerRater. In a 2013 survey, 91.5 percent of Internet viewers clicked on the first page of a web site; but fewer than 5 percent went on to a second page. Like other businesses, auto dealers want their establishments to be found on Page One.

Research by the Polk organization, cited by KBB's Alec Gutierrez, has found that 59 percent of research is on the web. Family and friends are consulted by 27 percent of shoppers, while 23 percent focus on TV commercials and 15 percent look to newspaper ads for information. Outdoor billboards and magazine ads are each important to 10 percent of respondents, while 9 percent pay attention to direct mail ads and 7 percent listen to car commercials on the radio.

Online shopping has its ups and downs, said Jack Simmons, dealer training manager for cars.com, during the CPO Forum in November 2013. People begin with excitement and go through a learning curve. During the process, shoppers move in and out of phases, for various reasons. Dealers know, too, that a growing number of customers are using smartphones, right at the dealership, to fact-check information they're told by a salesperson. "Internet shoppers are now smartphone shoppers," Simmons added. "We live in a society that wants it now. We want everything now."

Raj Sundaram, group president of dealer solutions at Dealertrack Technologies, reported on an eBay Motors survey, which discovered that 40 percent of shoppers access dealer sites with mobile phones. Not surprisingly, young people are more likely to rely on their phones. One-third of "millennials" research vehicles via mobile phone, but only 19 percent of shoppers in non-millennial generations do so.

Dealers nowadays are constantly trying to ease and shorten the shopping experience, which can actually run into months, not hours. KBB's Gutierrez said some customers are "spending months and months on a purchase," including "spending hours and hours online." KBB surveys have found that the average new-car shopper spends 10 hours online, versus 11.75 hours for used-car shoppers.

Total shopping time is 13.75 hours for new-car buyers, and 15 hours for those in the secondhand department. Of that time, used-car shoppers spend 6.5 hours on third-party web sites (not the dealer or manufacturer's site). But it's far from steady research. Gutierrez claims the process actually takes an average of five months.

Five months might seem far beyond excessive, but don't rush on research. Take your time. After all, you're selecting a product that you'll be using daily for years. An extra hour or two of investigation is almost sure to pay off later, in obtaining the best possible vehicle.

6

Which Vehicle to Buy

We all have "wants," and we all have "needs." Whether buying a car or any other commodity, decision-making entails a balancing of those two forces.

Unless you're rolling in bucks, or have an emotional attachment to certain vehicles, practical considerations need to be paramount. You can save thousands of dollars by choosing the most sensible vehicle for yourself and your family.

Being realistic, on the other hand, most of us tend to gravitate toward cars that look good, contain features we'd like to have, perform and behave in certain ways on the road – all factors that edge away from the strictly practical.

Ask yourself some critical questions:

- How old a vehicle would you consider? Would only a late-model satisfy? Or, would you rather pay less and drive home an older car?
- How important is luxury? Will "basic transportation" suffice, or would you be unhappy with a stripped-down model that lacks even the most basic comforts and pleasures? What about a compromise?
- How important is fuel economy? Will a basic subcompact do? Or, must you have a big sedan with a sizable trunk? If big SUVs and vans catch your eye, remember how much extra gas you'll be buying over the next few years.
- Will you be dissatisfied with anything other than, say, an SUV, or a crossover model? How many passengers normally ride along? If you're carrying more than five, you're limited to minivans and three-row SUVs. If you seldom have more than one passenger, a car with a minimal back seat might suffice. If a

larger vehicle is in the cards, will it fit easily into your garage or typical parking space?
- Do you crave sportiness, in either style or road behavior? Or both? What about high-performance? How much acceleration and taut handling is enough. Are you willing to pay a lot more to shave a few tenths of a second off a car's 0-60 mph acceleration time?
- Most important of all: How much can you afford? Is your credit good enough to finance a more costly model – and do you *really* want to? Obviously, the amount you are able to pay (or finance) should be determined early on.

All these considerations, and more, need to be pondered a bit before you begin shopping. Still, it pays to be flexible, particularly in terms of a particular make, model, and year. If you have your heart set on a certain vehicle type, you may be closing the doors to one that might provide nearly all those merits at a markedly lower price. Having one or two alternate choices in the back of your mind pays off, because you have a much larger selection of vehicles from which to make a final choice.

Are there specific features that you can't live without? Manual shift, say? Obviously, that limits the possibilities. But remember: the main goal is to drive home a car that you'll be happy to own.

At the CPO Forum in November 2013, Jack Simmons, dealer training manager at cars.com, advised that 94 percent of shoppers don't know what they want at first. Many wind up at a standstill: feeling overwhelmed, exhausted or discouraged.

At the same Forum, AutoTrader's Rick Wainschel showed a video of a woman who changed her mind along the way. She'd planned to buy a Prius, then found a Fusion Hybrid on AutoTrader. "She has a very non-linear journey," Wainschel explained. "For her, that journey is not a burden. It's a treasure."

It's a question of building, then manipulating a "consideration set," said cars.com's Simmons. Until the final decision is made, narrowing down to finding the right car for one's needs, a shopper's trajectory can easily switch back and forth, even in odd directions.

Let's hope our explanations help in your next quest to buy a secondhand car, narrowing down the possibilities with a minimum of fuss.

Vehicle type

Most likely, you already know which body style and category appeals the most, but here are the possibilities:

- **Four-door sedans** with a regular trunk come in subcompact, compact, midsize, or full-size models, with front- or rear-wheel drive (or in some cases, all-wheel drive).
- **Two-door coupes** may have either a minimal or adequate back seat. Coupes aren't nearly as common as in the past, especially in larger sizes. A number of automakers have taken to calling their sporty, stylish models "four-door coupes." They're not. They're shapely sedans.
- **Wagons** were once the mainstay of suburbia, but they've lost favor in recent years – though a modest comeback may be happening. Most current wagons are midsize or smaller. Early in 2011, Volvo announced that it would stop sending its last remaining wagon to the U.S. market – another sign of sagging wagon interest. Hatchbacks and crossovers have captured the hearts of many who might have leaned toward a wagon in the past.
- **Hatchbacks** are typically midsize or smaller, though a few bigger examples can be found. Some owners feel almost naked without a conventional trunk, but hatchbacks promise flexible storage capabilities. Far more common in Europe and elsewhere in the world, hatchbacks never quite caught fire in the U.S. market, with the exception of certain sporty versions.
- **Minivans** have declined sharply in popularity, prompting Ford and GM to abandon production a few years back. For years, minivans were the staple of suburban life, until they developed a stigma as "soccer mom" vehicles and began to be overtaken by small to midsize SUVs and crossovers. As a result, minivans are "now the grandparent car," says Ricky Beggs of *Black Book*; though oddly, minivan prices have been stronger than expected at times. Nearly all have three rows of seats, with seven- or

eight-passenger capacity. Five-passenger models are rarities now. Most minivans have sliding doors on each side, though some with a single slider can be found. Most minivans have front-wheel drive, but a few secondhand models have all-wheel drive. Four-cylinder minivans used to exist, but recent models are nearly all V-6 powered.

- **Full-size vans** are mostly sold for commercial use, but some larger families still love them. Vans may have rear-wheel drive, or possibly all-wheel drive.
- **Convertibles** have faded in popularity, partly because younger buyers aren't nearly as infatuated with soft-tops as their parents and grandparents were. So, the convertible "ends up being the third car" nowadays, in Beggs' view. They're no bigger than midsize anymore and could be front- or rear-drive, usually with a V-6 or even a V-8, though compacts are likely to be four-cylinder. Turbocharged engines, often found on sporty soft-tops, promise the vigor of a V-6 melded with the economy of a four-cylinder.
- **Sport-utility vehicles** (SUVs) have four conventional doors and a rear hatch (though some have fold-out cargo doors instead. Most are available with either two- or four-wheel (or all-wheel) drive, and could contain a four-cylinder, V-6, or V-8 engine. Traditional SUVs had a separate body and frame, but many switched to a unibody configuration in recent years.
- **Crossover SUVs**, often called simply "crossovers" or "crossover wagons," are the latest trend. They're more carlike in feel and behavior than a regular SUV, due in part to their unibody construction, though the latter lean more in that direction than in the past. The line between crossover and SUV remains somewhat blurred, but crossovers tend to be a little smaller than full-scale SUVs.
- **Pickup trucks** may be compact or full-size, with a handful of secondhand midsizes (such as the Dodge Dakota) around. Compacts usually have either a four-cylinder or V-6 engine. Full-size pickups could have a V-6 or a V-8. Pickups can be strictly basic or lavishly equipped, so the price range is enormous. Those with V-8 engines, in particular, are not the wise choice if fuel economy is paramount. Even V-8s with fuel-

saving systems, which shut off half the cylinders when cruising, are hardly renowned for thriftiness.

As we'll see in Part IV, some models within each category decline far quicker in value than others. For that matter, vehicles in certain *categories* depreciate at faster rates than others. Pickup trucks, for instance, have been retaining their values especially well lately, meaning they depreciate relatively slowly.

Vehicle age

Nearly all cars depreciate at a fairly steady rate as they age. Therefore, with only a few exceptions, the older it gets, the cheaper it becomes on the used-car market. On the other hand, modern-day cars are a lot more reliable and long-lasting than they used to be. So, a car with a few years on it might still have a long and reasonably trouble-free life ahead. Then again, it might not.

Average age of vehicles on the road has been growing steadily, helped by the 2008-09 financial turmoil that compelled many people to put off car purchases. A lot of them still haven't taken the plunge into a new (or newer) model. As of 2014, the average age is close to 11.5 years, which means plenty of cars and light trucks are way older than that.

Cars versus trucks

If utility tops your list of vehicle attributes, an SUV or pickup might be prudent. Gas mileage is nearly always less appealing with trucks, but quite a few of them now boast relatively carlike behavior. Many trucks don't feel very "trucky" anymore. Some can almost be mistaken for luxury cars. Distinctions between SUVs, crossovers, wagons, and even minivans have gotten hazy, so it doesn't pay to set your sights on one particular category.

A while back, trucks could be found for bargain prices. During the 2008-09 period when gasoline prices spiked, economy cars suddenly began to attract more interest, and their prices rose sharply. At the same time, trucks declined in value. Since then, the normal price gap between compact cars and full-size trucks has been restored, according to Tom Kontos, executive vice-president of customer strategies and analytics for ADESA (a major wholesale auction chain). Before long, full-size SUVs gained about $7,500 and full-size pickups rose by around $4,700, compared to compact cars. "SUVs and pickups have really come back," Kontos said.

Today, SUVs and pickups remain popular, even when gasoline prices start to rise. On the whole, fuel prices have been stable lately; and even when they increase, most of us don't expect that the per-gallon price will keep on escalating. We assume they'll reach a peak, then start dropping again. So, why steer clear of that fancy, bling-laden SUV or burly pickup that's captured our attention? Of course, one day we might be in for a big surprise, if that stable-price scenario fails to continue.

Popularity of pickups varies according to region, which means they're likely to be cheaper in some areas than in others. The Plains states have had the highest percentage of pickups in recent years, according to Experian Automotive. In Wyoming, about one-third of vehicles are pickups; in Texas, the proportion has hovered around 22 percent. Pickups have their fans even in urban areas, too, whether as ironic fashion statements or for strictly practical, everyday use.

"Some of the stigma associated with full-size SUVs, and less so with full-size pickups, has dissipated," said ADESA's Kontos. That's "created a more rational level of supply, [so now] there's not an overabundance of pickup trucks."

Vehicle size and passenger capacity

Size, vehicle type, and passenger/cargo space can be the principal deciding factors, overpowering other considerations. The Environmental Protection Agency rates a vehicle's capacity according to the number of seatbelts it contains. Be careful here, as some cars – not all of them compacts or smaller – have five official positions, but realistically can carry only four comfortably. In quite a few instances, even two in the back seat are too many.

Furthermore, the line between each of the four vehicle sizes is somewhat hazy. Some cars that are officially compact or smaller are surprisingly roomy, while others may be called mid- or full-size but fall short on spaciousness – especially in the back. Some are shockingly cramped, especially in the center rear position, where riders typically must endure a hard perch, restricted leg room, and scant head space. Even average-height folks are likely to scrape their heads on the roofs, if forced to sit in that center spot.

Ease of entry/exit is another factor to consider, as some seemingly sizable automobiles aren't as easy to get into as they look.

- **Subcompact:** what many consider as tiny, but some enjoy for maneuverability and fuel economy (and lower price). Most are four-cylinder with front-drive. Microcars (smaller than subcompact) are common in Europe; but apart from the cute little two-door Fiat 500, and the two-passenger smart fortwo, micro-size models are seldom seen in the U.S.
- **Compact:** four-cylinder or V-6, with fours gaining in prominence recently. Virtually all are front-wheel drive. Compacts make a nice compromise for singles and couples, as well as small families.
- **Midsize:** the family favorite, typically V-6. But here too, four-cylinders have become more prevalent in the past few years. Most are front-drive, but some have rear-drive (or all-wheel drive).
- **Full-size:** once the mainstay, now a shrinking segment – more the province of luxury makes. You can still find those traditional Ford Crown Victorias and Mercury Grand Marquis, though production halted some time ago. Equipped with a V-8 and rear-drive, but most family-focused big cars have been front-drive with a V-6 (or V-8), though the latter have been fading away fast.

Cargo volume

What type of cargo do you carry? Grocery bags? Big suitcases? Compare the luggage space's floor area and depth to your requirement. Note, too, how difficult it is to lift a suitcase – which might be heavy – over the bumper and lip to get into the trunk.

Hatchbacks can be handy, especially when their back seats fold down to add considerable cargo space. They're more flexible than a notchback model (with a regular trunk).

Still, many shoppers won't consider a car without a conventional trunk. Some trunks, even on relatively large cars, aren't as spacious as one might think. Not all are easy to load, either.

Most SUVs and crossovers have lift-up hatches at the rear, which can be difficult for older, shorter, disabled, or less-agile folks to reach when the lid has been raised. Only a handful of models, including the Nissan cube, have "refrigerator" style swing-out rear doors, which are a blessing for folks who have difficulty with raise-up liftgates.

Drivetrain layout

Front-wheel drive became almost the norm starting in the 1980s, until rear-drive began a comeback in the 21st century. Front-drive cars have a more compact, lighter-weight drivetrain and better slippery-road traction, making them more practical in wintry climates. Because more parts are packed under the hood, repairs can be more difficult and more costly.

Rear-wheel drive was used on almost all vehicles until the 1980s, and has achieved renewed popularity lately. Enthusiasts prefer rear-drive for its handling qualities, but winter traction is considerably less appealing than front-drive – even if traction control is installed.

Four-wheel drive can be part-time or full-time. Available on nearly all SUVs and most pickup trucks, 4WD improves traction considerably, especially on slick surfaces. Components are heavier and more complex, and 4WD vehicles are almost always less economical than 2WD. Sometimes, a *lot* less. Most recent systems are full-time, but many trucks with part-time systems should not be driven in 4WD when on dry pavement.

All-wheel drive gives the benefits of distributing power to all four wheels when needed, but operates automatically with no action required from the driver. That's because it's permanently engaged. AWD car and truck owners might not even realize they have such a system.

Powertrain: Performance versus fuel economy

The basic rule used to be simple: a small engine (four-cylinder) was more economical than a bigger one. That's still largely true, but the difference isn't always so great. Quite a few V-6s (and even some V-8s) have become significantly more economical to drive. Also, in a heavier vehicle, a bigger engine might actually be *more* frugal with gas because it's not struggling as hard. Then again, it might not.

High-performance models almost always consume plenty of gasoline, though here too, automakers have managed to improve their fuel economy. Many drivers, however, don't operate them in ways that deliver impressive miles-per-gallon. If you're one of those who are likely to push harder than average on the gas pedal, don't expect to achieve – or even approach – the gas-mileage estimates issued by the Environmental Protection Agency (EPA).

Plenty of cars, not all of them luxurious or high-performance, require premium-grade gasoline, which costs an extra 20 cents or more at the pump. Some automakers make premium (or mid-grade) fuel an option, recommending it for best performance but noting that the car will run acceptably well on regular, without causing harm.

Consider the type of driving you normally do, and whether you might need the benefits of a bigger engine only rarely, or regularly. On the highway, larger engines can deliver gas mileage that comes close to that of a smaller engine. In the city, that's a lot less likely. Some V-6 and V-8 engines continue to guzzle frightful quantities during urban commutes, or even in highway driving.

Import brands versus domestics

"At one time there was a great distinguishing area" between domestic and foreign cars, says Ricky Beggs, editorial director of *Black Book*. Not anymore.

Because so many import-brand automakers have factories in the U.S. (or Canada), there's no longer a clear-cut difference between import and domestic. Furthermore, parts may come from different countries than the locale where the car is assembled. Japanese makes still excel in perceived quality (and often in actual quality), but American-made models from those automakers differ little from their foreign-built counterparts. American-built cars from the "Detroit Three" also are far better in quality than in the past.

South Korean manufacturers (Hyundai and Kia) have been among the most-improved in recent years. Quite a few cars have been assembled in Mexico, where factories that might once have had questionable quality control have become considerably better.

Traditionally, Japanese and European brands have tended to depreciate more slowly, and therefore cost more. Lately, that gap has shrunk appreciably. Japanese brands have a history of relatively high resale value, as do Europeans. South Korean cars used to be among the fastest-depreciating, but that's been changing. Domestics, too, have improved considerably in retaining their value, though older examples are likely to be cheaper than a comparable import brand.

Base vs. step-up models

How important is price, compared to luxury and sportiness? For obvious reasons, a base model with few extras nearly always costs considerably less than a fully-loaded version. Maintenance costs might be lower, too, with fewer gadgets to go bad.

On the other hand, base-model cars aren't usually in high demand. So, if you plan to trade it in or sell it later on, a better-equipped model might be wiser. Many shoppers wind up with a compromise: a well-equipped example, but not top-of-the-line.

When searching for vehicles, look carefully at the lists of comfort/convenience items that are included with each trim level. Some of those lists look massive, but include a lot of features that are standard on every vehicle. Try to compare the equipment on a base model of a given vehicle with one or two of its more abundantly fitted versions: EX, LS, Limited, or whatever the manufacturer chose to call the higher-up trim levels. Look, too, for a list of options (and option groups) that are included with a car that interests you. Would you be paying extra for a lot of items that you don't really need, or want?

Corporate cousins

In the past, domestic automakers in particular had long lists of nearly-identical models issued by their various divisions. Mercury's Sable, for instance, was a close clone of the Ford Taurus. General Motors had the Chevrolet Cavalier and similar Pontiac Sunfire. Dodge and Plymouth models used to be nearly identical, such as the Dodge Omni and Plymouth Horizon.

During Used Car Week in November 2013, Eric Lyman, vice-president of editorial at ALG, compared two vehicles that are no longer produced, but were practically identical when offered for sale back in 1998-2002: the Honda Passport and Isuzu Rodeo. Study of transaction prices demonstrated that people were willing to pay 12.5 percent more for a Passport. Then, the average Passport sold wholesale at an auction for 20 percent more than a nearly-equal Rodeo. The reason was "confidence in the Honda brand," Lyman explained, even though the two were virtually identical.

Lyman's other example involved domestic trucks. Asked why they bought a GMC truck over a virtually-identical Chevrolet, "people even thought the steel was thicker" on the GMC unit.

Cousins aren't nearly as much of an issue anymore, especially after GM dropped its Pontiac brand and Ford abandoned the Mercury. But on the older used-car market, some of those nearly-identical models are still around. So, here's a list of common examples from a few years back:

Chevrolet Cobalt – Pontiac G5– Saturn Ion
Chevrolet Aveo – Pontiac G3
Chevrolet Cruze – Buick Verano
Chevrolet Equinox – GMC Terrain
Chevrolet Tahoe – GMC Yukon – Cadillac Escalade
Chevrolet Traverse – GMC Acadia
Chrysler 200 – Dodge Avenger
Chrysler 300 – Dodge Charger
Chrysler Town & Country – Dodge Grand Caravan
Ford Taurus – Mercury Sable
Ford Crown Victoria – Mercury Grand Marquis
Hyundai Accent – Kia Riio

Hyundai Tucson – Kia Sportage
Toyota Matrix – Pontiac Vibe

Note that some of the more recent "twins" aren't as identical as related models were in the past. Powertrains and basic body structure might be near-duplicates, but other differences could be considerable.

7

Looking for Luxury

Should you pay the price and sign up for a BMW, Mercedes-Benz, Audi, or other all-out luxury machine? What about shelling out a bundle of bucks for a high-end luxury sport model, such as a Maserati or Aston Martin?

Naturally, you'd get more amenities, at less cost than on a new car. Typically, a *lot* less. Some additional safety features might be included, true. But mainly, opting for the more posh motorcar is a matter of comfort and convenience.

Even low-budget new cars nowadays have a full complement of airbags, electronic stability control, and the possibility of, say, a rearview backup camera. No longer is it necessary to move way up the price scale, to Mercedes-Benz or BMW territory, in order to acquire such equipment. Or, to get a satisfactory set of safety features.

On the electronic entertainment front, it's another story. Move far enough into the luxury league, and your preferred automobile is likely to have top-end stereo with all the audio extras, power operation of nearly everything, and a full complement of connectivity features to help keep you in touch.

Sure, many of those extras can be found in midrange models; but they likely raised the price of those cars to levels that edge toward the luxury category. Or near-luxury, at least.

Luxury motoring is the choice for those who wish to be pampered and coddled while on the road, as if luxuriating in your easy chair at home, with sound quality rivaling that of many high-end residential systems. Luxury buyers can expect multi-position power seats, power lumbar support, pushbutton headrest adjustment, a full panoramic sunroof, and on and on.

Figured on a dollar rather than percentage basis, luxury cars typically decline markedly more in value than similar vehicles that cost less when new. Ricky Beggs, editorial director of *Black Book*, noted early in 2014 that luxury cars had been declining by an average of 14.5 percent, which was well above the figure for most mainstream models.

On the other hand, a lot of high-end motorcars are well known for holding their value well.

At age two or three, too, a big chunk of its depreciation has already taken place, absorbed by the car's first owner. Or, as is often the case in luxury levels, the person who *leased* it initially. Well-off folks generally lean toward leasing their luxury automobiles, rather than tie up appreciable amounts of cash in a vehicle that is inevitably a declining-value asset.

Rather than shell out the big bucks for one of the luxury editions, consider the possibility that an alternative make or model might offer nearly everything you desire, for a far smaller price. The primary question remains: Exactly what am I getting for those extra thousands of dollars, and how much do I really want those additional amenities?

8

Condition is Critical

No other factor is more important – or harder to assess – than a used vehicle's condition. Even the most thoroughly experienced experts know they can never be 100-percent certain.

Dealers, at least, have access to more information than in the past about vehicles they purchase for resale. Detailed condition reports, prepared at or for wholesale auction houses, can now give dealers accurate information about a given car's content and condition. Because that information is available, at least some of it might be passed along to the retail buyer, too. Detailed, uniform inspections and the condition reports that result can benefit everyone.

Otherwise, despite the vast amount of information available online, tangible facts about a car's condition and likely dependability is largely beyond the reach of shoppers. Vehicle History Reports, while invaluable, are limited in the amount and type of information they provide about an individual automobile. Yes, you can find out about a car's accident history (but not about accidents that were unreported to the police or an official agency). Maintenance records may (or may not) be available. Recall details for that model can easily be consulted. Data about owner experiences with that particular model can be found. But overall condition? That's where the used-car shopper is still taking a chance.

Logically enough, condition is even more crucial for older vehicles. Without question, cars have been getting older, too. Especially during the height of the 2008-09 "recession," owners started to hang onto their old vehicles longer, rather than spring for a new (or newer) model.

Trouble spots in specific models

Not only is it nearly impossible to gather information on the condition of an individual car, it's not that simple to find data about problem areas that affect certain makes and models. Consumerguide.com's used-car reviews have always included information on specific trouble spots that plagued certain car models. During 2013, however, the used-car portion of Consumer Guide's website was abandoned. As of summer 2014, it remains offline, though the company had posted a notice stating that used-car material might re-emerge at some point.

Unfortunately, not many other sources of information on specific trouble spots is available. Such information sources as Kelley Blue Book, NADA Used Car Guides, and cars.com offer plenty of helpful details, but little on likely defects in general, and nothing that pertains to any individual vehicle.

Even if available, and deemed reliable, such information applies only to a certain car model, not to a specific example of that model. No one can ever predict what will happen to a given vehicle; but awareness of potential weak spots (if any) can be helpful. Because vehicle quality has improved so much in recent years, it's fair to assume that the number of potential trouble spots, at least in late-model vehicles, isn't as great as in the past.

For many years, *Consumer Reports* has gathered responses from its readers regarding their vehicle experiences, to derive similar information in a different way. If a lot of respondents report trouble with a given model's automatic transmission, advise about unusual engine noises, or complain about performance, those figures are worth noting. Remember, though, that people are generally more likely to report on negative experiences than on positive ones; so statistics on problem areas cannot be assumed to reflect the entire population.

Consumer action groups often have information about problems that have been suspiciously common on specific models. Online forums about certain car models can suggest possible trouble spots; but in this instance, some participants may be biased in either direction. Fans of a particular model might report only favorable experiences. Others might enjoy "dissing" a certain model, for reasons of their own rather than truly based on actual occurrences of trouble. Like all customer reviews and evaluations, reports on trouble spots need to be considered with a grain of suspicion, rather than relied upon in full.

Importance of a Vehicle History Report

Availability of a history report is one of the main reasons why buying a used car isn't as risky as it used to be. These reports, which gather data from a variety of sources, provide details on a given vehicle's title history, reported accidents and damage, and whether it's been a personally-used vehicle (perhaps a one-owner). You can also learn when the car was purchased new, where it was owned, and the last reported odometer reading.

Many dealers post Carfax reports for some, if not all, of their vehicles – right on their web sites. Others may want you to pay to see the report, or first indicate that you're a serious potential buyer. With so many Carfax-connected online ads out there, you may as well concentrate on those cars that have one ready for viewing.

If nothing else, history reports let you weed out the undesirables early on. Shoppers spend an average of 11 hours searching for a used-car online, said senior process improvement manager Robert Grill during a 2014 Carfax webinar, "only to discover much of this time is wasted on a vehicle with the wrong history."

Grill further advised that 92 percent of used-car shoppers go online before buying. Though 60 percent of shoppers say they feel intimidated by the process, that figure used to be a lot worse: 90 to 95 percent claiming intimidation. Claiming 67 million carfax.com visitors, Grill suggested that 87 percent of used-car shoppers "know and trust" Carfax.

Among other useful facts, they can find out about accident history of a particular vehicle, its service and maintenance, number and type of owners; and where it's located. Not all of this information is available for every vehicle, however.

Shoppers can find cars listed for sale at the Carfax site, but no advertising is permitted. Shoppers interested in a particular vehicle are directed to that dealer's web site. Searchers can specify certain requirements, such as cars that have a Carfax history, that are one-owner, that were for personal use only, that include service records, or that had no accidents reported. Listings also show the odometer mileage and asking price.

Carfax is the best known, partly due to its often-heard advertising theme: "Show me the Carfax." However, other companies also offer similar history reports, including AutoCheck and Carproof.

Specific information on a Carfax report typically includes:
- Accident history (if any)
- Whether car has been personally-owned, rather than fleet-owned
- If it's a one-owner car
- Mileage on odometer (which may or may not be current)
- Maintenance and service records

Vehicle history reports are an integral part of the transparency world, said Cary Donovan, of the Sam Swope Auto Group, during Used Car Week in November 2013. They're just as important to dealers buying at wholesale, as they are to retail customers on the showroom floor.

If a history report isn't supplied automatically, ask for it. "We announce if a car has a clean Carfax," said Kirk Bechtel, from Mercedes-Benz Financial Services. If not, if a trouble spot or two has been revealed, the Carfax is not brought up unless the customer asks about it. Bechtel suggested that buyers will probably want a significant discount for a vehicle with a "bad" Carfax. Retail customers who are aware of a car's accident history are not going to be eager to pay anywhere near as much as they might for a less-flawed example of the same make and model.

Not every bit of information is available for every car. Reporting procedures on accidents vary by state, for instance, and not every state provides full information. Carfax explains that they're constantly striving to acquire even more information for their History Reports. If you come across one that appears to be incomplete, you always have the simple option of skipping that vehicle and moving on to another possibility instead.

Look for low-mileage

Mileage is another vital matter, even though modern automobiles can travel a lot more miles without mechanical troubles. Improved vehicle quality over the past decade means that even 100,000-mile-plus vehicles may warrant greater consideration.

Average vehicle mileage has been going up, though drivers are currently revealing a tendency to drive less. In 2013, the average car sold had traveled around 53,000 miles. Those that have gone through wholesale auctions typically have higher figures on their odometers.

In fact, every vehicle market class has shown higher average mileage in recent years. Mileage growth has been especially high for pickup trucks, vans, and SUVs.

So, how low should it be to qualify as low-mileage? The rule of thumb used to be about 12,000 miles per year, on average. In recent years, the average car has been driven more than 13,000 miles annually. So, just multiply that amount by the age of the vehicle, in years, to get the average. If the odometer you're checking shows a figure significantly lower, it's a low-mileage vehicle – assuming that the odometer reading is correct, that is.

Fraudulent figures

Odometer rollbacks, though illegal for decades, used to be common – especially on cars sold by questionable independent dealers. We recall a fellow for whom we worked long ago, who would buy a new car every two years. By that time, having been used daily for hard business driving, the car would have around 160,000 miles on it. After it was traded in for a new one, the dealer would arrange to turn back the odometer to 40,000 miles or so, claiming to prospective purchasers on his used-car lot that this was the actual mileage.

One automotive media person recalls watching the nefarious activities at a used-car dealership back in the Sixties or so, when a specialist was at work. Nothing would be seen of this fellow except for his feet, dangling out the car door as he tinkered with the odometer of one vehicle after another, transforming well-worn haulers into low-mileage beauties with a few twists of one of his tiny tools.

In 1986, the federal government took action to curtail this illicit activity, enacting the Truth in Mileage Act. Since then, secondhand vehicles have had to display a window label stating the correct mileage.

Rollbacks still happen, but not nearly as much – though a bit of a resurgence has been reported lately. In addition to severe legal penalties for such illicit behavior, modern electronic odometers aren't as easy to manipulate as their mechanical predecessors. Unfortunately, it's also more difficult to tell if an odometer has been subjected to tampering. Years ago, shoppers were warned to be alert for misaligned digits on the odometer, but no such evidence can be found on a digital mileage display.

Better yet, vehicle history reports can help you weed out cars whose mileage looks suspicious. If a vehicle was reported to have 60,000 miles on the odometer two years ago, but the gauge now shows 45,000, it's obviously either been rolled back, or it passed the hundred-thousand mark and reached 145,000. Either way, that sounds like a car to avoid. Carfax advises that the typical tinkered-with odometer has been rolled back by a whopping 50,000 miles.

9

Fuel Economy

Gas guzzlers can still be found on used-car lots, though in far fewer numbers than in the past. Thankfully, the era of cars that get 10 or 12 miles per gallon is long since over – though at least a handful of comparatively modern luxury cars and SUVs don't score all that much better. Even some ordinary-looking sedans don't get quite as thrifty mileage estimates as you might imagine. All the more so, if they contain an optional higher-power engine.

Plenty of publications and organizations that test-drive and review cars include data on gas mileage, presumably derived during their time on the road with that vehicle. A handful, such as TV's *MotorWeek*, strive to take their test vehicles around the same course, at similar speeds and under similar conditions. *Consumer Reports* is among the most meticulous of all, using a closed course for road tests. When figures are given by other publications, they should be considered only approximations, unless details of exactly how each car is driven are supplied.

Not that there's anything wrong with approximations, as long as they're derived during ordinary driving and not when seeking to eke out the highest possible fuel economy. Or, conversely, when driving overly aggressively, or in demanding conditions that may adversely affect gas mileage.

All those real-world test-drives have their place, but the U.S. Environmental Protection Agency is the only source of *complete* comparison data on fuel economy. Their figures are based on simulations rather than real-world driving. For years, critics charged that EPA estimates were overly optimistic, compared to real-world mileage figures; but they've become a lot more accurate in recent times. Even so, its numbers may be higher than you're likely to achieve in regular driving.

In addition to the fuel-economy estimates, the EPA's web site encourages car owners to report their actual fuel-economy figures in ordinary driving, as a comparison; but like customer reviews of any sort, the reliability of such reported figures is questionable. Not everyone knows how to assess and calculate miles-per-gallon accurately.

In 2013, the EPA began to offer simulated window labels for any car going back to 1984, taking the mileage estimates from its own database. Dealers or shoppers can obtain one for any model by going to the web site: www.fuel economy.gov. Look for the Used Car Label Tool.

Three estimated figures in miles-per-gallon are issued by the EPA: one for city driving, a second (nearly always higher) for highway operation, and a combined figure that covers a blend of city/highway use. Estimates vary by engine and transmission within each model. Body style and other differences may also have an impact. See www.fueleconomy.gov for complete data.

Traditionally, a car with an automatic transmission has consumed more fuel than the identical model with manual shift. That's often still the case, but not always. Automatics with six, seven, eight, and even nine speeds have emerged in recent years, typically more thrifty than the previous transmission, which had fewer gears. As a result, some automatic-transmission vehicles earn higher fuel-economy estimates than their stick-shift cousins.

Nearly always, too, the estimate for city driving is a lot lower than for highway use. One big exception to that rule involves hybrids, which run on a blend of gasoline and electric power. Most hybrid-powertrain vehicles achieve greater economy in urban driving than on the highway. Why? Because driving on city streets takes greater advantage of the fact that the gasoline engine usually shuts itself off at stoplights, thus consuming no fuel at all while the light is red.

Toyota's popular Prius, for instance, gets an EPA estimate of 51 miles per gallon in city driving and 48 mpg on the highway. The Ford Fusion Hybrid gets a 44/41-mpg estimate.

In contrast, a Toyota Camry with a regular gas engine and automatic earns a 25-mpg city/35-mpg highway estimate from the EPA, while a similarly-equipped gas-engine Ford Fusion gets a 22/34-

mpg estimate. Toyota's Camry Hybrid is estimated at 43 mpg in city driving and 39 mpg on the highway.

Some recent models have a start-stop feature incorporated into the transmission, which also shuts the engine off when stopped, yielding improved city mileage.

Plenty of additional information is available on the EPA's website (fueleconomy.gov), including:

- Access to all EPA mile-per-gallon estimates
- Mileage results submitted by ordinary drivers
- Gas mileage tips, and a Cost Calculator
- How to find the cheapest gasoline
- Fuel-saving calculators
- Best and Worst fuel-economy comparisons

Note, too, whether the car requires premium-grade (or mid-grade) gasoline rather than regular. As a percentage of total per-gallon cost, the difference isn't as great as it used to be, when gasoline cost a lot less. Still, a 20- or 30-cent difference for each gallon does add up. Quite a few automakers recommend premium fuel "for improved performance," but specify that regular will suffice. Sometimes, the difference is noticeable in acceleration; but often, not so much.

Several auto companies – notably Chrysler – have recommended mid-grade (89-octane) gasoline for certain engines. Here too, it may be recommended for best performance, but not necessarily mandatory.

How about a hybrid?

Is a hybrid right for you? Or even a pure electric car?

Not until the past few years have appreciable numbers of hybrid-powertrain vehicles reached the used-car market. Because of their long warranties on the battery pack and related powertrain components when sold as new, late-model hybrids should have many useful miles left. People used to worry about battery life in hybrids, but there's been little evidence that gasoline/electric cars are any more troublesome than those with conventional gasoline (or diesel) engines.

On the other hand, you might want to be more wary of an older hybrid, as those become available on the used-car market. Nothing lasts forever, and you don't want to have to pay for a whole new battery pack at some point. Otherwise, hybrids can be judged like any other automobile.

As of mid-2014, some three dozen hybrid models are available new. Also on sale are half a dozen plug-in hybrids, which can be plugged into an electrical outlet periodically to boost likely gas mileage further yet. Even more hybrids might be found on the used-car market, as several models have been dropped by their manufacturers in the past few years, including Ford's Escape Hybrid.

Details on several popular Hybrids that might be found at used-car dealerships are listed in Part VI, including average valuations and driving impressions.

Clearly, fuel economy is the biggest advantage of Hybrids. Fuel-economy estimates of some luxury hybrids don't differ all that much from their conventional counterparts; but for most models that are available either in regular or hybrid form, the difference is appreciable, as this comparison of 2012-model city/highway mpg estimates reveals:

Ford Fusion:
Gas engine – up to 23/33 mpg
Hybrid – 41/36 mpg

Kia Optima or Hyundai Sonata:
Gas engine – 24/35 mpg
Hybrid – 34/39 mpg

Electrics and CNG

Because electric cars in significant numbers didn't reach dealerships until late 2010, few are likely to turn up on used-car lots anytime soon. Best to let the original owners rack up some serious miles and a repair/maintenance history before considering a secondhand battery-powered car.

On the other hand, thus far, modern-day electrics have turned out to be rather notorious in terms of depreciating rapidly. Retained value (what it's worth after two years, say) of the Nissan Leaf has hovered around 35 percent of the original price, which is near the bottom of cars in general. That means you may be able to pick up a used electric car for a surprisingly low figure, compared to what they cost new.

Shoppers who like to "go green" have another option, but it's one that's rarely found on used-car lots. Since 1998, Honda has been selling a compressed natural gas (CNG) version of its Civic compact, but only on the West Coast. Only a few thousand have reached customers, so the number available secondhand has to be minuscule. Natural-gas vehicles have been around for a long time, though; some pickup trucks with CNG powertrains might be found here and there on used-car lots.

Data on Diesels

Though diesel-powered cars and trucks have gained favor in recent years, only a handful of manufacturers have been offering them in the U.S. market. In Europe and elsewhere in the world, diesels are a major part of the vehicle supply. Popularity in America has been a long time coming, due in part to problems with some American-made diesel engines – notably from General Motors – more than three decades ago.

In recent years, German manufacturers – luxury models like Audi, BMW, and Mercedes-Benz, but also Volkswagen – have led the diesel pack by far. Each of those automakers offers a selection of diesel models, equivalent to the gasoline-engine version in all but the engine. Other auto companies have made vague promises to start bringing their diesel-engine models, so popular in other countries, to the U.S. market as well. It's been a slow process, but finally a few are beginning to turn up, including the Chevrolet Cruze Diesel that debuted for the 2014 model year.

Shoppers used to scoff at diesels, claiming they were noisy and smelly. That's no longer true, and hasn't been for some years. You have to listen hard to hear the telltale "knock" of a diesel engine, and sniff intently to discern any odor. If you see any black smoke out the exhaust, it's almost sure to be barely existent. Diesels also tend to perform surprisingly well, due largely to the fact that they produce relatively large amounts of low-end torque, which translates to strong acceleration at lower speeds. Behind the wheel of most modern models, it's difficult to determine if that's actually a diesel engine beneath the hood.

As with hybrids, the big draw of a diesel is its fuel economy. Typical examples are shown below, compared to their gasoline-engine counterparts.

Volkswagen Jetta (automatic):
Gas engine (2.5-liter) – 24/31 mpg
Gas engine (turbo) – 23/29 mpg
Diesel – 30/42 mpg

Chevrolet Cruze:
Gas engine – 22/35 mpg
Diesel – 27/46 mpg

Unfortunately, only a few manufacturers have offered diesel engines to U.S. buyers, and most of those are premium German brands (Audi, BMW, Mercedes-Benz). Volkswagen is clearly the leader among more mainstream makes. Diesel fuel varies in price, but lately hasn't differed too much from gasoline in most areas.

10

Safety

Obviously, safety is as important on a used car as a new one. Probably more so, because the older car, logically enough, is more likely to experience some sort of failure eventually. Also, earlier models didn't have as many safety features installed on them, so it's even more vital that the ones which do exist operate properly.

Two kinds of safety devices are installed in automobiles: active and passive. Active systems require some sort of action by the driver before they come into play. In general, they help *avoid* an accident, by affecting steering or brakes.

Passive units become effective on their own, requiring no action on the driver's part. Rather than necessarily preventing an accident, they help minimize the effects of a collision when it does occur. Seatbelts and airbags are the most notable examples.

Antilock braking (ABS) has been standard on nearly all models for a number of years, but a few old non-ABS vehicles are still around on the used-car market. That wasn't true back in the 1990s, when ABS was an option at the lower end of the price scale, or not available at all on some budget-priced small cars. More recently, even the least-expensive cars have been equipped with antilock braking.

ABS helps prevent the wheels from locking up in a panic stop, especially on slippery pavement. With ABS, you're more likely to be able to steer around an obstacle in your path. We'd steer clear of non-ABS vehicles, especially in snowbelt states.

How does ABS work? By applying and releasing the braking pressure to each wheel, far more rapidly than a human foot could "pump" the brake pedal. Even more important, ABS can apply a different amount of braking pressure to each wheel, whereas ordinary brakes spread the force equally. When the greatest amount of force goes to the wheel that needs it most, the car is almost sure to halt more rapidly, especially on a slick surface, without skidding to the side. Drive an older car without ABS on an icy road, and you're sure to be convinced of its merits in a hurry.

Brake assist: Standard on recent models, this system helps the car stop faster in an emergency. When it detects that the driver is pushing harder than usual on the brake pedal, brake assist intensifies that action further yet. The system's computer might also accumulate data on the driver's habits, to provide more effective braking in an emergency.

Airbags: An airbag "war" had been taking place over the past few years, though it finally appears to have quieted down. Even some modestly-priced models of recent vintage contain six or more of them. At present, it looks like ten is the logical limit. Earlier cars have fewer airbags, as a rule, and that number might be sufficient.

Airbags are designed to inflate almost instantly during a collision. Because earlier airbags were shown to present risks of injury and even death when they deployed, modern airbags are less intense and designed to operate in stages.

Side-impact and side-curtain airbags came along in the 1990s, and are common among 21st-century vehicles. Side-impact airbags may be mounted in the seat or the door. Side-curtain airbags inflate and drop down from the roof, to protect occupant heads. Rollover-sensing airbags do just what their name suggests: detect the beginning of a rollover, and deploy to minimize harm to uccupants.

Recent models might also have a driver's knee airbag. General Motors has introduced a center-mounted airbag.

So, how many airbags do you and your family need to feel sufficiently safe? That's a personal decision, but in recent years most airbags have been standard rather than optional, so there's probably nothing to decide when shopping for a particular secondhand vehicle. The exception is rear-seat airbags, which have been optional on some luxury models, in particular.

Handling enhancements and safety assistants

Performance-oriented cars, in particular, are likely to be equipped with additional computerized helpers, intended to keep the vehicle stable and under control even during harder driving. Some were standard on a given model; others offered as options. Even using larger tires than standard for a given model may constitute a handling enhancement.

- **Electronic stability control** (ESC) is now installed on nearly all new automobiles, and soon will be mandatory on every one sold. On older models, it might have been unavailable or offered only as an option. Stability control makes use of computers to help maintain control during extreme steering maneuvers. When activated, it helps keep the car going in the intended direction, even if traction is dwindling.

- **Pre-collision systems:** Collision warning systems alert the driver of a likely impending collision, by detecting the changing relative position of the vehicle ahead. The system may also take action to impede or mitigate damage, if that collision does occur.

- **Lane Departure Monitor and Warning:** These systems monitor the lane markings on the highway being traveled, warning the driver of unintended edging toward, or abrupt movement into, an adjacent lane.

- **Lane Keeping Assist:** This is the next step beyond a lane departure warning, taking action itself to try and get the deviating car back on course.

- **Blind-spot Monitor:** Some drivers complain that blind-spot warnings are overzealous, signaling the presence of a vehicle in the car's "blind spot," invisible to the mirrors, even when no cars are nearby. It's true that some monitors are more likely to provide false warnings, but that's a lot better than failing to provide any warning at all of a car that's dangerously close on either side, yet unseen by the driver.

- **Adaptive Cruise Control:** Rather than simply maintain a pre-selected speed, adaptive systems detect the speed and movement of the car ahead, slowing your car down accordingly when it starts getting too close.

Safety Recalls

The National Highway Traffic Safety Administration (NHTSA) recalls hundreds of vehicles each year because of safety defects that have been discovered. Some recalls are initiated voluntarily by the manufacturer, or they can be ordered by NHTSA. Not all recalls are of equal seriousness by any means, but it's important to know if:

1. The vehicle you're considering has been recalled.
2. How serious those recalls were.
3. Whether this particular example has had all of its recalls remedied.

Recalls thundered into national attention early in 2014, when General Motors was charged with neglecting to order replacement of faulty ignition switches on the Chevrolet Cobalt and related Pontiac G5, despite having been aware of the problem long before those models went on sale in 2004. Investigators alleged that if any additional object was suspended on a chain that held the ignition key, the switch might fail at some point, causing the engine to shut off abruptly and the airbags to fail to deploy in an accident.

Having emerged from bankruptcy into profitability, GM was suddenly facing a public-relations nightmare, especially when it was alleged that the repair would have cost 57 cents per car. Thirteen deaths were attributed to the flawed ignition switches. As of this writing, in summer 2014, the case is far from settled, and GM faces a slew of lawsuits related to the finally-recalled vehicles.

Check www.safercar.gov to find out if a model you're considering has been recalled, and the reason for that action. A dealer for the make you're considering might be able to check the Vehicle Identification Number (VIN) and tell you if any open recalls still exist.

In August 2014, it suddenly became a lot easier to determine whether a specific vehicle has unrepaired recalls pending. Safercar.gov now contains a Search feature that lets you enter the VIN of a vehicle you'd like to buy, and find out immediately if all of its recalls have been addressed.

A surprising number of car owners neglect to have recalls corrected, even though all such repairs are free and must be performed by a dealer for that make. NHTSA estimates that only three-fourths of owners of vehicles subject to safety recalls get the work done, even though it's free. That leaves at least 25 percent of recalled vehicles unrepaired, totaling some 36 million cars, according to Carfax. Owners of older cars are even *less* likely to have them fixed.

Owners are supposed to be notified when a recall takes place, but not everyone receives such a notice – or understands its significance, if they do get one in the mail. Naturally, the buyer of a secondhand car that's been subject to one or more recalls isn't likely to ever see a notice of any kind.

To file a safety complaint, obtain publications, or inquire about up-to-date data that supplements the information at www.safercar.org, you could call the NHTSA Vehicle Safety Hotline toll-free: 1-800-424-9393 (366-0123 in Washington, DC). Hearing-impaired people may call 1-800-424-9153 (366-7800 in Washington, DC).

How do you find out if a particular vehicle has had its recall problems corrected? NHTSA does not provide such information, so you must contact the vehicle manufacturer or a dealer in that make. Be prepared to give the car's Vehicle Identification Number (VIN). That's the combination of numbers and letters embossed on a small, rectangular metal plate visible through the lower left corner of the windshield. The manufacturer's office might also be able to provide information on voluntary recalls or any service work that a dealer is required to perform without charge, and on service bulletins available to consumers.

Crash-test results

Every car sold new has to pass a U.S. Government crash test. Eventually, most models (except for some that are sold in limited number) also get a second crash test, which results in a star rating (score). Until 2011, ratings of 1 to 5 stars were given in four categories: frontal-impact (driver's side); frontal-impact (passenger side); side-impact (left) and side-impact (right).

Manufacturers strived for 5-star scores in each category. Because their scores had been improving so much, too many vehicle models were winding up with 5/5/5/5-star ratings, impairing the value of the rating system. Critics alleged that automakers were designing vehicles with the government crash test in mind, making revisions mainly (or solely) to achieve a higher score. As a result, NHTSA tightened the crash-test procedure, so fewer tested vehicles would get those top ratings.

In 2011, NHTSA modified its crash-test program, substituting more sophisticated dummies and adding a new side-pole test. Starting with 2011 models, the government crash test program provides three ratings of 1 to 5 stars (Frontal Crash, Side Crash, and an Overall rating). A Rollover rating also is provided.

Crash-testing includes:
- **Frontal crash** at 35 mph, into a solid barrier, with dummies belted.
- **Side Barrier collision** uses a 3,015-pound object, moving at 38.5 mph toward a standing vehicle, to simulate an intersection-type accident.
- **Side Pole collision** places the test vehicle (with a female crash-test dummy in the driver's seat) at a 75-degree angle; it's then pulled sideways, at 20 mph, into a pole.

In addition to the government-ordered crash tests, the Insurance Institute for Highway Safety (backed by the insurance industry) conducts its own testing, using different methods. IIHS testing includes five levels of crashworthiness:
- **Frontal Crash** with moderate overlap
- **Frontal Crash** with small overlap
- **Side Collision**
- **Roof Strength** test to assess rollover protection
- **Seats/Head Restraints** evaluation

Results of IIHS crash tests may be found at www.iihs.org. Ratings are specified as Good, Acceptable, Marginal, or Poor. Each year, IIHS awards a number of vehicles its Top Safety Pick status.

Look for both vehicle recalls and crash-test ratings at www.safercar.gov. A Search function lets you find recalls by entering the vehicle's year, make, and model. NHTSA considers availability of electronic stability control, collision warning, and lane departure warning systems when assessing the overall safety level of a vehicle.

Part III

Test Drive

11

Questions To Ask About the Car

Asking questions early in the sales process not only gives you information about a car that's tempting, but lets you rule out "bad apples" without wasting too much time and effort. Distinct questions need to be asked at each step.

Over the phone, before seeing the car

May as well save yourself the time and bother of making a trip to see a potential purchase, if it can be ruled out over the phone with a few probing questions.

- Do you own the car, or are you selling it for someone else (for private seller)?
- Asking price. You can also ask if it's negotiable or "firm."
- Is it properly titled? In what state, and in whose name? If the seller isn't the car's owner, a proper explanation is needed before even considering a purchase.
- What is the exact model (including year and trim level)?
- Are there any problems with the car? Have there been?
- Why are you selling it?

Don't expect a totally honest and complete answer to the last two questions, in particular. Just pay attention to how it's answered – hesitantly, emphatically, warily, etc.

From the previous owner (if possible)

A used car's former owner can be an invaluable source of information – provided that a dealer agrees to furnish that person's name and phone number. Some will balk; others will do it without even being asked. Check the glovebox for an owner's name on a service schedule, or other documentation that could have the prior owner's name on it.

If you can reach the prior owner, be brief but to the point. You might want to ask:
- How long did you own the car? If the person was the owner for a brief time, ask why he/she sold the car so quickly.
- When did you buy the car? The dealer's stated date should match the date on the title.
- Why did you sell it? The seller might have found a problem with the vehicle and was trying to unload it on someone else.
- Has it been in an accident? Cars that were in major accidents sometimes never "feel" right again, but lesser damage might have been properly repaired.
- Has the body been repaired or repainted? Is the car the same color as when the owner sold it? Maybe the dealer painted it quickly and cheaply to hide some flaws.
- Has it ever had any rust? Once a vehicle starts to rust seriously, almost nothing can be done short of costly body work. Fortunately, recent vehicles are far less prone to rusting than in the more distant past.
- How many miles were on it when you sold it? If there's a big difference from what the odometer shows, maybe the dealer has been using the vehicle for errands or driving it home at night. Service of this type can be especially hard on a vehicle, if it's treated with little respect. Extra miles might even suggest that the vehicle was resold and then returned by a dissatisfied buyer.
- Where was it driven, for the most part? City or highway? Several thousand highway miles can be equivalent to only a few hundred city miles. Highway miles tend to be kinder to a vehicle's moving parts.
- Has the car had regular maintenance? Where?

You don't want to be overly pushy or inquisitive, but all of this information is valuable. It will give you insight into the car's past, and help to determine if the dealer or salesperson is being straight with you.

During the inspection and test drive

- Where did the car come from (for dealer)? From the original owner as a trade-in? From a wholesale auction? Bought outright from the previous owner, for resale?
- Can I see a Carfax report (or similar vehicle history report)?
- What do you know about the car's past?
- Is it possible to speak to the prior owner? (if buying from a dealer)
- If you see any body damage or notice other flaws, ask about them.

If anything feels odd while driving the car, ask about that. Regardless of the answer, be prepared to walk away if you don't think you'll be happy with it.

During the negotiation

- What additional costs (fees, taxes, license, etc.) are involved, beyond the purchase price?
- If you're trading in your old car, exactly how much will you be getting for it? Don't let a salesperson mix the selling price of the "new" car with the offer for your trade-in.
- It's a typical practice to offer a figure below the asking price. That's expected. Making that offer too low, however, can be seen as insulting – especially to a private owner. Better to be realistic, leaving room to negotiate but not setting the stage for a battle.
- If the salesperson will not drop the price any further, it pays to ask if the dealership could offer any non-cash incentive to buy. Special financing? An accessory or two? Maybe even including a service contract.
- You can attempt to negotiate both the full price and the payment details, but don't expect much flexibility on the latter. Dealers ordinarily are limited by the rules of the lenders with whom they join forces.

Immediately after the sale

- Does anything else need to be done to conclude the sale?
- Who takes care of license plates, registration, insurance, and financing arrangements?
- Is there anything left to deal with after you've driven the car away?
- Whom do you contact with any questions that come up later?
- What form must the initial payment, made at purchase time, take? Cashier's check? Regular check? Some other way to pay?

Make sure you have all the relevant documents, and that you know the details of the warranty (if any), including what to do if a problem occurs.

12

Visual Inspection

So you've found a car you like, which looks good, at a price that's tempting. Before deciding to buy, you need to inspect it thoroughly, inside and out. Then comes the crucial Test Drive, to determine whether you'll be satisfied with the car's driving qualities, and if you and your family will be pleased to ride in it.

Even in this age of transparency and abundant information, used cars are always a gamble. An unpleasant surprise soon after a purchase is always possible. It sometimes happens to dealers, too, with cars that they're purchasing for resale – whether from a wholesale auction or a private seller.

Following these eight simple suggestions could at least help tip the odds in your favor:

1. Inspect the vehicle in daylight. Artificial lights (and rainy days) can hide too many defects in body metal. Faded paint can look glossy when wet, too, and raindrops might hide scratches or small dents. Sometimes, too, engines actually run a bit better on rainy days, because wet air is denser.

2. Allow enough time to make a thorough inspection, and then to take a comprehensive test drive. This is not a time to rush.

3. Bring a friend or relative along, in addition to your family. A third party might notice problems or trouble spots that escape your attention. Ask that friend to ride in the back seat during the test drive. Some sounds are better heard from back there.

4. Concentrate. Take your time. It's a good idea to take a few notes, so you don't have to rely on memory later on, when a final decision is being made. Ask plenty of questions of the salesperson or private owner. Whenever possible, try to ask questions that lead the seller to tell you more about the past life of the vehicle. Bear in mind, though, that a salesperson at a dealership might not have much personal knowledge of a particular vehicle that's offered for sale, even if it came as a trade-in.

5. Dress for the occasion. You might want to poke around the engine compartment – even if you know little about what makes a car go. It might be necessary to get down on the ground, too, to inspect the underside. Bring a flashlight along. Take note of any parts that look a little too new, considering the car's age; they could be a sign of a recent repair.

6. Don't rule out a car because of minor problems that aren't difficult or costly to fix – or little flaws that you can live with. Concentrate on any big defects.

7. Be thorough, but discreet. Neither dealers, salespeople, nor private sellers appreciate shoppers who spend hours probing every little detail, and asking questions with an aggressive or disbelieving tone in their voice.

8. If you're acquainted with a local service technician (what used to be called mechanics), ask that person to give the car a thorough inspection before you buy. Paying a fee for a neutral opinion is prudent, especially if you have any doubts. The peace of mind that fee buys could be the most valuable money you spend on your used-car purchase.

Because we've tried to be comprehensive with these recommendations for Inspection and Test Drive, the process might seem overwhelming. Remember, you don't have to follow every single step exactly as it's spelled out. They're all suggestions, not absolute requirements. So, exercise some restraint. Inspect and consider as many elements as you can, but you don't have to turn the whole process into an ordeal.

Start with the body

First, check for visible body damage: dents, dings, scratches, rust spots. Look, too, for less-obvious evidence that the car may have been in an accident, or is deteriorating abnormally.

After inspecting close-up, stand some distance back, and sight down the sides of the car from both front and rear. Wavy or rippled metal, uneven contours, crooked moldings, and poorly fitted panels suggest that body repairs have been made. Or, that such work needs to be done, to put the car in tip-top visual shape.

Do you see any mismatched colors, uneven textures, or paint overspray? Knock on body panels to detect spots where body filler may have been used to repair rustouts or dents. Those areas will lack the solid, ringing sound that's heard when tapping on metal. If an area looks suspicious, you might even want to touch a small magnet to that spot; it won't normally stick to plastic filler.

Naturally, if the car you're inspecting has any fiberglass or plastic body panels, the tapping and magnet tricks won't help.

What you want to avoid is a car that's received a quickie touch-up, over a basically unsound structure. Car bodies are far more corrosion-resistant than they used to be, but hidden rust remains a potential trouble spot, especially in regions where salt is used on winter roads.

Corrosion usually attacks first on the most vulnerable lower portions of the body: rocker panels, lower fenders, door bottoms. Check carefully along the inside bottom seams of the doors. Bubbles along a molding suggest rust beneath – a phenomenon that used to be common, but is far less so today, with modern protective techniques applied at the factory.

Be suspicious of anything that appears too clean or shiny, incompatible with the car's overall condition. New paint on an older car might be acceptable, but a late model should have its original finish.

Examine door handles, trim, and weatherstrips for telltale signs of paint where it doesn't belong. Quickie resprays may have omitted door pillars or underhood areas. Closer inspection may even reveal a visible "line" between old and new paint. Ragged weatherstripping, on the other hand, suggests overall neglect by the previous owner.

Crooked bumpers could point to a bent frame – or simply a flawed bumper. Don't automatically assume the worst. But check for uneven alignment of doors, hood, and the trunk lid or hatch. Doors should open easily and close without slamming. Sagging or sticking may signal a car that's been in an accident or has gone plenty of miles. Squeaks from doors and other areas are less of a concern, though not always easy to remedy.

Locks should work without fuss. Windows should roll up and down smoothly, without jerkiness. All glass should be free from serious cracks or scratches. A few tiny pits, or slight windshield scratching from defective wiper blades, may be acceptable. However, any scratch that catches your fingernail is probably serious enough to prompt a windshield replacement, sooner or later.

A fabric convertible top should fit tightly and operate smoothly. Its plastic rear window should be flat and clear, not creased and cloudy. Check for rust on the metal framework. For convertibles with solid roofs (known as retractable hardtops), see that the roof mates properly with the windshield header. With either type of retractable top, make sure the mechanism operates smoothly.

Open the trunk. Are the spare tire and appropriate tools inside? Inspect for rust along seams and under the mat.

Above all, be thorough, but don't insist on perfection. You won't find it on any used car.

Getting technical

If you're satisfied with the body condition, turn to the mechanical and electrical details. In addition to evaluating the car's running condition, you want to make sure it's safe. Many states conduct vehicle safety inspections periodically. In addition, some states allow troopers to inspect cars at random. Even if local authorities conduct no such inspections, do you really want to drive an unsafe vehicle?

An old test asks you to step to each corner of the car, in turn. Push down on the fender once, to test the reaction of the shock absorbers. The car should bounce upward only once, then settle to its original position. No unusual squeaks or banging should be heard, either. Modern cars don't always respond like earlier ones, but this quick test might still give an idea of suspension issues.

Next, get down on your hands and knees for a moment. (Aren't you glad you wore old clothes for the inspection?) Study the car from several angles. Does the car sit level? One corner lower than the others might suggest a weak or failing spring, or some other serious chassis/suspension problem.

Take a look at each tire, inspecting as much of its circumference as possible. All tires should be in good condition, without sidewall cracks or other significant imperfections. Uneven wear often is caused by over- or under-inflated tires. But it could also be due to improper wheel alignment, or even a bent front-end component. If tires on a recent model aren't all the same brand and style, the car might have higher mileage than the odometer suggests. Ask the owner or salesperson before moving forward.

Do wheels look bent in any way? Is there evidence of scraping around the perimeter of any wheel? That could suggest careless driving by the previous owner. Are all lug nuts in position and, as far as you can tell without picking up a wrench, tightened properly? To inspect steel wheels, you may need to pull off a wheel cover. Nothing special has to be done to inspect alloy (aluminum) wheels. If the car has locking lug nuts, be sure you receive the key if you buy the car.

Examine the exhaust system next. Peek underneath, as best you can. Surface rust is normal; holes in the metal are not. Slapdash repairs to a muffler or exhaust pipe are good reason to reject the car, since they suggest that the owner could have been neglectful and careless in other ways, too. If a particular spot looks questionable, tap the muffler or pipe with a metal instrument. A clear, ringing sound signals metal that's in good shape. Among other reasons to pay attention to the exhaust system, most areas nowadays require an emissions test, and a flawed exhaust system will probably keep a car from passing.

If you're at a dealership and anything doesn't look right, consider asking if the car can be put on a hoist, so you can get a clear view of the underside. NEVER crawl under a car that's held up by a jack.

Pay attention to fluids

Look closely at the ground below the car, for evidence of leaks. If the car is on a hoist, inspect the vehicle structure, too. A small amount of clear water at the front of the car is probably a result of condensation in the cooling system, and perfectly normal. However, actual coolant could leak from the radiator or its connecting hoses. Fluids can seep out of an automatic transmission (though this is less likely to happen with modern, sealed automatics). Oil might ooze from various spots on the engine. Gasoline could drip from fuel connections, the fuel pump, or the gas tank itself.

Brake fluid may escape from the master cylinder under the hood, the lines (tubes) that carry fluid to each wheel, or the connections. Each fluid in a car has a distinctive odor and/or appearance. If you plan to have a third-party mechanic inspect the car, take note of any leaks and pass along that information to him or her.

Ask about anything dangling loosely under the car. If the car is front-wheel drive and up on a hoist, check the rubber boots that surround the CV joints. The outer ones (at the inside center of each front wheel) are most prone to tearing, which suggests that the CV joint underneath might be damaged.

Moderate surface rust on the frame is normal in most parts of the country, but exaggerated accumulations are bad signs. Weld marks are worse yet. They could mean the car is a "clip," made up from separate vehicles that were severely wrecked. Beware!

Next, open the hood. Does it open (and close) easily? Inspect for leaks, frayed wires, battery cleanliness, and wear or cracks on belts and hoses. Make sure the engine is shut off before touching anything!

Pull out the oil dipstick. Engine oil should look just slightly dirty. Too much dirt reveals a lack of oil changes by the prior owner. If it's gummy or gritty, foamy or grayish, the engine may have serious problems. Prospective buyers used to be advised to check automatic-transmission fluid and other substances. Nowadays, many components are sealed for life, with the fluids inside; so there's nothing to be inspected. Rubber hoses, on the other hand, ought to feel firm, not spongy.

Loose-feeling fans used to indicate worn water-pump bearings, too. But fans on recent models aren't attached directly to the engine, so that little test wouldn't reveal much.

WARNING: Whatever you do, keep your hands away from fans, belts, or any other moving parts on the engine.

Checking the air filter is still a good idea. Replacements are cheap, but a clean filter is a good sign of proper maintenance.

13

Out on the Road

Never buy a car without an extensive test-drive. No exceptions! Even if you're getting it at a giveaway price, at least a few minutes behind the wheel are highly recommended, just to see if you'll be comfortable.

Yes, it's true that a growing number of people these days are feeling comfortable buying new or used cars online, without driving them. But most of us need to get the "feel" of a car we're considering before making a valid decision. A comprehensive test-drive is invaluable, just as it was in the past.

Most dealers are willing to allow prospective purchasers to take a drive, either alone or accompanied by a salesperson. Avoid dealers or private sellers who balk at a proper test drive, or give you a hard time.

Plan to do more than take the car around the block. Being realistic, don't expect more than 15 or 20 minutes; but try to make those minutes count. Don't let the salesperson distract you from concentrating on how the car feels and behaves – preferably in a variety of conditions, on different terrain, if that's possible to achieve.

Do you need a professional evaluation? If you're paying an appreciable sum, and you're just not sure after your own test drive, it may be worth paying for expert help. Years back, people often had a personal mechanic whom they trusted, who could inspect a potential purchase. Today, with most independent mechanics extinct, it's not as easy to find someone to provide an unbiased inspection. In some areas, third-party inspection services are readily available; but not everywhere. Best to check online, to try and find one in your neighborhood.

Behind the wheel

Climb in and get comfortable. Test drives are best undertaken alone; or better yet, with a friend or relative along. Being realistic, though, many salespeople and private sellers won't be too enthused about letting you take a car out by yourself, and will insist on accompanying you. Just make sure they don't talk too much, as you need to concentrate.

First off, does the seat feel comfortable? Supportive? Do all of its adjustments, whether manual or powered, work properly? Overly-soft seats, incidentally, can actually be more fatiguing than firm ones.

Can you see each gauge on the instrument panel, and reach all controls? Are they clearly marked? How is visibility in every direction?

Interior condition gives a helpful inkling of how well a car has been maintained. Upholstery should be clean, with no serious rips, cracks or lumps – worn only to a point appropriate for the car's age and mileage.

Seatbelts should be in good shape. Rips, tears, frayed webbing, or flawed anchorages are dangerous.

Theft of airbags has been a serious problem in recent years, so make sure there's no evidence that the airbags in this car have been tampered with.

Look for evidence that the prior owner was a smoker. In addition to unpleasant smells, smoke can loosen a headliner, weaken seat stitching, or even harm sensitive electronic parts.

Peek under the mats or carpet (if possible). Wet carpeting could indicate water leakage, a heater core leak, or even flood damage.

Brake, accelerator, and clutch pedals should work smoothly, without strange noises or binding. The gearshift lever should move easily into each position.

All controls, knobs, and switches should be clearly marked. None should be missing. The dashboard should have no missing parts or dangling wires. Worn or recently-replaced pedal pads suggest high mileage; so do obvious signs of wear on the steering wheel, seats, or armrests.

Check lubrication stickers on the doorjamb or windshield to see that the mileage indicated rings true with the odometer reading.

Startup time

Before starting the engine, look for the owner's manual. In addition to operating instructions, it contains data on maintenance, fluid capacities, and replacement parts. If there's no manual, ask why it's absent.

Try to start your test-drive when the engine is cold. If the engine is warm when you arrive, the seller could have been running it to hide starting difficulties or other problems.

See that all gauges and warning lights go on with the ignition switch, then go off or show normal readings once the engine is running. The engine need not start instantly, but should fire within a couple of seconds. If an elaborate starting ritual is required, be suspicious. You shouldn't have to pump the gas madly to keep the engine from stalling, a ritual that was common in motoring's olden days.

Some rack-and-pinion power steering units are prone to failure. One sign of impending trouble: When the car is first started after sitting for a long period, the power unit may provide no assist, so the steering wheel is hard to turn. As the power-steering fluid heats up, the power assist eventually returns, but the problem gets worse and worse. More and more recent models have electric power steering, eliminating this concern.

Some automatic transmissions suffer similar symptoms just before they give out altogether – all the more reason to make sure any car you test drive has a cold engine.

As the engine warms up, listen for pings, rattles, knocks, grinds, vibrations, or squeals. Abnormal sounds could signal anything from major mechanical ills to relatively minor problems, such as a slightly sticky valve lifter. An odd "clicking" noise could indicate worn valves that require an expensive repair. Cars with overhead-camshaft engines use timing belts that may grind or clatter before they are about to fail.

Get out and open the hood so you can listen and look more carefully. Note any strange odors. Watch the engine for new leaks. Then get down on hands and knees again to peek under the chassis.

Turn off the engine and check again. A late-model car shouldn't leak anything, although a few drops of water from the air conditioner is not ordinarily abnormal.

Back inside, try all controls: wipers/washers, inside and outside lights, horn, turn signals, power seats and windows. Turn on the radio, heater, and air conditioner.

The brake pedal should go down only an inch or two and feel firm, not spongy – even after holding it down for half a minute or so. Be sure the brake lights work.

Turn the steering wheel lightly back and forth with two fingers. An inch of free play is normal; more could mean worn parts. As you turn the wheel through its entire travel, it should not "clunk" or bind. A growing number of recent models have electric power steering, with no mechanical connection between steering wheel and road wheels.

After the engine is warm, stomp on the gas pedal once or twice and look out the back for smoke coming from the tailpipe. Blue smoke signals oil burning that could mean an imminent engine overhaul. We don't see that much anymore. Black smoke is unburned gasoline and reveals fuel-system problems. White smoke that disappears after warm-up is normal condensation; but if it persists after the engine is warm, it could suggest an internal coolant leak – a serious and costly problem.

The engine should idle smoothly. Stab the gas pedal to see that the engine responds without hesitating, then returns to idle. Listen for loud, rumbling noises or hissing that may indicate leaks.

If you smell exhaust inside the car, something is seriously wrong. Black, gummy deposits in the tailpipe are a clue that the engine is burning oil. Dry deposits may reveal fuel-system ills.

Turn the engine off. It should restart at least as easily as it did when cold.

On the move

Two rules need to be remembered on the test drive: One, drive carefully. Two, take all the time you need. Don't agree to that two-minute spin around the block.

Get a license plate or other authorization for your test drive, but sign no paper: it could be a sales contract. Dealerships often ask to photocopy your driver's license before handing you the keys. When you're finished, though, ask to get that copy back. Identity Theft is a big problem, and thieves love to get ahold of your "numbers."

Before pulling away, see that the parking brake works and is strong enough to hold the car. This is particularly important if the car has a manual transmission.

Drive slowly at first to get the "feel" of the car. An automatic transmission should shift smoothly, without jerking, slurring, or hesitation. A manual gearbox should shift easily, without grinding or stiffness; the clutch must engage and disengage without grabbing or chattering.

Many stick shifts are balky or stiff, making gear changes a chore; others are known to be silken smooth. Don't forget to try Reverse gear.

Drive over smooth and rough pavement. Hit a few bumps. Sail over railroad tracks, if possible. Get on a highway and run the car up to speed.

Check it out in city traffic. Listen for groaning noises from the front end that get louder or quieter when going around turns or over pavement swells.

Accelerate hard on a clear road. Response should be quick and confident. Back off and hit the gas again. There should be no "flat spots" or hesitation. The car should track straight, without vibration or pulling to the side.

Brakes should grab evenly, not pull to one side. Slow to 10 or 15 mph on a flat surface, watch for traffic, then hit the brakes hard. Squeals, vibrations, or swerving mean problems. The pedal shouldn't feel spongy. Pedal pulsation is normal only under hard braking, when the anti-lock brakes engage.

Is the car too noisy inside? Are there serious blind spots in any direction?

Take some tight turns and corners. Ease through some sharp curves. Anywhere you go, the car should feel stable and secure. On straightaways, a tendency to wander from side to side, or unresponsive steering, suggests worn components and clearly impairs driving ease. Excessive bouncing over bumps could indicate worn shocks or other suspension woes. Does the steering wheel turn easily enough for parallel parking?

If the car is front-wheel drive, slow to walking pace and make tight left and right turns. "Clunks," ticking noises, or rattles up front typically indicate worn CV joints or other serious maladies.

After your test drive, re-examine the gauges and warning lights. Low oil pressure or above-normal coolant temperature could point to the need for a major overhaul. Listen to the engine again. Hard driving sometimes amplifies intermittent noises. Check for leaks one more time.

Restart to see how the engine fires when hot. If the engine fails to start quickly, there could be a major problem.

If the engine didn't run well or made suspicious noises, don't fall for the old adage that "it just needs a tune-up." Modern cars rarely improve magically with a quick fix. In fact, there's very little to be "tuned" anymore.

Tell the seller that you won't consider the vehicle until they either have the problem fixed or your mechanic takes a look. If the seller balks, it's not worth the gamble. After all, there are plenty of other cars to choose from.

Part IV

Dollars and Sense

14

Down to Dollars

Now that you've picked out one or two cars worth serious consideration, what's next? Determining the price, of course. You should already have gotten an asking price. Now, if you're up to it, this is the time to get ready to negotiate.

Many people hate the idea of bargaining, while others take it as a challenge. At the CPO Forum in November 2010, Brian Benstock, head of Paragon Acura in Queens, New York, reminded dealers that the "biggest fear of consumers [is] that they don't want to make a mistake."

In any case, a bit of bargaining is expected, but never obligatory. After all, no dealer would refuse to sell at the asking price. Besides, recent surveys show that the amount typically knocked off through negotiation isn't always all that great.

Remember, too: Paying a little more than the next person might bring you a car you really like, which is hardly a disaster.

Transparency by dealerships, as we've already seen, includes fair market-based pricing. "Consumers love it," said Kraig Quisenberry, from the DCH Auto Group, at the 2013 CPO Forum. "We love it."

Quisenberry cites Amazon and Costco as good examples. "We don't want to get too cheap," he admitted to the Forum audience, "but we want a fair price" for anything. "Customers respond to fair market-based pricing," he added.

"You're paying a little bit more" for a given automobile than you might have six or seven years ago, said Ricky Beggs, editorial director of *Black Book*. During recent years, however, quality has improved greatly, so "they last longer."

David Nelson, from the Hendrick Automotive Group, advised dealers that their retail vehicles need the "right price on Day One." But after some time passes, they should make adjustments if a car doesn't sell. Customers who aren't in a hurry might wish to take advantage of such adjustments, by looking over a dealer's selection periodically and picking out those vehicles that have been on sale for a while. Naturally, it pays to be prudent, though. There just might be some tangible reason why a given car hasn't sold after several weeks on the lot.

Realistic expectations

Are dealers really willing to bargain down prices from valuations in a guidebook, or supplied by some other third-party information source? Alec Gutierrez, senior market analyst at Kelley Blue Book, cited a survey that showed 46 percent of dealers took a third-party valuation and either accepted it (35%) or improved upon it (11%). It's worth a try, but don't expect miracles. Gutierrez also noted that consumers often have misinformed, unrealistic expectations.

"Consumers don't understand" the pricing terms out there, he explained, confusing such figures as suggested retail price, trade-in value, and private-party value, while trying to get the final selling price of the car they want as low as possible. "In their head, they're creating a range," he said. After being educated a bit, consumer priorities typically shift a lot, and they "value transparent pricing tools."

Used-car economics is actually quite simple: the value of any vehicle (any age or condition) is determined by supply and demand. When used cars are plentiful, prices tend to go down. When they're in short supply, prices tend to rise. The same holds true for particular types of vehicles: late-models, big trucks, subcompacts, or anything else.

Note, too, that in general, used cars purchased at a franchised dealership for that brand sell for more than those bought elsewhere. Then again, they're more likely to be trade-ins, originally purchased at that dealership and perhaps serviced there regularly.

Don't expect a lot of bargains in today's used-car marketplace. Late in 2013, Eric Lyman of ALG noted that transaction prices for used vehicles were at an "all-time high." Moving into 2014, prices have generally remained at or near record levels.

Best advice: Don't be in too much of a hurry. Shop competing sellers/dealers, to compare prices on similar vehicles. Initial steps, at least, can be done online these days, reserving an actual visit for those vehicles and dealers that are most tempting. When you make that actual visit, pay attention to whether you'd feel comfortable buying from this particular dealer (or private seller). If not, think twice – even if their price appears to be the most attractive.

15

Used Car Valuations

Assessing the value of a used car isn't so easy. Valuations are volatile, variable, seasonal – and most important, uncertain. Even when calculated by the most knowledgeable experts, based upon the most valid data, they're never more than estimates and predictions for the near future.

Successful dealers don't buy cars for sale because of their wholesale price at an auction, or from any other source. Rather, they base their purchase price on how much they *expect* to get for that car from a retail customer – including a suitable profit. A car priced low in the auction lane is no bargain unless the dealer's representative is certain it will sell promptly at an acceptable retail price.

"There is a ceiling on what a customer will pay for a used vehicle," said Ford's Linda Silverstein at the 2010 National Remarketing Conference. Specifically, it's when that used-car figure approaches that of a comparable new model. It happens.

Over the past couple of years, said Cary Donovan during 2013 Used Car Week, a surprising phenomenon has occurred. As competition among dealers heightened and the supply of desirable vehicles dwindled, plenty of examples came to light of dealers paying close to retail figures, when buying *at wholesale*. Sometimes, *even more* than retail. Obviously, nobody can make a profit that way, or even pay the dealership's overhead. Even expert buyers, it seems, can get carried away in the frenzy of rising prices and intensified competition for cars to resell.

Depreciation and resale value

Depreciation is a measure of the amount of value a vehicle loses as it ages. The moment a new car is driven away from the dealership, it becomes secondhand and loses a substantial portion of its worth, just minutes earlier. Some models take a big hit right off the bat; others suffer less in that initial burst of depreciation. Models that have been in high demand, such as BMW's Mini Cooper, Toyota's FJ Cruiser, or a Chevrolet Corvette ZR-1, lose a far smaller percentage of their initial value.

Naturally, the rate of loss eases after those early moments. Cars lose value fairly steadily – though not linearly – during their journey toward old age and, eventually, the crusher.

Resale value is, simply, the amount a secondhand car will bring, when sold to a retail customer. *Retained* value is similar, but not the same. It means a *predicted* value, indicating how much of a new vehicle's initial cost will be left when it's sold as a used car three, four, or more years later. If a car worth $20,000 when new is estimated to retain 40 percent of its value at age four, it will then be worth $8,000. Unless that initial estimate was mistaken, of course. Nothing is perfect when estimating depreciation.

Residual value is the figure assigned to a new vehicle by such services as ALG (Automotive Lease Guide) and Kelley Blue Book (KBB). It's intended to predict how much that vehicle will be worth when it's two, three, four, or five years old. Either a percentage or a dollar value might be supplied. Residual value isn't the same as retained value, but they're similar; so, residual values often are used to get a rough idea of how fast a given model has depreciated, or how quickly it's likely to do so in the next few years. As of mid-2014, ALG advised that the average new vehicle retained 54.6 percent of its initial value after three years.

Quick-depreciating models can be good bets

You can make the principle of depreciation work in your favor, by looking for models that lose their value more quickly than the average. Beware, though: you don't want a car that's sunk fast for a tangible reason, such as a known trouble spot.

Honda and Toyota, for example, are well-known leaders in reliability. As a rule, they tend to depreciate more slowly than average – thus costing more on the used-car market. A growing number of competitors, seeing substantial quality improvements in recent years, are nearly as likely to provide many miles of additional useful service, but at a lower purchase price. Why? Because they lose value more rapidly during their early lives. In some cases, a *lot* more.

European-brand models tend to depreciate slower than average, retaining their value quite strongly. Luxury-level Euro-brands generally lose value quite slowly. But so do some moderately-priced German models – led by BMW's Mini Cooper, which is one of the slowest-depreciating cars on the market. Strictly in terms of price, that would make these models weaker values, especially since they may also cost more to repair later. Yet, certain shoppers are happy to pay more, simply because they appreciate European engineering.

Domestically-built cars have traditionally depreciated more rapidly than the average. So have South Korean models. That could make them better bets when secondhand, simply because they tend to cost less than a comparable Japanese model. However, the gap between Japanese- or European-brand vehicles and those made in the U.S. or Korea has been narrowing fast lately. In other words, domestic models are holding their value better now than in the past – but still not necessarily as well as some foreign rivals.

Lately, the used-vehicle market has seen considerable difference between cars and light trucks, in terms of depreciation rates. Four out of five of the vehicles with the greatest amount of annual depreciation have been cars, said Ricky Beggs, editorial director of *Black Book*. Therefore, in general, cars are likely to be cheaper on the retail sales lots, while truck buyers should expect to pay more than they might have had in mind.

Wholesale vs. retail and loan valuations

Wholesale is the amount a dealer pays for a vehicle, whether purchased at an auction, taken in trade, or bought outright from a private seller. Whenever you trade a car in at a dealership, you'll get the wholesale amount – or less. If a trade-in has too many miles on it, or is in mediocre condition, a dealer isn't going to pay any published price for it. Those figures are based on vehicles with a typical number of miles on the odometer, in either Average, Good, or Clean condition.

Retail is approximately the highest amount an individual shopper can expect to pay at a franchised new-car dealership. The difference between wholesale and retail covers the dealership's expenses and profit. That's how they make their money.

Especially during the past couple of years, with new-car sales sagging, dealers have counted on used car sales (as well as service work and income from financing) to make enough to stay in business. Typically, there's a greater profit margin in used cars than new ones.

The third figure you may come across is Loan Valuation. Somewhere between wholesale and retail, it's the amount a bank or other financial institution might be willing to loan toward a purchase.

Published "retail" figures tend to be on the high side, partly because they're basically "asking prices." They're what the dealer would *like* to get, but might not succeed in obtaining.

As a rule, cars cost less at independent dealerships (the ones that don't also sell new vehicles). Least expensive of all is the one bought from a private party. But there are plenty of exceptions to each of these rules. Sometimes, the best overall value to be found, and the one offering the greatest peace of mind, is at a franchised dealership – including one that sells the same make of car that you're considering.

Because consumer advocates and advisers push so hard on demanding the lowest possible price for everything you buy, it's easy to lose sight of the concept of value. The most desirable automobile (or any commodity) isn't necessarily the cheapest one. Value is a mix of benefit and cost. Both factors need to be considered for any purchase, if you want to avoid "buyer's remorse" after the sale.

Dealer price vs. private-seller price

Most guidebook valuations assume that you're buying from a dealership. Traditionally, private sales have been cheaper, whether you're buying from someone you know or from a stranger.

They're still a good choice for lower-priced vehicles. But buying private can be risky when you're paying tens of thousands of dollars. Too much could go wrong, unless you know the seller really well; and even then, troubles are hardly unknown.

Sadly, even some basically honest folks manage to turn into veritable bandits when selling a used car. With a private seller, too, you normally have no recourse after the sale. Happy or not, it's yours.

Trading in your old car

Most new- and used-car buyers trade in their old car. It's easy, and usually covers all or most of the down payment on the new vehicle.

However, dealers typically make more profit on used cars than on the sale of new ones. Therefore, they have a strong incentive to offer as little as possible for your old car.

Before signing any contract, make sure you know exactly how much is being paid for your trade-in. It's all too easy to mix the trade-in figure with the selling price of the "new" vehicle, making it difficult to discern which is which. In the notorious past, dealers commonly offered unrealistically high prices for trade-ins, but then managed to jack up the price of the car being purchased. Such practices are less common today, but they still happen. If the figures are properly spelled out on paper, it won't happen to you.

Most important, if at all possible, avoid trading a car before it's paid for. If you do, the dealer could pay off your old loan, use any residual value as a down payment, then write another loan for the new car – with ample profit for himself. Again, some of these dubious practices from the past haven't quite disappeared, even in this age of increased transparency.

One advantage to trading your old car in to a dealer is that you could lower the amount of sales tax on your new purchase. If your old car trades in for $2,500, that money is subtracted from the retail price of the newer vehicle, reducing its sales tax base by that amount. State and local sales tax laws vary, however, so don't count on this difference unless you investigate first.

Remember, a dealer will only give wholesale value – or less – for a used car. Sell it yourself and you might be able to get actual retail value. Or at least, an amount closer to that figure. If the dealer is giving you more than fair value for your car, chances are they're making up the difference somewhere else in the deal.

Either way, find out, at least roughly, how much your car is worth before you start shopping. Used-car price guides, available at public libraries, tell you the price your car is likely to fetch at retail, and the price a used-car dealer would pay at wholesale.

Going through a few used-car sales sites online can give you some idea of what certain models appear to be bringing at present; though remember, those figures you see are "asking prices," not "transaction prices." Also, you can take a look in the classified section of newspapers, or online, to get a general idea of prices.

If you don't trade, the only alternative is selling that old car yourself. Private sales used to be a wholly acceptable alternative, but the world is more complex and laden with pitfalls nowadays.

Be wary. Weigh the extra money you might get by selling it yourself against the time spent, and against the risk of inviting strangers to your home to see the car. Not to mention, allowing them to test-drive it.

There is one traditional alternative: Ask friends if they know anyone who's interested in your old car.

Resale Values: High and Low

Group One contains examples of cars that tend to sell for relatively high amounts secondhand: well above average, having depreciated only moderately. In Group Two are examples of cars that tend to depreciate considerably *more* rapidly than the average, and therefore sell for comparatively less when used.

Group One:
Recent Models with
High Resale Value
Acura MDX
Audi A5
Audi Q5 and Q7
BMW M3, X3, and X5
Chevrolet Camaro V-8
Chevrolet Silverado Crew Cab
Ford Super Duty pickup
Honda CR-V and Fit
Infiniti EX and FX
Jeep Wrangler
Lexus IS
Lexus GX, LX, and RX
Mini Cooper
Nissan 370Z coupe
Toyota FJ Cruiser
Toyota Land Cruiser
Toyota Tacoma
Toyota Tundra Crew Max
Toyota Venza
Volkswagen Touareg TDI

Group Two:
Recent Model with
Low Resale Value
Cadillac DTS
Cadillac STS
Chevrolet Aveo
Chevrolet Express van
Chevrolet HHR
Chevrolet Impala
Dodge Avenger
Dodge Charger V-6
Ford Econoline van
Hyundai Accent
Jaguar XK
Kia Rio
Kia Sedona minivan
Mercury Grand Marquis
Mitsubishi Endeavor
Mitsubishi Galant
Suzuki Grand Vitara
Suzuki SX4 (some models)
Volvo C70 convertible

16

Guidebooks

How to Use Them Most Effectively

Two primary guidebooks are available to retail shoppers: *Kelley Blue Book* and the *NADA Used Car Guide*. Both can be found at many libraries. Each company has a web site that provides valuation information, but the printed versions include all car models in handy form.

Regular guidebooks cover car and light-truck models going back eight years or so. Early-model editions, with values dating as far back as 1946 and even earlier, also are available.

Kelley Blue Book: Published since 1926, Kelley Blue Book (www.kbb.com) gives three figures for each model: "Auction Value" (wholesale), Suggested Retail Value (asking price – a "starting point for negotiation."), and Wholesale Lending Value (the amount a financial institution might lend on that car). Cars are evaluated in Fair and Good condition. List price (when new) also is supplied, along with equipment schedules and a mileage chart. KBB has led the way in providing add-on figures for used cars that have been certified.

NADA Used Car Guide: Issued by the National Automobile Dealers Association, these Guides show Retail and Loan figures for vehicles in Clean condition, plus Trade-in (wholesale) values in Clean, Average, and Rough condition. Also available are the original Manufacturers Suggested Retail Price (MSRP), equipment add-on figures, and suggested mileage adjustments. The NADA price guide website is www.nadaguides.com. Add-on amounts for certification also are listed.

Dealers also use the *Black Book,* issued by a division of Hearst Business Media Corp. *Black Book* dates back to 1955. In fact, many consider it the "bible" of the used-car business. If you happen to come across a monthly edition, wholesale values are given in Clean and Average condition, plus Market Value at auction. You'll also find Retail figures in Clean and Average condition, but they're multipliers (derived from the wholesale amount) that "represent an acceptable price by the seller."

Guidebooks for dealer use also are issued by *Galves* and *Red Book*, but they're popular mainly in certain parts of the country.

Consumer Guide provided used-vehicle valuations to consumers for three decades, initially in print and later online (www.consumerguide.com). Rather than specific figures for each car model, Consumer Guide published approximate ranges, which gave a useful "ball park" idea of what you could expect to pay. Unfortunately, Consumer Guide ceased to publish its used-car guide online in mid-2013, but might (or might not) revive it at some point.

How guidebooks assign values to used vehicles

Used almost entirely by dealers who need wholesale valuations of car models, the *Black Book* has been around since 1955. Ricky Beggs, the senior vice-president editorial director, recently gave a synopsis of how *Black Book* editors come up with their figures, which nowadays are updated daily.

"Every year when a new model year vehicle is announced," Beggs said, "we take the information showing the exact model and trim levels and all of the available optional equipment and packages." Additions and Deductions are determined, reflecting items that warrant additional value once they get into the used market, and others that take value away if they're not present on the vehicle. Based on their experience and knowledge, the editors come up with a First Value figure.

Mainly, however, *Black Book* reports used-vehicle market values "as they occur ... through auction results." Editors study results of thousands of actual sales, every day. Every week, *Black Book* survey people attend more than 60 wholesale, dealer-only auctions around the country. Survey personnel inspect vehicles at the auction site, noting year, make, model, trim level, engine size, transmission type, drivetrain configuration, equipment, color, mileage, and "appraised condition." They also record the actual sale price.

Editors themselves attend at least one auction each week, and observe many more online, to get a feel for the market. Attending actual auctions lets them see reactions of buyers and sellers, talk to auction personnel, and get opinions from the auctioneers as to which vehicles are "hot" and which are "struggling."

Meanwhile, results of thousands of vehicles sold at wholesale are transmitted to *Black Book* by remarketers, leasing companies, and financial institutions. All the gathered data contribute to the analysis that results in published figures.

A lot of copies of *Black Book* are still printed, Beggs added, updated weekly or monthly. But "printed guidebooks are going away," supplanted by information sent to iPhones, Androids, and other digital devices. Because dealers benefit from having the latest data, the ability to get current figures in seconds, right at your fingertips, is hard to resist.

17

Factors that Affect Used Car Prices

What the retail customer winds up paying for a car results from a mix of several important factors. Each one can make the average price of a given model rise or fall – sometimes slightly, sometimes substantially. Taken together, they can make an enormous difference.

Vehicle condition is the Number One factor in assessing value, because it helps predict the amount of useful (hopefully trouble-free) life that might remain in the car. Guidebooks are quite specific about this, providing figures that represent a vehicle in a stated condition: perhaps Excellent or Clean, Good, and Average. Of course, one observer's "clean" might qualify as merely "good" to someone else, and vice versa. But those who evaluate used cars for a living have become quite expert at assigning the proper condition ranking.

Mileage and odometer readings are used to modify the basic valuation. In fact, some guidebooks provide specific charts with figures that should be added to or subtracted from the regular valuations, for a car that has significantly less or more mileage than average for a vehicle of that type and age. For a year-old car, up to 15,000 miles (or a little higher) is considered normal; a two-year-old can have up to 30,000; a three-year-old, up to 40,000 or so. Mileage higher than these figures usually begins to reduce the value.

As already described, unscrupulous used-car dealers have a long history of "rolling back" odometers that showed high mileage, to give the impression of a low-mileage vehicle – which could then sell for more. Lax titling laws in certain states actually made it easy to roll back an odometer, get the title adjusted accordingly, and sell the car elsewhere.

Such odometer "adjustments" are a lot less common nowadays, particularly since vehicle history reports include odometer information; but they still happen. The recent shortage of clean, low-mileage late-model automobiles could be a temptation for unethical sellers. If a vehicle appears to have traveled a lot farther than its odometer suggests, be wary.

Certification, described in detail in Chapter 4, provides "peace of mind" to buyers who might worry about a car's potential reliability, but it comes at a price. Kelley Blue Book provides estimated add-on figures for certification, but most valuation sources do not. In 2010, Tony DiPanni, a sales director for SmartAuction, estimated the average amount of extra cost for certification was around $1,300. Other experts, commenting more recently, have suggested different added-cost figures, but nearly all of them are substantial. Evidently, many customers value that "peace of mind" quite highly, and are willing to pay amply for it. Used-car guidebooks have even been including average add-on figures for certification, for specific models.

Market conditions cannot be overlooked, either. The overall economy has an impact on the types of vehicles people want. "In hard times, there are a lot more 'need' buyers," said veteran used-car dealer Jack Fitzgerald at the National Remarketing Conference. "There is a vast need for basic transportation," added Larry Dorfman, speaking for the CarMark independent certified pre-owned program.

Special models cost more, too: limited editions, low-production cars, those that attract collectors and enthusiasts, and so forth. Still, many that sound "special" really aren't all that unique or in-demand. Countless special-editions have been issued over the years as promotional devices, to stimulate interest when new-car sales weren't meeting expectations. In addition, many were simply local or regional "specials" (perhaps given a distinctive name) that aren't necessarily worth more than a plain old example when the car becomes secondhand.

Cars with **top-level trim or option packages** also warrant higher prices, near or even a bit above the high end of the scale for a given model. One often-seen example: Eddie Bauer editions of the Ford Explorer.

Supply and demand means a slow-seller might go for below the wholesale price. Conversely, a popular late-model may command the retail figure or more, even stretching toward the car's original Manufacturers Suggested Retail Price (MSRP) when it was brand-new. In general, too, prices tend to decline in summer. All the more so in 2014, following unusually high average selling prices earlier in the year.

Patience sometimes pays off, if you're not in a hurry and can take the time to stop at a dealer's lot periodically. The era of keeping cars on the lot indefinitely rather than cutting the price is largely gone. Dealers don't like to keep cars too long, taking up space with no monetary return.

If a car doesn't sell in 14 days, said dealer Kevin Nachbar at the CPO Forum in 2010, he might drop the price by $1,000. If it was still there after 30 days, perhaps $1,000 more. After 60 days, Nachbar figured there was probably no profit left.

"The longer the car sits, the more it depreciates," added Subaru's John Manchini. Most dealers will try to wholesale that hard-to-sell unit to another store, or send it to a wholesale auction. But an offer from a retail customer that would have been rejected a month ago, just might sound more tempting when the car is reaching the end of its logical life on the sale lot.

"What's popular new tends to be what dealers and consumers are looking for used," says Tom Kontos, executive vice-president of analytical services at ADESA (a major auction chain). "As popularly equipped" is what dealers look for in the wholesale auction lanes; and therefore, what's most likely to wind up in the front row at a dealer's lot. Dealers will seek out, for instance, an LT Malibu over a less-abundantly equipped LS version. Customers are well advised to consider both trim levels and popular options, when making a buying decision.

18

Equipment and Options

Every car model has a list of standard equipment: items that were installed on every one that rolled off the assembly line when that model was new. Most new cars also had a list of options that could have been installed at extra cost. Honda has long been one of the exceptions, simplifying the new-car buying process by eliminating most extra-cost options.

If you ever plan to resell the used car you're planning to buy, make sure it has the features that virtually everyone expects to find there. Even moderately-priced vehicles these days are expected to have at least basic air conditioning, power locks and windows, and cruise control. Many are considered practically "stripped" if they lack a few other items as well.

Naturally, a car costs more if well-equipped, either because it's a step-up trim level or contains a selection of options. Equipment levels have grown in recent years, too; even for lower-cost cars, a basic model usually has more equipment than did its predecessor from a few years earlier.

Unfortunately, it's difficult to tell whether any tangible amount has been added to a used car's asking price for additional equipment. It's not like buying a new car, where every item and option group has a specific retail price in dollars. Used-car price guidebooks do include a list of add-on amounts, to be included if a specified option is on a particular car. But the lists only include major items. Some pricing folks at dealerships follow such guidelines; others are less rigorous, simply coming up with a total price as the car stands. No point worrying too much about any additional cost you might be paying for a better-equipped car, as long as you're satisfied with it as a whole.

Here are some features that might be worth seeking:

- **Option packages (Sport, Luxury, Technology, etc.):** If it includes items you really want, and that a future owner might also appreciate, a named option group is worth paying a little extra for – but not a fortune. Trouble is, it's hard to tell if a car has a special option package on it, unless you find an original equipment list and compare it to the existing car's actual features.
- **Leather upholstery:** Not everyone cares for it, but for a luxury or near-luxury automobile, lack of leather can be a drawback if you wind up selling it later. Typically, leather is used for the seating surfaces, not necessarily for the entire upholstery. Leather-wrapped steering wheels aren't likely to cost extra, but do add a classy touch to many car interiors.
- **Alloy wheels:** No need to pay a considerable sum for the fanciest wheels around, but attractive alloys look better than steel wheels with separate covers and shouldn't add much (if anything) to the price. A lot of cars, including moderately-priced models, have had alloys as standard equipment, at least on higher trim levels.
- **Premium (step-up) sound system:** People do love audio nowadays, and the systems developed by such companies as Bose, Bang & Olufsen, and harman/kardon can be most appealing. Best not to be overly tempted by one of the very top systems, which could add a substantial sum to the price of a car – though far less than when the car was purchased new.
- **Sunroof or moonroof:** Even if you're not fond of them, lack of one can restrict the prospects for reselling later (depending on the model).
- **Power seats:** Not worth paying a lot extra on a moderately-priced car, but they're undeniably handy compared to the controls for some manual seats. Multiple-way power seats with a memory have become a lot more common in late-models, though not everyone feels they're necessary.
- **Connectivity:** A growing number of shoppers won't even consider a late-model car that lacks suitable cell-phone connectivity, Bluetooth, and various "apps" that bring the Internet experience to the road. If you're one of them, find out early on if the car has everything you'll want, and can work with

the latest smartphones or other devices. USB ports and iPod interfaces are almost expected in late-model vehicles.
- **Navigation system:** Not everybody wants or needs satellite-based guidance, but those who favor "nav" systems would feel deprived without it. Expect to pay several hundred dollars extra for a factory-installed system.
- **Sport suspension:** Drivers who enjoy a taut feel when cornering or on winding roads will gravitate toward used cars with a sportier suspension than the base setup.
- **Turbocharged engine:** In addition to heightened performance, turbos can be more efficient than their regular counterparts, unless driven aggressively.
- **All-wheel drive:** Drivers in the snowbelt know the advantages of AWD on slippery roads, and most are more than willing to pay extra for it. AWD can be helpful in less wintry climates, but it's less essential.
- **Cruise control:** Most recent cars have cruise control as standard, but it's been an extra-cost option for some lower-priced models. In addition to convenience on the highway, cruise control can actually improve gas mileage a bit.

And here are a few that you might *not* want:
- **Panoramic sunroof:** Some people love these; others can't stand them. Do you really want the sun shining down on you all the time? If not, make sure there's an inner shade that can cover the entire sunroof area, blocking the sun's rays.
- **DVD/Blu-Ray video entertainment:** For family-oriented vehicles, such as minivans, video is a worthwhile bonus. For other cars and trucks, it's not expected and therefore not worth paying extra. Still, a lot of regular passenger cars, and especially SUVs, in recent years have been fitted with video. So, the add-on cost might not be all that great.
- **Manual transmission:** If you enjoy shifting gears, fine; but except for a sporty car, a manual gearbox seriously limits the number of potential buyers later on. And that means less chance of getting a good price for the car.

- **Pushbutton start:** Many folks love it; others almost detest it. Gradually, it's become almost standard on a lot of models. On a used car, it shouldn't cost extra – or at least, not much.
- **Heated (and ventilated) seats:** Plenty of folks in colder (or hotter) climates can barely survive without these; some others wouldn't pay a nickel for either one.
- **Satellite radio:** Now called SiriusXM, it's a subscription service with a monthly fee, in contrast to regular broadcast radio. Check the list of channels before agreeing, to make sure there's enough to interest you and your regular passengers.
- **Remote starter:** Urban dwellers who fret about thieves might frown at the idea of starting an engine before the driver is present. Suburbanites, on the other hand, often like the convenience of having the car warmed up a bit before they enter, especially on chilly mornings.
- **Rain-sensing wipers:** These would be a fine idea if they were invariably accurate. Despite the fact that such systems have been around since the Fifties, some turn the wipers on when only a few raindrops have appeared, and fail to do so as soon as the rainfall starts to escalate.
- **Steering-wheel radio controls:** Some drivers use these constantly; others are barely aware of their existence, preferring to adjust the radio the old-fashioned way.
- **Automatic stop/start:** It's hard to criticize a system that helps boost gas mileage in city driving, but a surprising number of automatic stop/start systems – even when installed on high-end cars – operate with a startling lack of smoothness. Some are downright jerky. When operating properly, they shut the engine off when the car is stopped (like a hybrid), and start it up again as soon as you touch the gas pedal or the clutch.
- **Paddle shifters:** Because operation of most automatic transmission has improved considerably in recent years, the need to override its gear-changing actions is less than it used to be. Driving enthusiasts still tend to like them, but most others will use the paddles a few times, then forget all about them. One exception: they can help in mountainous terrain, allowing you to keep the car in a lower gear when going downhill.

- **Head-up display:** Projecting the car speed into the windshield may be either a big help or an annoying hindrance. Certainly, these displays make it easy to remain aware of your speed; yet, a lot of drivers seem to dislike them.

Factory-installed vs. dealer-installed and aftermarket accessories

Options that were installed at the factory as the vehicle was built are the ones that can add value to a used model. (Naturally, that's a "plus" for the person selling a car, but not so appealing to the one who's buying it.) Guidebooks include auxiliary figures that need to be added to the basic valuations, when a car has more equipment than might be expected. But those figures only apply to factory-installed equipment.

Dealer-installed extras seldom add much, if any, value to a used vehicle. At least, not unless they're official factory items that can be installed readily after a car is delivered to the dealer.

Aftermarket accessories, installed by the owner or a third party, rarely make any notable difference in used-car valuations. In fact, they can be a detriment to a car's overall appeal, and therefore to its selling price.

Modern technology in late-model cars

The newer a car or light truck is, the more likely it is to have a selection of high-tech features. Some are valuable safety features that may be worth having, or provide useful comfort/convenience that will be appreciated. Other complex, high-tech extras qualify mainly as additional items to go bad, sooner or later.

- **Electronic Stability Control**, or **Electronic Stability Program:** Little by little, this definite safety "plus" has made its way onto a large number of vehicles, either standard or as an option, though few vehicles more than a couple of years old will have it. They're sometimes referred to as antiskid systems.
- **Blind-spot alert:** Safety experts and plenty of drivers who've tried it wonder how they've managed to survive without a blind-spot warning. If you've ever experienced the sudden appearance

of an oncoming vehicle, right in your blind spot, you know how valuable this system can be.
- **Rearview backup camera:** Critics say people shouldn't rely on a video image for backing up, and they're right; but these can be a big help. Drive with a backup camera for a while, and you might wonder how you ever got along without one.
- **Parking Assist:** Sensors that warn when you're getting too close to a vehicle ahead or behind are another option that some consider unnecessary, and others love. Mostly offered on more expensive cars, at least initially, these don't necessarily add much (if anything) to the secondhand price. Available for front and/or rear, this feature can prevent significant front- or rear-end damage, especially on cars whose front end sits low to the ground. It doesn't take much of an impact against a stretch of curbing or an unseen post to cause damage that's costly to fix.
- **Parallel-parking helper:** So far, only expensive cars from a few manufacturers have these. Most of us are able to manage without it, and auto-parking cars need a rather sizable space to back into hands-free. As social critic Calvin Trillin wrote when these first came along, in New York City you need to be able to back into a space with only inches to spare, whereas these systems typically require six feet or more.
- **Navigation system:** Here, too, many people come to rely on their "nav" system, while others wouldn't pay *anything* extra for it. They cost a lot as new-car factory options (though prices have dropped somewhat in the past year or two), and can add a fair amount to a used car's price, too. Aftermarket navigation systems are far less costly, and add little or nothing to the value of a car. With late-model cars, voice recognition is expected in the navigation system.
- **Pre-Collision system:** Warning of a collision is clearly in the best interest of every driver. Availability of frontal collision warning systems has been growing substantially.
- **Adaptive Cruise Control:** By monitoring how close you're getting to the car ahead, and slowing your car down as needed, this safety feature can handily prevent a collision.
- **Adaptive Headlights:** Linked to the steering system, adaptive headlights alter the pattern they make on the road ahead. In

curves, this could spell the difference between seeing an object in your path and running into it. Still, adaptive headlights haven't received nearly as much attention as other available safety systems.

How important are such safety features as electronic stability control and blind-spot warning systems? "A vehicle has to have" most of these, in order to compete in today's marketplace, says Ricky Beggs, editorial director of *Black Book*. From the dealer's perspective, a well-equipped vehicle "might sell quicker" and "bring more dollarwise," because people want those kinds of features. Less-equipped models might be considered "bland," and unable to "stand out." Stripped down far enough, they rank as mere "transportation."

Low mileage and abundant comfort/convenience equipment translate to "highly-sought-after vehicles," added Juan Flores, trade-in marketplace director at AutoTrader.com.

19

Negotiating the Final Price

Dealing with a dealer and/or salesperson doesn't have to be the ordeal that so many of us expect it to be. Not everyone has gotten the transparency message, but dealers are increasingly disposed toward a more customer-friendly sales encounter, where talking price doesn't have to be an ordeal. Maintaining a non-adversarial tone, they realize, works out better in the end for everyone.

Besides, the customer has the ultimate weapon right at hand: he or she can simply walk away if the final figure isn't acceptable. Or, if anything else about the encounter is troubling.

Remember, though, the initial figure you're given by a salesperson, or see advertised, is an "asking price." Let's not forget that the dealer is in business to make money. That means including a passable profit in the final amount that you'll be paying. That's the reality.

Whether you're facing a dealer's salesperson or a private party, you'll probably choose to negotiate, at least a little. Word of advice: Determine your top acceptable price before starting to negotiate, but keep it to yourself, stay focused, and just see what happens.

How about One-Price?

A surprising number of dealers have turned to single-price, no-bargaining used-car sales. Others have occasional one-price sale days. Sounds like paradise to some shoppers, but only if that no-haggle price isn't excessive. A one-price transaction is appealing only if the non-negotiable price is acceptable to you. A dealer's claim that "You can't overpay" or "You get only the best price" hardly proves that the stated figure is a reasonable one.

Probably the biggest and best-known of the "one-price" dealers, which permit no haggling, is the chain of CarMax used-car dealerships. Some dealerships that turned to one-price selling a few years back have reverted to the traditional way, convinced that their customers would rather "bargain" than accept a take-it-or-leave-it figure.

Bargaining basics

Enroute to making the final decision, don't let a salesperson steer you toward a more expensive vehicle; or one with unwanted features. Don't reveal how attracted you are toward a specific vehicle, either. Salespeople are trained to take advantage of cues.

No matter how crafty you think you're being, the salesperson probably has seen it all and can be craftier yet if he or she chooses. You're not going to beat him.

If you have a trade-in, it's generally best not to say so until you get a firm selling price on the car you're buying. An overzealous dealer could "inflate" your trade-in's value by manipulating the selling price. That's been the traditional warning, at any rate.

If you see evidence that you're working with a more modern dealership, which values transparency and fair pricing, revealing the existence of a trade-in earlier in the process might not be such a bad idea. As long as you can find out exactly what's being allowed for it as a trade-in, keeping it hidden until the last moment isn't as essential.

If you're not satisfied with the asking price, and the seller rejects your opening offer, many shoppers immediately begin to point out all the car's shortcomings, real and imaginary. Nitpicking every possible flaw and defect in a vehicle, striving to knock the price down little by little, isn't as effective as some folks think, and is more likely to make the seller defensive. All you're likely to do is make the seller – whether dealership or private – defensive, and determined not to reduce the price any further.

Besides, if the car has a tempting price and appears to be in excellent condition, best not to try *too* hard to knock that price down. After all, someone else might turn up at any moment and snap it up.

Naturally, it never pays to get argumentative, either. If you reach an impasse and the final asking price is still too high, just thank the seller for his or her time and walk away. The seller might even come back at the last second with a lower figure. If not, you might want to check back in a few days. If the car is still there, chances are you can knock the price down a bit more. And if time isn't important, check again after a week or two.

Dealers don't like to keep cars on their lots any longer than necessary, so if it's still unsold, they might be amenable to yet another offer. There's a limit, though. Dealers have to make a profit, so don't think you can snatch away all or most of it by sheer negotiating will.

At a dealership, the salesperson you've been talking with seldom has full authority to conclude the sale. Instead, he or she will state a price. If you make a counteroffer, he'll take that figure to the sales manager. Most likely, it will be rejected. (At least, that's a familiar step in the traditional, well-tested sales process that was well-honed back in the 1950s.) The rejection may even take a fair amount of time to be relayed to you, however – a delay designed to make you think it was a tough decision

Then, the salesperson typically makes an offer somewhere in between. If you make another counteroffer, that, too, is submitted for approval or rejection. The process continues again until an approval is finally granted – or not. In traditional sales practice, the goal was to wear down the hapless customer, and keep him or her from leaving.

When you've decided on a car you want, putting down a deposit is usually essential; but don't do it unless you really intend to buy that car. If a dealer or a private party wants a deposit and you're not absolutely ready to make a decision, politely decline. If they insist, it's probably not a good idea to buy from that person.

Trying to get a deposit back can be a hassle, if not an impossibility. If you do leave a deposit, either by check or cash, be sure to get a receipt. Ask for a written statement that if a problem comes up, or you decide against the car, you can get that deposit back.

Some sellers will balk, so you may have to decide whether it's worth risking the deposit money. Needless to say, it's prudent to make it as low as possible, just in case something falls through and you have to take a loss.

One old trick could still happen today: dealers have been known to show the customer what appears to be a contract for the deposit, but is actually an agreement to buy the car. Ancient high-pressure gimmicks never go away entirely.

Salespeople and dealers have long been notorious for trying to keep a reluctant customer in the showroom or on the sales lot, trotting out even more inducements to buy – and buy right now. If he or she leaves the premises, it's presumed that the customer is lost forever, and won't return. "I know we hate be-backs in this world," said Jack Simmons of cars.com to an audience of dealers during 2013 Used Car Week. But many do come back, he advised. Once again, modern-thinking dealers won't insist on abiding by the shady old "rules" of the auto-sales game.

20

Warranties and Service Contracts

What's called the FTC Buyers Guide, developed by the Federal Trade Commission under its Used Car Rule, is posted on the window of every used vehicle to be sold by a dealer. Among other information, it specifies whether the vehicle is to be sold "as is" or includes a warranty. It also spells out what percentage of the repair cost the dealer is agreeing to pay, under the warranty (if there is one).

Except for certified pre-owned (CPO) vehicles, used cars – especially older ones – don't often come with a worthwhile warranty. Most have none at all. When they do, warranties tend to be short-term and perhaps packed with loopholes.

Three questions take precedence with any warranty:

1. Exactly what is warranted and what's not?
2. How long does the warranty last?
3. Who backs it up? The dealer? A third-party organization?
4. If it's backed by anything other than the original manufacturer, do they have a good reputation?

You also need to find out where any needed work must be done, and how it's arranged. Must you pay for a repair and then be reimbursed? Or will the dealer take care of all the details. Find out *now*, and then hope you never need to use it.

Note: Vehicles sold in Maine and Wisconsin have a different version of the Buyers Guide. Each Buyers Guide warns that spoken promises are difficult to enforce, and recommends that you get every detail spelled out in writing. They also advise that, contrary to what some customers believe, there is no legal right to cancel a contract, once it's signed: no three-day "cooling off period," or any other way out.

Do you need a Service Contract?

You'll probably be encouraged to sign up for one. Why? One big reason: Service contracts are generally high-profit items, for which the dealership gets a significant commission.

A service contract is an extra-cost item, not included in the purchase price. Rather than a warranty, it's actually an insurance policy, which covers repair work that may be needed at some point, for major mechanical failures.

Service contracts are issued by a third-party company and cost hundreds of dollars, if not thousands. They cover repairs for a specified period of time, likely with a deductible that you must pay for every repair done. The choice of available "plans" can be confusing.

Most emphatically, as with warranties, find out who does the actual repair work. Is it the dealer? A certain repair shop? A choice of shops? Find out if a repair can be done right away, when it's needed, or if you have to deal with the insurance company first.

Be sure you know who is actually issuing the contract, too. Make certain you know who to contact, should repairs be needed.

Ask about the *deductible*, which is the amount you will have to pay for each repair, regardless of the actual cost of that work. Find out about cancellation policies, and whether a refund would be available.

Remember, too, service contracts primarily cover major components that aren't likely to fail during the coverage period. Are they worth the price? Some people say yes; others wouldn't touch a service contract. If the price sounds unusually high, think twice about whether you really need it. Sometimes, it's wiser to just take a chance.

Don't be surprised if you're contacted later by one or more service-contract companies. They can be quite persistent.

Typical new-car factory warranties

For later-model cars, the original factory new-car warranty is probably still in effect and can be transferred to you, as the next owner. If you choose to buy a Service Contract, make sure it doesn't duplicate what that factory warranty continues to cover; and be certain you know how to get that coverage transferred to your name.

New-car warranties in recent years have generally covered comprehensive (bumper-to-bumper) repairs for a period of 3 to 5 years, or 36,000 to 60,000 miles (whichever comes first: time or mileage). Powertrain coverage – for the engine, transmission, and drivetrain components, which actually make the car run – is typically for a longer period and a greater number of miles. Some powertrain warranties are good for as long as 10 years or 100,000 miles; others, only 4-year/50,000-mile. Those tiny two-passenger Smart cars have shorter warranty coverage than any other make sold in the U.S.

New cars also are covered for corrosion damage, sometimes for as many as 100,000 miles (or unlimited), or anywhere from 3 to 12 years.

For information on specific makes, see the Manufacturer New-Car Warranties chart below. For additional, detailed information on service contracts, go to the Federal Trade Commission website (www.ftc.gov) and look for Buying a Used Car.

Manufacturer New-Car Warranties

New-car warranties issued by, and backed by, the manufacturer of a vehicle have two elements:
Basic provides limited bumper-to-bumper, comprehensive coverage.
Powertrain covers only the powertrain components (engine, transmission, etc.).

Each is issued for a specified number of miles or number of years, whichever comes first. A basic warranty for 3/36,000 miles is valid for 3 years after the initial purchase, or until the car has been driven for 36,000 miles (whichever happens first). Basic warranties have no deductible (no amount that must be paid by the owner, to have repair work done). Powertrain warranties may have a deductible.

Basic warranties transfer automatically to the second owner of a vehicle, and to any subsequent owners, until the age or mileage limit is met. Powertrain warranties are intended for the initial owner, but might be transferable to a second owner, typically only after payment of a transfer fee.

Acura: 4/50,000 basic; 6/70,000 powertrain
Audi: 4/50,000 basic and powertrain
BMW: 4/50,000 basic and powertrain
Buick: 4/50,000 basic; 5/100,000 powertrain (2007-12, 5/100,000 powertrain)
Cadillac: 4/50,000 basic; 5/100,000 powertrain
Chevrolet: 3/36,000 basic; 5/100,000 powertrain
Chrysler: 3/36,000 basic; 5/100,000 powertrain (2007.5-09, lifetime powertrain)
Dodge: 3/36,000 basic; 5/100,000 powertrain (2007.5-09, lifetime powertrain)
Fiat: 4/50,000 basic and powertrain
Ford: 3/36,000 basic; 5/60,000 powertrain
GMC: 3/36,000 basic; 5/100,000 powertrain
Honda: 3/36,000 basic; 5/60,000 powertrain

Hummer: 4/50,000 basic; 5/100,000 powertrain (U.S. sales ceased after 2010)
Hyundai: 5/60,000 basic; 10/100,000 powertrain
Infiniti: 4/60,000 basic; 6/70,000 powertrain
Isuzu: 3/50,000 basic; 7/75,000 powertrain (U.S. sales ceased after 2008)
Jaguar: 4/50,000 basic and powertrain (2011 only, 5/50,000)
Jeep: 3/36,000 basic; 5/100,000 powertrain (2007.5-09, lifetime powertrain)
Kia: 5/60,000 basic; 10/100,000 powertrain (2008-up)
Land Rover: 4/50,000 basic and powertrain
Lexus: 4/50,000 basic; 6/70,000 powertrain
Lincoln: 4/50,000 basic; 6/70,000 powertrain
Mazda: 3/36,000 basic; 5/60,000 powertrain
Mercedes-Benz: 4/50,000 basic and powertrain
Mercury: 3/36,000 basic; 5/60,000 powertrain (U.S. sales ceased after 2011)
Mini: 4/50,000 basic and powertrain
Mitsubishi: 5/60,000 basic; 10/100,000 powertrain
Nissan: 3/36,000 basic; 5/60,000 powertrain
Pontiac: 3/36,000 basic; 5/100,000 powertrain (U.S. sales ceased after 2010)
Porsche: 4/50,000 basic and powertrain
Saab: 4/50,000 basic and powertrain (U.S. sales ceased after 2012).
Saturn: 3/36,000 basic; 5/100,000 powertrain (U.S. sales ceased after 2009)
Scion: 3/36,000 basic; 5/60,000 powertrain
Smart: 2/24,000 basic and powertrain (2012-up: 4/50,000)
Subaru: 3/36,000 basic; 5/60,000 powertrain
Suzuki: 3/36,000 basic; 7/100,000 powertrain (U.S. sales ceased after 2013)
Toyota: 3/36,000 basic; 5/60,000 powertrain
Volkswagen: 3/36,000 basic; 5/60,000 powertrain (pre-2009, 4/60 basic; 5/60,000 powertrain)
Volvo: 4/50,000 basic and powertrain

A manufacturer's warranty could be voided for any of several reasons:
1. Flagrant misuse of the vehicle, resulting in damage.
2. Damage caused by natural disasters.
3. Evidence of tampering of the car's odometer.
4. If vehicle is totally wrecked and then rebuilt, issued a salvage title.

5. Failure to perform proper maintenance. What's proper is debatable, but all work does not necessarily have to be done by the selling dealership.

21

Financing

Of all vehicles financed in 2013, more than 62 percent were used, according to Experian Automotive. The average amount financed has been rising – especially for used vehicles, which approached $18,000 in late 2013. As a comparison, the average *new-vehicle* buyer financed $27,612 – nearly $10,000 higher.

Average monthly payments came to $352 for a used car, versus about $471 for a new one, according to Experian. Even in this age of low interest, the average used-vehicle buyer had to pay an interest rate of 8.7 percent (annual percentage rate, or APR), for a loan term of 61 months. That interest rate was just about twice the average paid by new-vehicle buyers.

"There's good financing available, at good rates," said Ricky Beggs, editorial director of Black Book, during a phone interview early in 2014. "It's all about payment. You've got to have a payment that's less."

Ever since the 1950s, when installment buying became an integral part of the burgeoning suburban culture, Americans have been basing their car purchases largely, if not completely, on the amount of down payment and monthly payment. If asked, a lot of people wouldn't even know how much their car had actually cost, in cash.

In the recent past, Beggs observed, it typically took about three-fourths of the loan term for the borrower to get into an equity position with his or her vehicle. That's the point where the vehicle is worth as much as is still owed on it. These days, it tends to happen sooner. Yet, plenty of hapless owners find themselves "underwater," owing more – often, a lot more – than their vehicle is worth.

Credit investigations used to take time. Not anymore. With so many online services available, loans can often be approved in a matter of minutes.

Just over 21 percent of used-car buyers get loans from a finance company, according to Experian. Banks get 35 percent of that market, and credit unions account for nearly 21 percent. Credit score makes a huge difference, though. Finance companies account for more than 94 percent of loans issued to shoppers who don't fall into the Prime category.

Banks traditionally have been the most restrictive in terms of deciding who will be granted a loan (and how much), and who will be denied. At the other end of the scale, finance companies have often been notorious for granting credit to nearly anyone – but charging near-usurious interest rates for that privilege. Credit unions may be the best choice, for shoppers who belong to one.

A few years ago, financing an automobile was more difficult. According to Tammy Darvish of Darcars, a Washington, D.C. dealership group, financing was the biggest challenge. "Finance companies are looking for far more equity," Darvish said at the 2010 National Remarketing Conference.

Credit history counts most

Used-car buyers have different credit needs than those who buy new. According to Experian Automotive, the average credit score in late 2013 for a new-vehicle buyer was about 715, versus 646 for those who buy used.

Experian divides credit applicants into five categories: Super Prime (people with a top credit score); Prime; Nonprime; Subprime; and Deep Subprime. As expected, those in the latter category aren't exactly sought-after by most credit grantors, because their credit scores fall far below the average.

As a convenience, Experian splits people into just two groups: Prime and Nonprime. Of total used-vehicle buyers in late 2013, 35.8 percent fell into one of the Prime brackets, while 64.2 percent ranked Nonprime or lower.

Subprime credit began to loosen in 2010, according to the Manheim Used Car Market Report, for shoppers with FICO credit scores under 570. Even though credit scores are assessed and provided to lenders by several companies (TransUnion, Equifax, and Experian), they're all often called FICO scores.

Credit scores affect interest rates and terms, as well as the amount that can be loaned. In late 2013, the average customer with nonprime credit obtained financing for $17,712, while subprime buyers could get a loan averaging $15,858. At the bottom of that scale, those with Deep Subprime credit could finance $14,410 – provided they were granted a loan at all.

Shopping within your means

Reach beyond what you can afford, or sign up for monthly payments that you are unable to keep up, and you might be visited one evening by the "repo man." Finance companies traditionally have a higher rate of vehicle repossessions than other credit grantors.

Repossessions dropped by at least 7.5 percent in 2010, according to Tom Webb, chief economist for Manheim auctions. "Consumers have done a good job of paying their auto loans," he explained at that time. A troubled debtor might walk away from his or her home loan, but make the car payments. "Both markets are totally driven by monthly payment," Webb added.

After dipping to 0.4 percent of total loans outstanding in 2012, repos rose back up to 0.62 percent in 2013 (on par with the 2011 figure); then up further to 0.68 percent. Finance companies, which typically face more delinquencies, endured a repo rate of 3 percent (a massive jump from the 1.78 percent rate they had a year earlier).

Before facing the indignity of the repo man, a debtor becomes delinquent, failing to make payments on time or skipping them completely. Late in 2013, about 2.2 percent of loans resulted in delinquency by 30 days or more. Those who wound up delinquent by 60 days or more accounted for 0.52 percent of total loans in effect.

What you want to avoid is the risk of going "underwater" or "upside-down," meaning you owe more on your car than it's worth. That's the likely outcome when you make a subpar down payment, and monthly payments weren't high enough to yield equity in the vehicle.

Extended-term financing is on the rise. Loan periods are getting longer. For customers with Deep Subprime credit (the worst), according to Experian Automotive, the average term in late 2013 was 56 months (up from 51). About 54 percent of loans were for terms of more than 60 months – up from 45 percent in 2011. But it could be worse: Canada does 100-month terms.

Eric Lyman, of ALG, pointed out during 2013 Used Car Week that people are more likely to make a car payment than their mortgage payment. Why? They simply need that car to go to work. So, the house payment can wait.

More loans for the credit-challenged

Financing continues to expand, with more people able to secure loans, said Melinda Zabritski, senior director for Experian Automotive during her presentation of data for the first quarter of 2014. Leasing continues to grow, Zabritski noted, accounting for more than one-fourth of new vehicles that find homes. Shoppers with less-ideal credit scores, falling into subprime categories, are more likely to get financed than they would have a year or two earlier. Monthly payment and interest rates have "jumped" in the higher-risk segments, Zabritski added, but credit-challenged folks are getting loans of some sort: often from a finance company or at a Buy Here-Pay Here dealer.

Only 35 percent of used-car loans were issued by a bank. Credit unions and finance companies each accounted for about 21 percent of the total, while BHPH dealers directly financed 15.3 percent of the used-car buyers.

Credit scores have been falling for some time, for both new- and used-car buyers. The average for new-vehicle buyers in the first quarter of 2014 was 714 (down from 722 a year earlier). For used-car buyers, the average actually went up a bit: from 637 in 2013 to 641 in the current year. Shoppers who were granted leases on new vehicles, incidentally, had an average score of 721 (down from 731 a year earlier), and 70 percent of them scored in the Prime or Super Prime category.

More than 94 percent of loans issued by finance companies go to persons with subprime credit, while more than 90 percent of BHPH dealers' loans are subprime. Banks, in contrast, issue less than half of their loans to buyers with non-prime credit.

Though buyers with less-than-prime credit are the ones more likely to become unable to make their payments, delinquencies have been fairly stable lately. The 30-day delinquency rate in January-March

2014 was 2.24 percent, down from 2.36 percent a year earlier. For finance companies, on the other hand, 4.6 percent of loan customers were 30 or more days behind with their payments. Banks had a 30-day delinquency rate around 2 percent, while only 1.2 percent of loans issued by credit unions were 30 days behind.

Geography makes a difference in delinquency. According to Experian, the states with the worst records are in a belt through the southeast: Mississippi, Louisiana, Alabama, Georgia, and both Carolinas. Best records for delinquencies go to states in the upper Midwest, along with Washington, Oregon, and Utah. Overall, only 0.63 percent of debtors are 60 days delinquent with their car loans, though repossessions rose from 0.5 percent in early 2013 to 0.68 percent a year later. Again, finance companies are considerably more likely to "repo" the cars they've loaned money: that rate rose from 1.78 percent in early 2013 to a hefty 3 percent in the first quarter of 2014.

Making car loans available to shoppers with shaky credit histories is risky, but subprime lending has been a growth industry. In its quarterly financial summary of the industry, Experian Automotive stated that in the first quarter of 2014, the volume of subprime car loans was 15 percent higher than it had been a year earlier. In mid-2014, CNW Research determined that the number of subprime buyers had grown by 25.5 percent during the previous year. Those in the group of lowest credit scores rose by 23.6 percent during that year.

Critics have charged that the growth in subprime auto credit echoes the excesses of the subprime mortgage fiasco that caused plenty of turmoil a few years back, leading to big-bank bailouts. Early in August 2014, *The New York Times* reported that federal prosecutors were investigating subprime auto lending; particularly, the practice of "packaging" questionable loans into large blocks that are sold to investors. When we first heard the term "securitization" at a nonprime financing conference a decade or so ago, we had no idea what it meant. Since then, it's grown almost exponentially, luring investors with the promise of particularly high returns.

General Motors' finance subsidiary (GM Financial), among the biggest participants in subprime auto lending, was served with a subpoena related to its securitization practices dating back to 2007, before the company's filing for bankruptcy and subsequent bailout.

Investigators wondered if investors knew about the questionable creditworthiness of car-buyers who'd been given the loans. Dealers were even alleged to have falsified income and employment information on some loan applications, to increase the likelihood of acceptance by a lender.

Subprime financing vs. standard rates

Interest rates vary widely according to credit rating, Experian's Melinda Zabritski said. Deep Subprime buyers of used cars paid an average APR (Annual Percentage Rate) of nearly 18.6 percent in late 2013, versus 14.5 percent for Subprime customers and only 8.5 percent for those with Nonprime credit.

Those on the prime side of the equation pay even lower rates. Experian found that the average used-vehicle buyer with Super Prime credit paid only a 3.5 percent APR. Prime shoppers averaged a 5.1 percent rate.

Example: For comparison, let's take a customer who buys a car for $18,000, paying $3,000 down. He or she is therefore financing $15,000, for, say, a 60-month term. If this buyer can get a loan at 5.9 percent APR, he'll pay about $2,358 in interest over the entire period. With a loan at 8.9 percent APR, the interest total jumps to $3,639. A borrower with subprime credit obtains an average APR of 14 percent, which translates to $5,941 in interest paid. If this person is in *deep* subprime territory, paying 18 percent, the total interest paid would be a whopping $7,854. That's $6,722 more in interest than the buyer who obtains a 2.9-percent loan will pay. Monthly payments in these examples range from $269 for the 2.9-percent loan to $381 for that 18-percenter.

Increasing the amount of your down payment is among the best ways to reduce your total outlay for credit. Especially if you're steering toward a higher interest rate, reducing the amount to be financed makes a substantial difference in what you'll be paying over the loan term. Obviously, though, folks with subpar credit histories are the ones least likely to have surplus cash at hand for a down payment. According to the National Independent Automobile Dealers

Association, the average down payment for a used vehicle is $1,328, with an average loan term of 41 months.

Subprime bottomed in 2009 before starting to rise, said Raj Sundaram of Dealertrack Technologies, and as of mid-2014 is still not at pre-recession levels. About 30 percent of loans now are high-risk. Between January 2010 and late 2013, the number of subprime lenders went from about 650 to near 1,200 (up 75 percent).

In 2008-09, "money dried up," Sundaram explained. The loan approval rate, which had been in the 30 to 40 percent range, sank to a mere 4 percent. Now, it's back around 20 percent. Loan periods are lengthening, too: "That clearly is troubling."

During 2010, availability of credit improved in the lower tiers, according to Manheim. As a result, many dealers said the customers who proved hardest to finance were those in *near-prime* status, rather than those at the bottom of the pile. Experian advised that subprime car loans had increased by 15 percent in early 2014, compared to the figure a year earlier. Later in 2014, CNW Research reported that the number of subprime purchasers had risen by 28.5 percent.

Much of the subprime growth is in the "higher credit score ranges," Experian's Zabritski said. "Banks have creatively grown their share of subprime financing." Two-thirds of web shoppers who fill out online credit applications have subprime credit scores.

On the whole, monthly payments have been flat, though payments for subprime buyers have shown a "steady increase," Zabritski said. The average used-car buyer with Deep Subprime credit paid $371 per month in late 2013.

Washington, D.C. leads the used-car pack in terms of the number of subprime sales, with 48.6 percent, according to the Consumer Credit Database. Nevada is next with 43.5 percent, followed by Florida, Georgia, and Mississippi. In South Dakota, on the other hand, fewer than one-fourth of sales are to subprime customers.

"Lenders are realizing that auto loans have lower risk than other consumer lending, especially mortgages," said former NADA Chairman Stephen Wade a few years back. "As a result, dealers are seeing more credit flowing to nonprime vehicle buyers."

During one session at Used Car Week in November 2013, several groups of people in the subprime business got together to discuss relevant issues. "There should be no more high-fives when you gave a consumer a higher rate than deserved," or engaged in other deceptive practices, one member reported to the full audience. The "glaring problem is trust." A third participant suggested that it "all boils down to F&I [finance and insurance] departments," which are "forcing the poor consumer into bad deals."

One participant simply warned: "Let's just try not to play Wizard of Oz, smoke and mirrors.... What's good for the dealer isn't necessarily good for the customer."

Buy Here–Pay Here

If you're in serious credit trouble, your only recourse may be a Buy-Here-Pay-Here dealership – the kind that occupies a lot plastered with signs promising "Easy Credit," "We Finance Everyone," and "Everybody Drives." Many BHPH dealers also make a point of having salespeople speak the languages of people who reside in the area, with big signs proclaiming that capability.

There's been a "general deterioration of credit quality across the entire population," according to the Manheim Used Car Market Report. Many who could have qualified for a conventional loan in the recent past have had to rely on dealer financing or BHPH car lots. Still, Buy-Here-Pay-Here dealerships have often been the "only game in town" for the credit-challenged. Because BHPH customers inevitably are the likeliest to default on their automotive debt, those dealerships charge high interest rates and are geared toward customers who cannot qualify for conventional loans.

BHPH dealers are the ones most likely to use technology to prod reluctant debtors into making their monthly car payments. Technological methods include Payment Reminders, Payment Assurance Devices, and GPS Tracking.

The starter-interrupt is a Payment Assurance Device. When a borrower is sufficiently delinquent to prompt forcible action, the dealer or lender can, essentially with the push of a button, prevent the engine in the borrower's vehicle from starting. Once the payments are resumed in a satisfactory manner, the lender can release the device, allowing the car to run normally again. As a safety factor, the devices are not meant to the stop the engine once it's running; they take effect only when it's stopped. Of course, that could mean it's in front of the borrower's home – or, perhaps, in a parking spot with a time limit. So, the borrower could be in for even more trouble than expected, if the device is activated.

As its name suggests, GPS Tracking allows the lender to determine where the vehicle is located, using the same sort of technology employed in navigation systems and with cell phones. Before installing a GPS device, the lender must obtain written consent from the borrower. As Corinne Kirkendall, of PassTime, admitted during a webinar on payment-related devices, that person must "knowingly surrender the rights of privacy." In order to get the car, of course, a credit-challenged borrower either accepts the indignity of a starter-interrupt or GPS tracking, or doesn't get to drive.

In several states, use of GPS Tracking is illegal without such consent, or prohibited entirely. Wisconsin, for one, has declared it an unfair collection practice, as well as an invasion of privacy. No federal law limits or prohibits GPS Tracking or Payment Assurance Technology.

According to the National Independent Automobile Dealers Association, 12.4 percent of BHPH dealers use payment reminders, 21.2 percent installed starter-interrupt devices, and a whopping 66.4 percent turn to GPS tracking for customers with questionable credit. From their perspective, these methods are necessary, because one-fourth of BHPH sales turn into "bad debts."

Once you're in the BHPH category as a car-buyer, you don't have to remain there indefinitely. In a BHPH webinar, Brent Carmichael, of NCM Associates, said he advises dealers to look at customers who are nearly paid-up on their car, paying on time; perhaps, on the next go-round, they can be upgraded to a *better* car.

All dealers – BHPH, regular independent, and franchised – are affected by the recently-established Consumer Financial Protection Bureau, which emanated from the Dodd-Frank Act of 2012. The CFPB is authorized to enforce financial protection laws, create and enforce new protection rules, monitor the credit-granting industry, and supervise certain financial institutions. One of its primary goals is elimination of discriminatory lending practices, which cause people in certain ethnic or other groups to pay higher rates than would otherwise be the case.

Financing Glossary

When discussing financing at the dealership or with a representative of a lending organization, you probably will (or should) hear most of these terms:

- **Amount financed:** The actual dollar amount you're borrowing to buy a vehicle, not including finance charges.
- **BHPH (Buy Here-Pay Here):** A dealership that specializes in low-end vehicles, selling to customers with flawed credit histories.
- **Co-signer:** Person with a better credit rating, who signs the loan contract as a guarantor that the creditor (borrower) will pay; that person will be held responsible if the car-buyer defaults on payments.
- **Credit insurance:** Optional insurance pays unpaid balance on loan contract if you die; or monthly payments, if you become disabled.
- **Credit score:** A three-digit number that gives lenders a quick appraisal of your credit status, and likelihood of making payments on time. Three major credit-reporting agencies issue credit scores (Expedia, Equifax, and TransUnion), using different criteria. All of them, collectively, are generally referred to as FICO scores.
- **Credit report:** A document containing information about your residence, bill-payment history, employment, lawsuits, bankruptcy, and other factors; that information is sold to potential lenders, employers, insurers and others who wish to evaluate your creditworthiness.
- **Dealership financing:** Credit obtained directly through the dealership, though the contract is typically sold to a bank, finance company, or credit union.
- **Deficiency balance:** The amount you still owe on a loan after you've stopped making payments.
- **Default judgment:** A legal determination that a person is in default – has not paid – a specified amount.

- **Direct lending:** Credit obtained from a bank, finance company, or credit union, for the purpose of purchasing a vehicle; the amount received is then used to pay for the vehicle at a dealership.
- **Down payment:** The amount of cash that you give to the seller at the time of purchase, plus the value of your trade-in (if any).
- **Finance charge:** Cost of the credit that's obtained, in dollars; this figure is added to the dollar amount of the actual vehicle loan, to determine the total amount to be paid over a stated period of months.
- **Fixed rate:** A loan where the interest rate remains the same through the entire term of the contract; auto loans are nearly always fixed-rate, as opposed to variable-rate.
- **Guaranteed Auto Protection (GAP):** Optional insurance that pays the difference between the amount you still owe on a vehicle, and the amount an insurer would pay, if the vehicle is stolen or destroyed.
- **Interest rate:** Annual Percentage Rate (APR) of interest that you will be paying over the life of the financing contract.
- **Loan Term:** A period in months, during which you are required to make regular payments.
- **Monthly payment:** The amount you are expected to pay each month, for the term of the loan.
- **Negative equity:** Situation whereby the amount still owed on a vehicle is higher than the market value for that vehicle; debtors with negative equity are said to be "underwater" or "upside-down."
- **Repossession (repo):** The practice by lenders or their representation of taking a car back if the borrower has failed to make payments properly.
- **Securitization:** Situation whereby a lender sells your loan contract, grouped with dozens or hundreds of others, to a larger organization that makes the entire group available to investors. Traditionally, borrowers knew who held their contract; but securitization is common nowadays, and investors anticipate high interest from such "bundled" loan contracts.
- **Total of payments:** The total amount paid on a loan contract, in dollars, after the final monthly payment is made.

For additional information on financing, go to www.bankrate.com (Autos section); or to the Federal Trade Commission (consumer.ftc.gov).

Online payment calculators, such as those found at bankrate.com and cars.com, let you determine how much you'll be paying in interest by "plugging in" the amount to be financed, loan term, and APR. Best to be prepared, even before applying for a loan, experimenting with various figures.

22

Insurance

Unless you're a first-time car buyer, you probably have insurance on your current vehicle. Do you need more coverage for the "new" one? Different coverage?

How much do you need? Almost certainly, more than is *required* in your state. Mainly, be sure you're fully covered as you drive the newly-purchased car away from the dealership or the private seller. Accidents can happen – and do – moments after a sale has concluded.

Remember, car insurance has two basic elements:

1. Liability and Property Damage, covering the other car and its occupant, if involved in an accident.

2. Collision coverage, dealing with damage to your own car.

Liability coverage for that other car (which is what you *must* have) has three elements:

1. An amount Per Person.
2. A larger amount Per Accident.
3. A separate amount for Property Damage.

If your old car has had only minimal coverage – covering only the other people and the vehicle in an accident, with nothing for your own car – you may want to opt for collision and comprehensive, especially if the vehicle you're buying is considerably newer. If you're financing the car, collision/comprehensive coverage may be required by the lender.

Naturally, if you've caused accidents and/or been convicted of moving traffic violations, you can expect to pay considerably more. Lowest rates generally go to drivers with no tickets or accidents on their records. However, today's insurance companies also consider factors that have little or nothing to do with your driving record, such as residence address and employment history, to assess a premium.

Some factors affecting your premium

Like all insurance companies, auto insurers rely on a combination of factors to determine how much your premium will be. Most of them have little or nothing to do with actual driving, and critics argue that those factors should not be taken into account. Nothing is likely to change anytime soon, despite the proliferation of hard-sell ads and e-mails that try to convince policyholders that they're currently paying too much for their auto coverage.

These are the primary factors that are considered:

- Age: Historically, young drivers pay considerably more than older ones.
- Gender: Women generally get better rates than men – and girls can insure cars for far less than teenage boys.
- Marital status: Being married helps keep the rate down.
- Driving record: Obviously, this one belongs in the consideration list, though minor infractions or accidents that were someone else's fault should not result in increased premiums.
- Residence location: They call it "redlining," which means actuaries map locations in an urban area where the risk of accident or damage is considered to be greater, and charge higher premiums for those who happen to live there.
- Where car is garaged or kept: Park on the street rather than an enclosed garage, and you're likely to be charged more.

Traditionally, single males under 25 pay significantly higher rates than other drivers, simply because statistics reveal that they're involved in more accidents. Married men can expect to pay less than single men, and women generally are charged less. A few states do not permit rate differentials based on sex or age. People who live in dense urban areas can expect to pay more. Often, a *lot* more.

Only Hawaii does not permit insurers to consider age, gender, or amount of driving experience when setting rates.

If you have more assets and income than the average person, you're especially in need of higher coverage – perhaps including a "personal liability umbrella" policy in the amount of $1 million or more.

Premiums vary according to the type of car and model, too, and even according to engine size. Pick a high-performance model, and you'll be paying considerably higher premiums, regardless of how it's driven. The year of the car can make a difference, too.

Installation of certain safety features might lower the premium a bit. Accepting a higher deductible for some portions of insurance coverage usually lowers the premium cost, but you're gambling that you won't have to come up with those dollars yourself at some point.

In the past few years, insurers have been urging customers to allow the installation of electronic tracking devices, which are supposed to let the insurance company know how safely you drive. If your driving meets a certain standard, the premium may go down (though not necessarily by much). In exchange, you're giving up some precious freedom: namely, the freedom not to have your actions monitored at all times.

Insurance shopping

Shop for insurance quotes, online or over the phone. Getting quotes from several insurers used to be a tedious process; but nowadays, the number of companies willing and eager to provide them is overwhelming. Most likely, your e-mail in-box is full of offers from insurance companies to slash your rates. Remember, a company that pushes so hard to attract new customers expects to make an abundant profit from those who succumb. Better to stick with insurers you've dealt with before, or that you've found yourself.

Once you determine the vehicle or vehicles you're interested in, ask your insurance representative to advise you as to what impact that vehicle will have on your overall premium. Should this change be greater than anticipated, ask why. Ask if other similar cars are rated the same, or if a change in engine size (such as, a 4-cylinder vs. V-6), model, or year of the car would make a significant difference.

Ask what impact driving record, deductibles, anti-theft devices, future age changes, experience level, marital status, children, garaging, and/or location might have on your overall premium cost.

Be certain your insurance representative or company is knowledgeable in these areas. Ask about the claim-handling procedures of the company you're with, and what you might expect should a loss occur. A particular insurance company may have low rates, but a confusing and difficult claim procedure. Is saving a few dollars worth the added time and trouble?

Insurance laws and practices differ from state to state. Coverages that may be readily available in one area or under one set of circumstances may be dramatically affected by seemingly minor changes.

Your policy coverages may not be exactly as described above, so it's important that you discuss these items with your insurance representative.

Finally, you may find a much cheaper rate at one particular, possibly unfamiliar, insurance company. This is not always good news. Like any other organization, an insurance company just might be here today, but gone tomorrow. If you're unfamiliar with a company, check them out through the Chamber of Commerce or the Better Business Bureau in your area before you give them any money.

23

Concluding the Car Purchase

Dealers and their employees are adept at wearing down customers, so they don't get away without buying. It's common for a customer to deal with several people during the transaction. One person might greet you at the door. Another shows you the car you ask about. Yet another turns up suddenly, to try and close the deal. Waiting in the wings is the sales manager, ready to approve (or disapprove) the transaction.

Dealership F&I (Finance and Insurance) people tend to whip through their portion of the transaction, presenting you with a flurry of documents to sign and (supposedly) scrutinize. We all know that we're supposed to read everything on a contract before signing. In reality, not many people get past the first few words – if that. Do the best you can to make sure all the details are correctly stated, and *never* sign a contract that has any blank spaces.

That F&I person isn't necessarily trying to befuddle you (though some might). They're just accustomed to doing this every day, failing to recognize that even an expert shopper can easily get lost in the maze of paperwork.

Be sure to get every detail in writing. Double-check all figures and calculations, remembering that even the most honest people can make errors. Remember, oral agreements are useless. If anything bothers you, insist that the F&I person – and anyone else you deal with – slow down. Above all, remain calm and pay attention.

Contract, Bill of Sale, and Title

At any dealership, you'll be signing a sales contract, which is a standard form. Just make sure all the details are *exactly* as you understood them when talking to the salesperson, manager, and any other involved parties. If anything doesn't look right, clarify it now.

If you're paying cash, you should get a form stating that the car's title will be in your name alone. Most likely, the actual title will be mailed to you later, from the state's offices.

Persons who finance a car won't get a clear title to the vehicle until it's paid for. Just make sure you have appropriate papers signifying that the vehicle is legally yours – with the proviso that a bank, credit union, or finance company may hold the actual title for the next few years.

When you're financing the car through the dealership, even closer scrutiny of all paperwork is mandatory. Make sure the loan amount, monthly payments, and every other stated figure add up as they should.

Private sales are typically concluded with a simple Bill of Sale; but if you have any doubt, make sure that's sufficient in your state. Ask at the Department of Motor Vehicles.

A Bill of Sale can be handwritten or rolled out of a printer. Make two copies. Each should be signed by both the buyer and the seller, and each party should keep one copy.

Best advice: Don't sign anything until you're *certain* that you're ready to buy. And you're not ready until you know *exactly* what you're buying, and how much (in total) you are going to pay for it.

Don't hesitate to ask questions about anything you don't understand, or that's unclear. It doesn't hurt to bring a friend or relative along, just to keep you from saying "yes" to a deal that has not yet been fully clarified, or which has potential trouble spots.

What to watch for before you sign

Make a final check of the car's title. First of all, be sure the Vehicle Identification Number (VIN) on the title matches the VIN on the car. It's stamped onto a rectangular plate, affixed to the driver's side of the dashboard (near the windshield base). Consisting of a 17-character combination of letters and numbers, VINs can be read from outside the car.

The 10th symbol in the VIN specifies the car's age: X=1999; Y=2000; 1=2001; 2=2002; 3=2003; 4=2004; 5=2005; 6=2006;

7=2007; 8=2008; 9=2009; A=2010; B=2011; C=2012; D=2013; E=2014. F=2015.

Inspect the title carefully, to make sure there's no evidence of alteration or erasure. Most titles specify if there's a lien against the car (meaning someone still owes money on it). If there is, walk away. Don't complicate your life with a car whose title is in jeopardy, even if the selling price is irresistible.

Should you trade-in your old car?

Statistics on the number of people who trade in their old cars when buying a new (or newer) one appear to be hazy. Veteran used-car expert Ricky Beggs, editorial director of *Black Book*, estimates that about 65 percent of shoppers do so. It's a majority, at any rate, compared to those who sell their old car privately.

You can usually get more for your old car in a private sale, but the process isn't nearly as easy or wise as it used to be. Do you really want a stream of shoppers turning up at your doorstep? How do you collect the money if a sale is consummated? Not many people bring sufficient cash along, except for the cheapest cars, and you're hardly in a position to arrange financing.

For a low-priced car, it's still a possibility. For more costly ones, the extra cash you could make probably isn't worth the added frustration, not to mention the various risks and dangers.

Therefore, most buyers trade in their old car to the dealership where they're buying a new one (or in this case, a *newer used* model). Before doing so, do a little research to find out what the old car might be worth, taking into account that the *most* you're going to get is "wholesale" value. A trade-in will probably cover the down payment on your next vehicle – or most of it, at any rate.

Remember, though, that dealers make more profit on sales of used cars than of new ones. All the more so nowadays, with new-car profit margins slimmer than in the past. Therefore, they won't be inclined to offer impressive amounts for trade-ins, even though they need those trades badly, to keep their stock of used vehicles at desired levels. If your trade-in is a clean late-model with low mileage, you should be able to get a satisfying sum for it just because such vehicles are in high demand, and likely to be for the next few years.

Don't try and trade in a car that's not paid for. That's asking for serious financial woes.

An old warning still holds: If a dealer offers more than reasonable, fair value for the car you're trading in, you can be pretty sure he's making up for that generosity at some other point of the deal.

"Everybody wants to hold the trade to the end, and then surprise us with it," said Craig Belowski of Acton Toyota in Littleton, Massachusetts, speaking at the 2013 CPO Forum. "We're not surprised."

PART V: Resources

A: How to Read the Ads
B: Test Drive Checklist
C: Manufacturer-backed CPO Programs
D: For More Information...
E: Used Car Buyer's Checklist
F: Sample Bill of Sale

A

How to Read the Ads – Online and In Print

Used-car advertisements aren't what they used to be. Newspapers, for one thing, carry far fewer ads than in the past, now that so much consumer information has moved online. In print, you're likely to find more used-car ads in giveaway "trader" publications than in a daily newspaper.

Online, a host of automotive information services provide access to used cars for sale – whether at dealerships or from private sellers. AutoTrader.com may be the leader, but you could easily spend days running through the ads on one site after another.

Not all ads are sufficiently informative, but on the whole they've improved. At the 2010 National Remarketing Conference, Kevin Nachbar of the McCarthy Auto Group advised dealers to provide "relevant information. No spin, no hype. Get rid of the car lingo." He further suggested: "Don't waste people's time. They don't have it."

Online ads tend to be packed with photos, but use caution here. Even the best digital photo can conceal a lot of imperfect body surfaces, not to mention trouble spots that are not visible from outside.

Clutter and confusion

Because ads compete for attention in an increasingly-crowded marketplace, clutter is the norm. We're all bombarded from morning to night by pleas to buy some product or service. In an attempt to bulldoze past the clutter, advertisers often turn to extremes: meaningless claims, redundant statements, intimidating inducements, all stuffed into a barrel of hype.

How can we, as consumers, be expected to separate the few useful messages from the mass of words and images we confront? Especially since the vast majority of ads are of no interest at all to us. In this sense, the Internet has made things worse, allowing advertisers to assault us with a constant flurry of promotions, whether via websites or e-mail, Twitter or texts.

Plenty of automobile dealers continue to miss the point, too, filling their ads with lists of features and standard equipment, amplified by shrieking verbiage that's likely to "turn off" more readers than it attracts. Vehicle photos and even videos are abundant on both dealer and third-party websites, but they convey far less information to prospective buyers than dealers seem to think. Details that are most important to the potential customer are seldom discernible to online readers/viewers, no matter how many photographic views of a car – differing only slightly from each other – are posted.

Modern dealers know that used-car ads should make it clear why a particular vehicle stands out from the crowd. Because every used car is different, those differences need to be stated clearly. Instead, the reader is often left hanging, unable to discern why this compact car or full-size pickup is worth a look and perhaps a test-drive, while another one might not be.

What's wrong with this ad?

13' MODEL SONIC WITH 13K MILES!!!
Manual Transmission!!! Superrrrrrrrrr MPG!!!
2013 CHEVROLET SONIC LS 4-DR SEDAN
ONE OWNER CAR!!! Features: Manual
transmission, Ac, 1.8 liter 4-Cylinder,
Cloth interior, RED!!! RED!!! RED!!!
HOT COLOR!!! and MUCH MORE!!!!
Exceptional buy... New body style, very nice!!!
Under Factory Warranty!!! COME IN NOW!!!

In the ad above, a fair amount of information is helpful to shoppers; more than in many ads, actually. Yet, some elements are not helpful (led by the excessive exclamation points):

Superrrrrrrrrrrr MPG! Who says it's super? How much does it really get?
LS 4-door sedan: Specifying trim level is important.
1.8-liter 4-cylinder: Important; but only if there's another engine choice.
13K miles: Among the most important figures of all.
One-owner car: Absolutely vital, if true
Manual Transmission: A fact that definitely needs to be stated up front.
Red! Red! Red! Hot Color: One "red" will do, and not everyone deems it "hot."
Under factory warranty: Excellent fact, though most late-models are still covered.
New body style: What does this mean? Is the 4-door new? Was this model redesigned?
Punctuation: Shortened form of 2013 is '13, not 13'.
Exceptional buy: Obviously, that's a matter of opinion.

Patrick McMullen, vice-president of MAX Systems, advises dealers to forget about features and equipment that apply to every example of a given model. A long list of standard equipment provides no useful value to the shopper. Instead, helpful ads should simply answer the question: How does this individual vehicle differ from all the similar ones that might be available in a given area?

Admittedly, some ads are intended mainly to draw interested parties into a dealership, rather than supply details on specific vehicles. But when they're meant to be the initial step in selling an actual car or truck, they'd better contain information that counts, not just a bunch of useless fluff.

According to McMullen, the goal is to "create robust listings" that answer tangible questions:

1. Is this the right car for me? Nearly every shopper is, or will be, considering several vehicles; so he or she needs reasons to put this one near the top of the list.

2. Is this a fair price? It may or may not be the lowest price around, but experts agree that what today's shoppers really seek is a fair figure.

3. Am I buying a lemon? That's a word we don't hear so much anymore; but in the used car field, shoppers are still worried about driving home a car that might quickly fail.

4. Why is this car better than all the others I've seen online? Again, you need specific reasons, not vague, dull, or overly dramatic words.

5. Why should I buy from this dealer?

McMullen cautions against descending into "chintzy dealer speak." Skip the allegedly clever but meaningless phrases, he advises, such as: "So clean you can eat off the floor mats." Retail customers need real, relevant facts. They include:

- Crash-test rating, when new. If it was 5-star, say so.
- Carfax details. Most buyers would rather have a car that was never in an accident, so emphasize that fact if it's true. Same thing if it's a one-owner car.
- Priced $000 Below Kelley Blue Book (assuming that discount off the "book" figure is true, of course).
- Certified pre-owned model. Is it certified as part of a manufacturer's CPO program? By a third-party organization?
- Statements made in published test drives when the car was new.
- Months/miles remaining on original new-car warranty (if applicable).
- Gas mileage estimate. Stickers that show original EPA estimates are available at fueleconomy.gov.
- How this model scored in J.D. Power quality ratings, when new.
- Any awards or accolades that were given to this model.
- Details of options and packages installed on the car when new.
•

Listings should be "educational in nature," McMullen concluded in his webinar on advertising. "If we as dealers aren't educating," the customers aren't going to buy.

Used-Car terms and abbreviations

• **Lo Mi** – Low mileage (but exactly how low is it?).

- **No Money Down** – Inevitably, you'll be paying more in monthly payments.
- **Cert** – Certified pre-owned (CPO).
- **We Finance Anyone** (or similar wording) – If true, the selling price is likely to be sky-high, to accommodate that decision.
- **Recon** (reconditioned) – May include mechanical work, but most often the focus is on appearance detailing: touching up nicks, dents, scrapes, to give the car a clean look.
- **As Is** – Sold with no promises as to running condition, with no recourse if a problem occurs. Not a wise choice, no matter how cheap the car may be.
- **Base Model** – Least expensive version of a given car model, with minimal equipment and few (if any) accessories; most likely, also has the smallest engine. Used to be called "strippers."
- **Book Price** – Valuation found in one of the major used-car price guidebooks (Kelley Blue Book, NADA, Black Book). Wholesale and retail price figures vary among the guidebooks; so naturally, a dealer is more likely to pick the one with the highest amount shown for the model you're considering.
- **Doc Fee** – Documentation fee, charged by dealers for doing the paperwork related to the purchase, including the title and license applications. Some dealers absorb certain extra charges, as the cost of doing business.
- **Fixed Price** – Instead of being open to negotiation, in the traditional way, some dealers assign a no-bargaining-permitted price to each vehicle offered for sale.
- **Highline** (or Premium) – Terms used for a luxury or near-luxury vehicle, priced well above the average.
- **Loaded** – Vehicle with a full complement of optional equipment installed. Guidebooks generally suggest an add-on price for certain options, to be added to the basic retail figure.
- **VIN** (Vehicle Identification Number) – The 17-digit number found on the upper dashboard of every vehicle manufactured. Digits 1-3 indicate the manufacturer; 4, the restraint system; 5-7, the line, series, and body type; 8, engine type; 9, a check digit with no significance to the shopper; 10, model year; 11, assembly plant; and 12-17, the sequential production number of that particular vehicle.

Many more terms can be found, though abbreviations aren't quite as common as they used to be, when newspaper classified ads were the dominant means of advertising used cars.

B

Test-Drive Checklist

Inspection
o Body damage: dings, dents, scratches, rust.
o Evidence of an accident.
o Evidence of superficial or imperfect body repair.
o Corrosion of any sort: far less likely than in the past, but still a serious concern.
o Windows and doors work properly.
o Glass condition.
o Tire condition, and presence of a spare tire.
o Exhaust system (seen underneath the vehicle).
o Evidence of fluid leakage.
o Condition of engine oil and coolant.
o Upholstery condition.
o Lubrication stickers (to confirm regular maintenance and vehicle mileage).
o Lights all work properly.

Startup
o Engine starts easily; no unusual sounds, and no ritual required.
o Driver's seat feels comfortable and roomy; passenger seats, too.
o Gauges are easy to read at a glance.
o No visibility issues (blockage by headrest, etc.).
o Pedals work normally.
o No noise or vibration at idle.
o No hesitation or roughness at idle.
o No smoke emanating from tailpipe or elsewhere.

On the Road

- Overall feel: no jerking, hesitation, looseness, tendency to wander, etc.
- Automatic-transmission's gears change smoothly.
- Manual transmission easy to shift; well-behaved clutch.
- Acceleration smooth and adequate.
- Straight-line tracking: no pulling to the side.
- Brakes quiet, bringing vehicle evenly and promptly to a halt.
- No odd noises underneath the vehicle or under the hood.
- No odd steering sounds when turning.
- Nothing unusual shown on oil-pressure or other gauges (if any).
- Engine restarts easily, when warmed up and after a drive.

C

Manufacturer-backed CPO Programs

Almost all manufacturers offer a certified pre-owned vehicle program. Certification programs backed by the manufacturer cover vehicles that are no more than four to seven years old, with no more than 50,000 to 85,000 miles on the odometer (eight years and up to 100,000 for Porsche models). Many vehicle ages are measured in model years, but some count age by calendar year. All programs include a step-by-step inspection, with a specific number of points to examine.

Warranties vary considerably in duration and coverage. Some begin when the used CPO vehicle is purchased. Others start with the car's original sale date, when it was new. There may be a comprehensive warranty for a stated period, and a powertrain warranty that covers a longer time frame. Warranty coverage also may vary, according to the age of the vehicle.

Many programs include Roadside Assistance. Some offer a return/exchange program, with specific requirements that must be followed. GM vehicles include a 3-day/150-mile Customer Satisfaction Guarantee program. Acura models may be exchanged within 3 days. Mercedes-Benz allows 7 days or 500 miles.

An extended warranty, beyond the terms of the CPO program, is usually available at extra cost. Some programs offer special financing for CPO vehicles.

Virtually all CPO vehicles include a vehicle history report – typically supplied by Carfax. Nissan and Infiniti have their own history report.

Note: Comprehensive data on factory-backed certified programs may be found at www.intellichoice.com. All CPO program details are subject to change at any time.

Several makes listed below are no longer manufactured, including Hummer, Mercury, Pontiac, Saab, and Saturn. Certified pre-owned examples may no longer be sold, but information is provided below for anybody who happens to own one.

ACURA
Maximum Age: 6 years
Maximum Mileage: 80,000
Inspection Points: 150
Additional Warranty Coverage (months/miles): 12/12,000 comprehensive, 12/30,000 powertrain (coverage for earlier models may differ)

AUDI
Maximum Age: 5 years
Maximum Mileage: 60,000
Inspection Points: 300+
Additional Warranty Coverage (months/miles): 24/50,000 comprehensive

BMW
Maximum Age: 5 years
Maximum Mileage: 60,000
Inspection Points: 200
Additional Warranty Coverage (months/miles): 24/50,000 comprehensive

BUICK
Maximum Age: 6 (current model year plus up to five previous model years)
Maximum Mileage: 75,000
Inspection Points: 172
Additional Warranty Coverage (months/miles): 12/12,000 comprehensive, 60/100,000 powertrain (from original in-service date)

CADILLAC
Maximum Age: 5 years
Maximum Mileage: 50,000
Inspection Points: 172
Additional Warranty Coverage (months/miles): 24/20,000 comprehensive, 24-month powertrain (12-month for earlier models)

CHEVROLET
Maximum Age: 6 (current model year plus up to five previous model years)
Maximum Mileage: 75,000
Inspection Points: 172
Additional Warranty Coverage (months/miles): 12/12,000 comprehensive, 60/100,000 powertrain (from original in-service date)

CHRYSLER
Maximum Age: 6 years
Maximum Mileage: 75,000
Inspection Points: 125
Additional Warranty Coverage (months/miles): 3/3,000 comprehensive, 36/64,000 powertrain (2010 and newer models, 24-month)

DODGE
Maximum Age: 6 years
Maximum Mileage: 75,000
Inspection Points: 125
Additional Warranty Coverage (months/miles): 3/3,000 comprehensive, 36/64,000 powertrain (2010 and newer models, 24-month)

FIAT
Maximum Age: 6 years
Maximum Mileage: 75,000
Inspection Points: 125
Additional Warranty Coverage (months/miles): 24/30,000 comprehensive

FORD
Maximum Age: 6 (current model year plus up to five previous model years)
Maximum Mileage: 80,000
Inspection Points: 172
Additional Warranty Coverage (months/miles): 12/12,000 comprehensive, 12/40,000 powertrain

GMC
Maximum Age: 6 (current model year plus up to five previous model years)

Maximum Mileage: 75,000
Inspection Points: 172
Additional Warranty Coverage (months/miles): 12/12,000 comprehensive, 24/64,000 powertrain

HONDA
Maximum Age: 6 years
Maximum Mileage: 80,000
Inspection Points: 150
Additional Warranty Coverage (months/miles): 12/12,000 comprehensive, 24/40,000 powertrain (coverage for earlier models may differ)

HUMMER (US sales ceased after 2010)

HYUNDAI
Maximum Age: 5 years
Maximum Mileage: 60,000
Inspection Points: 150
Additional Warranty Coverage (months/miles): 120/100,000 powertrain (total)

INFINITI
Maximum Age: 4 years
Maximum Mileage: 60,000
Inspection Points: 100
Additional Warranty Coverage (months/miles): 24/40,000 comprehensive, 12/30,000 powertrain

JAGUAR
Maximum Age: 5 years
Maximum Mileage: 60,000
Inspection Points: 150
Additional Warranty Coverage (months/miles): 24/50,000 comprehensive

JEEP
Maximum Age: 6 years
Maximum Mileage: 75,000
Inspection Points: 125

Additional Warranty Coverage (months/miles): 3/3,000 comprehensive, 36/64,000 powertrain (2010 and newer models, 24-month)

KIA
Maximum Age: 5 years
Maximum Mileage: 60,000
Inspection Points: 150
Additional Warranty Coverage (months/miles): 60/40,000 powertrain

LAND ROVER
Maximum Age: 5 years
Maximum Mileage: 60,000
Inspection Points: 150
Additional Warranty Coverage (months/miles): 24/50,000 comprehensive

LEXUS
Maximum Age: 6 years
Maximum Mileage: 70,000
Inspection Points: 161
Additional Warranty Coverage (months/miles): 36/100,000 comprehensive

LINCOLN
Maximum Age: 6 (current model year plus up to five previous model years)
Maximum Mileage: 60,000
Inspection Points: 200
Additional Warranty Coverage (months/miles): 24/50,000 comprehensive

MAZDA
Maximum Age: 6 years
Maximum Mileage: 80,000
Inspection Points: 150
Additional Warranty Coverage (months/miles): 12/12,000 comprehensive, 24/40,000 powertrain

MERCEDES-BENZ
Maximum Age: 6 years
Maximum Mileage: 75,000

Inspection Points: 155+
Additional Warranty Coverage (months/miles): 12/50,000 comprehensive

MERCURY (US sales ceased after 2011)
Maximum Age: 6 (current model year plus up to five previous model years
Maximum Mileage: 80,000
Inspection Points: 172
Additional Warranty Coverage (months/miles): 12/12,000 comprehensive, 12/40,000 powertrain

MINI
Maximum Age: 5 years
Maximum Mileage: 60,000
Inspection Points: 197
Additional Warranty Coverage (months/miles): 24/50,000 comprehensive

MITSUBISHI
Maximum Age: 5 years
Maximum Mileage: 60,000
Inspection Points: 123
Additional Warranty Coverage (months/miles): 60/60,000 comprehensive, 10/100,000 powertrain

NISSAN
Maximum Age: 6 years
Maximum Mileage: 75,000
Inspection Points: 125
Additional Warranty Coverage (months/miles): 3/3,000 comprehensive, 30/64,000 powertrain (24-month for newer models)

PONTIAC (US sales ceased after 2010)
Maximum Age: 6 (current model year plus up to five previous model years)
Maximum Mileage: 75,000
Inspection Points: 172
Additional Warranty Coverage (months/miles): 12/12,000 comprehensive, 24/64,000 powertrain

PORSCHE
Maximum Age: 8 years
Maximum Mileage: 100,000
Inspection Points: 111
Additional Warranty Coverage (months/miles): 24/50,000 comprehensive

RAM
Maximum Age: 6 years
Maximum Mileage: 75,000
Inspection Points: 125
Additional Warranty Coverage (months/miles): 3/3,000 comprehensive, 36/64,000 powertrain (2010 and newer models, 24 months)

SAAB (US sales ceased after 2011)

SATURN (US sales ceased after 2009)
Maximum Age: 6 (current model year plus up to five previous model years)
Maximum Mileage: 75,000
Inspection Points: 172
Additional Warranty Coverage (months/miles): 12/12,000 comprehensive, 24/64,000 powertrain

SCION
Maximum Age: 7 years (current year plus up to six model years)
Maximum Mileage: 85,000
Inspection Points: 160
Additional Warranty Coverage (months/miles): 12/12,000 comprehensive, 24/40,000 powertrain

SMART
Additional Warranty Coverage (months/miles): total, 12/100,000 or 24/100,000, depending on model year

SUBARU
Maximum Age: 5 years
Maximum Mileage: 80,000
Inspection Points: 152
Additional Warranty Coverage (months/miles): 12/40,000 powertrain

SUZUKI (US sales ceased after 2012)

TOYOTA
Maximum Age: 7 years (current year plus up to six model years)
Maximum Mileage: 85,000
Inspection Points: 160+
Additional Warranty Coverage (months/miles): 12/12,000 comprehensive, 24/40,000 powertrain

VOLKSWAGEN
Maximum Age: 6 years
Maximum Mileage: 75,000
Inspection Points: 112
Additional Warranty Coverage (months/miles): 24/24,000 comprehensive

VOLVO
Maximum Age: 6 years (current year plus up to five previous model years)
Maximum Mileage: 80,000
Inspection Points: 130+
Additional Warranty Coverage (months/miles): 24/50,000 comprehensive (coverage for relatively new models may be lower)

D

For More Information

Information Resources
www.kbb.com (used-car valuations)
www.consumerreports.com (reliability surveys)
www.cars.com (general information)
www.usedcars.about.com (general information and trends)
www.nadaguides.com (information and valuations from National Automobile Dealers Association Used Car Guide)
www.autotrader.com (vehicle sources and information)
www.carfax.com and www.autocheck.com (vehicle history reports)
www.iihs.org (crash tests from Insurance Institute for Highway Safety)
www.safercar.gov (government 5-star crash tests and safety recalls)
www.fueleconomy.gov (government fuel-economy estimates)
www.intellichoice.com (CPO information and details)
www.consumerguide.com (used-vehicle reviews and valuations): availability ceased in mid-2013; may be revived at some point.

Online used-car sales:
In addition to major third-party advertising services (www.autotrader.com, www.cars.com, www.kbb.com), various other online sources of secondhand vehicles have sprouted up, and will continue to do so.

Third-party certification:
POADA certification: www.carmarkcertified.com
NIADA certification: www.niada.certified.com
Motor Trend: www.motortrendcertified.com
Carmax: www.carmax.com

Enterprise Car Sales: www.enterprisecarsales.com/certified-used-cars-for-sale

Dealer groups
National Automobile Dealers Association: www.nada.org
National Independent Automobile Dealers Association: www.niada.com

Manufacturer Web Sites:

Acura: acura.com
Audi: audiusa.com
BMW: bmwusa.com
Chevrolet: chevrolet.com
Chrysler: chrysler.com
Dodge: dodge.com
Fiat: fiatusa.com
Ford: ford.com
GMC: gmc.com
Honda: honda.com
Hyundai: hyundaiusa.com
Infiniti: infinitiusa.com
Jaguar: jaguarusa.com
Jeep: jeep.com
Kia: kia.com
Land Rover: landroverusa.com
Lexus: lexus.com
Lincoln: lincoln.com
Mazda: mazdausa.com
Mercedes-Benz: mbusa.com
Mitsubishi: mitsubishicars.com
Nissan: nissanusa.com
Porsche: porsche.com/usa
Ram: ramtrucks.com
Smart: smartusa.com
Subaru: subaru.com
Suzuki: suzukiauto.com (for warranty issues)
Toyota: toyota.com
Volkswagen: vw.com
Volvo: volvocars.com/us

E

Used Car Buyer's Worksheet

Getting the figures down on paper in an organized manner can help a lot in determining what you will be paying, and what you're getting. Always insist that the dealer or his representative explain each fee that's tacked onto the final price; don't agree to pay them until you understand what they are.

Beware of contracts that offer promising terms but include a "balloon" payment at the end of the loan period. It could amount to thousands of dollars, payable in one lump sum.

Sample Bill of Sale

Year _____ Make _____
Model _____
Body Style _____

Selling Price (what you've agreed to pay for car) $ _____
Add: Taxes (state and/or local) $ _____
Add: License fees $ _____
Add: Additional fees and costs $ _____

Total Price To Be Paid $ _____

Subtract: Trade-in Allowance (if any) $ _____
Total Amount Due $ _____

Subtract: Down Payment (cash) $ _____
Amount to be financed $ _____

Interest (total to be paid) $ _____
_____ months at _____ percent APR (annual percentage rate)
(_____ monthly payments of $ _____ each)

Total Amount To Be Paid Over Life of Contract $ _____

F

Sample Bill of Sale

I, _____
　　　　　　　(seller's name)
of
_____
　　　　　　　(seller's address)
hereby sell to
_____
　　　　　　　(buyer's name)
of
_____
　　　　　　　(buyer's address)
one _____ _____
_____
car (or truck), with Vehicle Identification Number
_____

Vehicle is sold As Is and As Shown, with clear title,

for the sum of $ _____, paid in full in cash (or check)

Signed
_____
　　　　　　　(buyer)
Signed
_____
　　　　　　　(seller)
Date
_____

Sample Bill of Sale

Dealers have their own paperwork, of course: plenty of it. When buying from a private seller, however, a simple Bill of Sale usually suffices. If in doubt about anything, though, it's always wise to consult a lawyer before signing even the simplest document.

Part VI

Popular Used Cars

**Descriptions, Specifications,
& Quick Reviews by Category**

**Complete with Average Valuations
(2007-2013)**

Subcompact Cars
Compact Cars
Midsize Cars
Full-size Cars
Minivans
Compact Crossover/SUVs
Midsize Crossover/SUVs
Full-size SUVs
Sporty Cars
Hybrids
Electric Cars

Best-Selling Popular-Priced Models

In each vehicle category, we've selected some of the top-selling models when they were new, plus some that appear to be especially popular as used cars. Generally, if a car was popular when new, it's a desirable model when secondhand as well. Also included are several that are somewhat unique, or have an enthusiastic following, even if sales were not huge.

This edition of the Buyer's Guide focuses on mainstream models. Selected premium and luxury models are scheduled to appear in later editions.

In the charts below, unless otherwise specified, all specifications and other details apply to 2012 models. Notable changes to the powertrain in prior (or subsequent) years are indicated in the text.

Please note that Driving Impressions were obtained when the specified model was new. Some opinions stemming from those test drives may not apply fully to equivalent used models.

Before moving on to the individual models, two final topics need to be addressed.

Best Bets (and worst bets)

Which specific factors make a car a good (or bad) buy? Any number of publications issue "Best Buy" lists, though not as many for used cars as new ones. Don't expect any of them to have "the answer" for you.

Everybody's different when it comes to car purchases. Don't pay too much attention to *anyone's* list of Best Bets. What's satisfying to you might annoy the next person, and vice versa.

For instance, most Toyotas have long-standing reputations for dependable and long, trouble-free lives. Even after Toyota's troubles in 2010, over the manner in which recalls were announced, the company's reputation remained largely intact. Some shoppers won't consider anything else; or limit their possibilities to, say, Toyota and Honda – another perennial contender for top reliability as well as thrifty driving. Still, those makes typically cost more, and don't appeal to everyone.

Similarly, quite a few folks won't have anything other than a strictly-domestic automobile. Others see all European makes as superior. Their preferences – and those of evaluators who compile those "best" lists – don't mean a thing unless that vehicle just happens to look good and feel good to you. At the used-car lot you're Number One, and every other opinion is secondary.

Types of cars that might be best avoided

Lists of cars to shun used to be extensive; but not so much anymore, now that car quality has improved across the board. For obvious reasons, those most likely to have been driven hard would be unwise: high-performance or ultra-sporty models, and those that appeal most to teenagers and 20-somethings.

What about makes and models that no longer exist? We have more of those nowadays, with the recent disappearance of such makes as Pontiac, Saab, Saturn, and Mercury. Ordinarily, now-extinct cars that were made by General Motors, Ford, or Chrysler can still be serviced at dealerships for a related make. Because these "orphan" makes generally tend to be cheaper than makes that still exist, they can be good values.

Minivans and wagons aren't as popular as they used to be, but could be good values *because* of that fact. If they're not in high demand, their prices tend to gravitate toward the lower end.

Convertibles used to be considered automatically suspicious, assumed to be driven by younger, perhaps less-careful folks. Nowadays, soft-tops are more likely to be in the hands of middle-aged men, whose more aggressive driving habits might (or might not) be behind them. Furthermore, modern convertibles differ little in quality from comparable coupes or sedans, and their mechanisms stand up better than those of their ancestors. Leakage past fabric roofs used to be a worry, too. However, many of today's convertibles are actually retractable hardtops, with metal roofs. Those mechanisms can be quite complex, but sealing is far less of a problem.

In the past, convertibles tended to cost considerably more than a comparable coupe or sedan, Today, the differences are often surprisingly slight.

When fuel prices are high, gas guzzlers tend to lose value – fast. That's what happened a few years back, when gas topped $4 a gallon and appeared ready to reach $5 or more. A lot of people parked their non-thrifty SUVs for the duration, and those on sale sank dramatically in value. Some folks captured them at bargain prices – but they'd soon be paying plenty for all the fuel they consumed.

As soon as gas prices began to ease, buyers quickly lost interest in the frugal, fuel-efficient models that had shot upward in popularity. We tend to forget in a hurry, when the situation changes. And things can change mighty fast in the car business.

Finally, accept the fact that any used car can go bad – either quickly or later on. That's the chance you take when buying secondhand. And it doesn't pay to get distraught if it happens.

Just about every owner of a string of used cars has wound up with a "lemon" once or twice – including the "experts." That's the name of the used-car game, and you just need to move on if it happens to you. Warranties and inspections ease the mind, but nothing is ever for certain, even though the risk factor has diminished a lot since the bad old days.

Pricing Notes

All valuations shown were effective in mid-2014, subject to additional depreciation beyond that time. Wholesale and retail prices of used cars have been even more volatile than usual lately, hitting record highs late in 2013. but they're expected to ease somewhat during the second half of 2014,

Valuation ranges for each year are for a car in Good (Clean) condition, sold at a dealership. Vehicles sold by private parties are likely to be priced lower, though the difference nowadays isn't always as great as people tend to think.

The lower figure for each year is for the least-costly version, typically with an automatic transmission but few (if any) extras. The upper figure denotes a fairly well-equipped model in the top trim level. In many cases, separate valuations are provided for individual trim levels, or for a group of trim levels (such as LX, EX). If a vehicle is equipped with one or more option groups, and/or a sizable selection of individual options, the price can increase substantially. Except for sporty models and some trucks, a vehicle with a manual transmission usually costs a bit less than one with automatic.

Like all valuation predictions for used vehicles, the figures shown here are estimates. All are subject to change – whether slightly or appreciably – in accord with market conditions later in 2014 and into 2015. Rather than relying on them as predictors of what a given make and model is likely to cost at a dealership, all published valuations are most useful for comparison purposes:

1. Comparing different makes/models in a vehicle category that interests you (such as 2012 Honda CR-V versus 2012 Ford Escape).
2. Comparing prices for a specific model at various ages (2012 Honda Fit versus 2011 Fit, for instance).
3. Comparing prices of low-end and step-up version of the same vehicle (for example, 2012 Ford Mustang V-6 coupe versus 2012 Mustang GT (V-8) coupe.

Where's it from?

"Made in" indicates the assembly point, though parts could come from other factories across the world. Many cars are built in more than one factory, often in several countries, which may or may not export products to North America. Assembly locations are always changing, too, as manufacturers move production to a different plant (often to cut costs), or build a brand-new facility. In short, determining exactly where a particular model was made, over a period of years, isn't nearly as easy as it used to be.

SUBCOMPACT CARS

Honda Fit

Description: Subcompact, front-wheel-drive four-door hatchback. Sold in Base or Sport trim.

History: Introduced for 2007, Honda's Fit hatchback was reworked for 2009. A battery-powered Fit EV joined for 2013, intended for lease rather than retail sale.

Powertrain(s): 1.5-liter four-cylinder engine, developing 117 horsepower and 106 pound-feet of torque. Five-speed manual or five-speed automatic transmission.

Specifications: 161.6 inches long, on a 98.4-inch wheelbase; 66.7 inches wide and 60 inches high. Curb weight, about 2489 pounds. EPA fuel-economy estimate (2012): 27-mpg city/33-mpg highway with manual shift; 28/35 mpg with automatic.

Driving Impressions: [2009 model] Impressively refined, especially for a subcompact, the Fit delivers a confident and solid feel on the road. Reacting adeptly to driver requests, delivering fuss-free handling, the Fit behaves as nimbly as any smaller car and better than most. Untroubled by most pavement imperfections, the suspension reduces trouble spots to a minimal level of annoyance. Little correction is needed on straightaways. Acceleration from zero is reasonably brisk. Pushing hard on the gas to pass or merge produces less-impressive response, but it's on par with this class. Few small cars are as quiet when idling, and the sound while accelerating is pleasantly refined. Paddle shifters on Sport model operate with such subtlety that it's difficult to discern whether a gear change has taken place.

As in many smaller cars, a manual gearbox can extract more energy from the engine than an automatic transmission. Honda's five-speed manual benefits from a loose-operating, easy-to-use shifter. Front seats are comfortably cushioned, with adequate headroom. Backseat legroom is reasonably good, but falls short of Nissan Versa's space.

Rear headroom is better, with ample toe space. Visibility is helped by large mirrors, but thick rear pillars hinder views. Blue dash-markings on the large speedometer are helpful when sunlight makes instruments difficult to read. Other, deep-set gauges aren't as easy to see.

Made in: Japan

Average Retail Value
2007 Fit: $7000 – $7700
2008 Fit: $7800 – $8700
2009 Fit: $8700 – $9700
2010 Fit: $9800 – $11,000
2011 Fit: $11,000 – $12,200
2012 Fit: $12,400 – $13,600
2013 Fit: $13,900 – $15,000
2013 Fit Electric: Marketed on 3-year lease

Toyota Yaris

Description: Subcompact front-wheel-drive four-door sedan or hatchback.

History: Introduced for 2007, Yaris was redesigned for 2012 with new styling and longer dimensions. Latest version provides up to 68 percent more cargo room than prior generation, plus more headroom. Offered as two- or four-door hatchback, or (until 2012) four-door sedan. Three trim levels: entry-level L, value-priced LE, and sporty SE (hatchback only). Each recent Yaris contains nine airbags, including a driver's knee airbag.

Powertrain(s): 1.5-liter four-cylinder engine, developing 106 horsepower and 103 pound-feet of torque. Five-speed manual or four-speed automatic transmission (LE is automatic-only).

Specifications: 153.5 inches long, on a 98.8-inch wheelbase; 66.7 inches wide and 59.4 inches high. Curb weight, about 2295 pounds. Fuel-economy estimate (2012): 30-mpg city/38-mpg highway with manual shift; 30/35 mpg with automatic.

Driving Impressions: Even with an automatic transmission, the early

Yaris sedan was a lovely performer, managing fairly spirited acceleration, downshifting promptly and effectively. Except for mild noise when accelerating moderately, the engine was hardly noticed, snarling only as it approached 6000 rpm. Ride comfort on smooth roads ranked several cuts above the small-car norm, as its suspension absorbed much of modest bumps. Tight turns yielded considerably less body lean than expected, as the Yaris maneuvers smartly and crisply. Center-mounted gauges take some getting used to. Abundant glass assures good visibility. Backseat legroom is scant if the front seat is pushed rearward very much, though the center perch isn't the worst. While the backseat is comfortable enough, legroom is scant if the front seat is pushed rearward very much at all. In the center rear, many occupant heads will touch the roof, but the hard perch isn't the worst. In the early liftback, a simpler dashboard with no tachometer is easier to read. Engine noise was more noticeable on acceleration than the sedan exhibited.

Clearly scoring above the early Yaris in most respects, the 2013 model comes across as a pleasant little machine. Acceleration suffers just a little of typical microcar sluggishness at start-up. Once it catches hold, acceleration is actually quite brisk. Automatic-transmission operation is very good: smooth and prompt; with no abrupt moves, hardly noticed. Engine slightly buzzier than some while accelerating; but at idle, only minimally bothersome. While underway, becomes quite quiet nearly all the time. Maneuvering smartly, as subcompacts should, Yaris is almost fun to drive. Although ride is nothing to exclaim about, it's on par for this class. Only fairly harsh bumps register, and not by much. Surprisingly, the driver enjoys plenty of room. Getting into rear is a challenge, even for the reasonably agile.

Made in: Japan or (recent models) France

Average Retail Value
2007 Yaris: $6000 – $7100
2008 Yaris: $6800 – $8000
2009 Yaris: $7700 – $9000
2010 Yaris: $8700 – $9800
2011 Yaris: $9800 – $11,000
2012 Yaris: $11,200 – $12,700
2013 Yaris: $12,700 – $14,500

Nissan Versa

Description: Subcompact front-wheel-drive four-door sedan or hatchback.

History: Introduced for 2007, the Versa sedan was redesigned for 2012. A new Versa Note hatchback debuted for 2014.

Powertrain(s): 1.6-liter four-cylinder engine, developing 109 horsepower and 107 pound-feet of torque. Five-speed manual gearbox or continuously variable transmission (CVT). Sedan, starting in 2012, used 1.8-liter engine, developing 122 horsepower and 127 pound-feet of torque; with six-speed manual, four-speed automatic transmission, or CVT.

Specifications: [hatchback] 169.1 inches long, on a 102.4-inch wheelbase; 66.7 inches wide and 60.4 inches high. Curb weight, about 2693 pounds. Sedan is 175.4 inches long, on 102.4-inch wheelbase. EPA fuel-economy estimate: Pre-2013 hatchback, pre-2012 sedan: 27-mpg city/36-mpg highway with manual; 28/34 mpg with CVT. Sedan starting in 2012, 26/31 mpg with manual, 24/32 mpg with automatic, 28/34 mpg with CVT.

Driving Impressions: In one particular attribute, Nissan's smallest car has trounced the competition since it first appeared as a 2007 model. That attribute is backseat space, especially legroom.

[2012] Versa suffers a somewhat growly engine when accelerating, but quiets down nicely at speed. Acceleration is entirely satisfactory: not exactly enthusiastic, but no need to worry when passing or merging. Nissan's CVT works fine, and you seldom feel the transition between modes. Very easy to drive, the sedan stays on course well, requiring minimal correction. It's also quite nimble for a small family car. Confident steering feel is coupled with good feedback. Ride quality is especially pleasing, seldom even approaching harshness. The suspension isn't especially taut, but yields impressive stability for a compact; plus, it's unfazed by most road imperfections. When it does respond, it does so promptly and effectively, softening the rougher edges adeptly. Rear headroom is abundant and legroom huge, though toe space could be a tad taller. The front is spacious and comfortable, though a bit snug. White-on-black gauges are big and easy, but the orange-lit trip odometer not so much.

Made in: Mexico

Average Retail Value
2007 Versa: $5900 – $6900
2008 Versa S: $6800 – $8300
2008 Versa SL: $7600 – $8400
2009 Versa: $6500 – $7300
2009 Versa S, SL: $7600 – $8700
2010 Versa: $7500 – $8300
2010 Versa S, SL: $8800 – $10,300
2011 Versa S: $8700 – $9700
2011 Versa SL: $11,500 – $12,500
2012 Versa S: $10,200 – $11,000
2012 Versa SV, SL: $12,000 – $14,000
2013 Versa S: $11,800 – $12,700
2013 Versa SV, SL: $13,500 – $15,000

Chevrolet Sonic/Aveo

Description: Subcompact front-wheel-drive four-door sedan or hatchback. Three Sonic trim levels have been offered: LS, LT, and LTZ.

History: Sonic was introduced for 2012, as a replacement for the Aveo, which had debuted as a 2004 model. An RS trim level was added to the Sonic for 2013. For 2014, the Sonic could have a rearview camera, lane departure warning, and forward collision alert.

Powertrain(s): Sonic uses a 1.8-liter four-cylinder engine, developing 138 horsepower and 125 pound-feet of torque. Five-speed manual or six-speed automatic transmission. LT/LTZ models may have 1.4-liter turbocharged engine, rated 138 horsepower and 148 pound-feet. Aveos held a 1.6-liter engine, rated at 103 to 108 horsepower.

Specifications: Sonic sedan is 173.1 inches long, on a 99.4-inch wheelbase; 68.3 inches wide and 59.7 inches high. Curb weight, about 2721 pounds. Hatchback is only 159 inches long, on the same wheelbase. EPA fuel-economy estimate (2012): 26-mpg city/35-mpg highway with manual; 25/35 mpg with automatic. Turbo, 29/40 mpg with manual; 27/37 mpg with automatic.

Driving Impressions: Chevrolet's Korean-built Aveo, launched for 2004, was a basic subcompact that failed to stand apart from rivals. Its Sonic successor is substantially more refined and capable.

[2009 Aveo] Early Aveos qualified as fuel-efficient but rather humdrum people-carriers. By 2009, with a stronger engine, the Aveo accelerated with some spirit (even with an automatic transmission), behaved impressively on the road, steered nimbly, and rode with a comfort level beyond its size class. Actually fun to drive, Aveo remained a basic car, but one with a dash of personality – especially in hatchback dress. Chevrolet's automatic transmission delivers prompt, crisp gear changes as it helps deliver acceleration that's more linear than typical of subcompacts. Absent from Aveo is the telltale sound of a subcompact's struggling engine as the car picks up speed. The buzziness that characterized earlier engines has largely disappeared, too. A manual gearbox isn't necessary to get the most out of this engine. With automatic, there's little need to fear entering an expressway on-ramp. Still, attention must be paid when merging or lane-changing. Choppy ride quality has been a penalty of short-wheelbase subcompacts. Even when rolling over railroad tracks or harsh pavement, an Aveo5 hatchback retains its composure. Not all was ideal. Throbbing vibration could be felt while the Aveo5's engine was idling. Doors sound a trifle tinny, though the car feels solid overall. Front-seat space was adequate, rear leg space marginal, though headroom is better.

[2012 Sonic] Chevrolet did it right with the Sonic, which hasn't always been the case with the company's smaller cars. Test-driving an LTS hatchback with the 1.8-liter engine and automatic, the only flaw was some road noise: specifically, light tire whine on some surfaces. Exceptionally easy to drive, the Sonic needs little correction to stay right on course. The ride is quite easygoing; with only a hint of typical small-car feel, which means an occasional bump hits just a bit hard. Recovery from such jolts, however, is smart and painless. Enthusiastic and spirited response to the gas pedal is another bonus. In fact, a Turbo model with manual shift didn't feel that much swifter, held back by a bit of lag when pushing the pedal hard.

A large digital speedometer is easy to read; the dial ahead of the drive is the tachometer. The comfortable driver's seat has a relatively long bottom for a small car, and the dashboard layout is undeniably distinctive. Occupant space is plentiful, including abundant headroom. Views ahead and all-around are superior. Even in the back, seating is roomy and comfortable, including the center position, which is only slightly perchlike – markedly better than in most cars these days, including some larger ones.

Made in: (Aveo) South Korea; (Sonic) Michigan, USA

Average Retail Value
2007 Aveo hatchback: $3300 – $4400
2007 Aveo sedan: $4300 – $5200
2008 Aveo: $3900 – $4600
2008 Aveo LS, LT: $4900 – $5900
2009 Aveo: $5000 – $6300
2010 Aveo: $6400 – $7800
2011 Aveo: $8000 – $9200
2012 Sonic LS, LT: $10,200 – $11,700
2012 Sonic LTZ: $12,000 – $13,000
2013 Sonic LS, LT: $11,700 – $13,500
2013 Sonic LTZ: $13,800 – $14,800
2013 Sonic RS: $16,000 – $17,200

Ford Fiesta

Description: Subcompact front-wheel-drive four-door hatchback or four-door sedan. Hatchbacks came in SE and SES trim; sedans in S, SE, and SEL. For 2013, a Titanium edition replaced the SES and SEL. A performance hatchback version debuted for 2014.

History: Introduced to the U.S. for 2011 after several years on sale elsewhere in the world.

Powertrain(s): 1.6-liter four-cylinder engine, developing 120 horsepower and 112 pound-feet of torque. Five-speed manual or six-speed automatic transmission.

Specifications: [hatchback] 160.1 inches long, on a 98-inch wheelbase; 67.8 inches wide and 58 inches high. Curb weight, about 2537 pounds. Sedan is 173.6 inches long, also on a 98-inch wheelbase. EPA fuel-economy estimate (2012): 28-mpg city/37-mpg highway with manual; 29/40 mpg with automatic.

Driving Impressions: [2011 model] Frisky might be the word to describe the road behavior of the little Fiesta, which has a sportier demeanor than the typical subcompact. PowerShift automatic transmission manages to extract some seriously spirited performance out of the small Fiesta engine, marred only by a shockingly noisy exhaust. Gear changes are quite curt, each accompanied by that blip of unnecessary sound. But they yield some impressive performance, both from a standstill and when passing or merging. Nimble and Euro-style in handling, Fiesta flaunts responsive steering, coupled with a tantalizing steering feel. Visibility is fine all-around, and the driver faces a distinctive dashboard. Unlike some small cars, Fiesta is easy and inviting to shift with a manual transmission. Gearshift lever flicks neatly and mates with a well-matched, easy-engaging clutch.

With either transmission, Ford's European-themed subcompact qualifies as lovely in nearly every respect. Despite short seat bottoms, the driver gets an enjoyable position, though right leg might touch the center console. Unless the driver sits well forward, back-seat space is snug. Rear legroom is scant, and some heads might touch the roof. Center-rear occupant's head might tap the overhead light.

Made in: Mexico

Average Retail Value
2011 Fiesta S, SE: $9100 – $10,500
2011 Fiesta SEL, SES: $10,200 – $12,000
2012 Fiesta S: $10,000 – $11,000
2012 Fiesta SEL, SES: $11,200 – $13,200
2013 Fiesta S, SE: $11,000 – $13,000
2013 Fiesta Titanium: $13,500 – $14,500

Additional Subcompact Cars

Chevrolet Spark (new for 2013); Kia Rio and Hyundai Accent (closely related); Mazda2; Mitsubishi Mirage (revived recently); Nissan cube (boxy and roomy, launched in 2009); Scion xD; Suzuki SX4; smart ForTwo (2-passenger).

COMPACT CARS

Ford Focus

Description: Compact front-wheel-drive four-door sedan or four-door hatchback. Four trim levels offered in 2012: entry-level S, SE, SEL, and premium Titanium.

History: First introduced for 2001, Focus was redesigned in 2008, and again for 2012. An electric version debuted in 2012, too.

Powertrain(s): [2012 model] 2.0-liter four-cylinder engine, developing 160 horsepower and 146 pound-feet of torque. Five-speed manual or six-speed automated manual transmission.

Specifications: [hatchback] 171.6 inches long, on a 104.3-inch wheelbase; 71.8 inches wide and 57.7 inches high. Curb weight, about 2920 pounds. Sedan is 178.5 inches long, on the same wheelbase. EPA fuel-economy estimate (2012): 26-mpg city/36-mpg highway with manual; 28/38 mpg with automated manual.

Driving Impressions: Though the 2008-11 Focus generation could be seen as a bit of a step backward, substantial improvement marked the 2012 model, including greater fuel-efficiency. Steering has a more European feel: confident, poised, in control, easy to maneuver. Ride quality scores as good, though not perfect; Focus does hit the occasional bump a bit hard. Suspension is tauter than expected, which is okay on smooth roads but can yield a lumpy ride on lesser-level pavement. Acceleration is energetic from a standstill, and almost as strong from 35 mph or so; but there may be some delay for the automatic to decide what to do. Quiet-running overall, Focus is subdued during acceleration.

Hooded gauges are easy enough to read, but controls are cryptic on busy-looking dashboard. Even turning on the radio can be a challenge. Visibility is fine all-around. Front space is ample enough on somewhat hard but highly supportive, amply-bolstered seats; but seatback adjuster is hard to reach and operate, and outer door handles might pinch small fingers. Foot room is good in rear, but leg space marginal and headroom so-so. The center tunnel is a major obstacle, though the center rear seat is actually less uncomfortable than most. Rear-seat entry isn't so easy.

Made in: Michigan, USA

Average Retail Value
2007 Focus: $5300 – $7000
2007 Focus S hatchback: $4700 – $5500
2008 Focus S: $5800 – $6700
2008 Focus SE, SES: $6500 – $8000
2009 Focus S: $7100 – $8000
2009 Focus SE, SES, SEL: $8000 – $9200
2010 Focus S, SE: $8400 – $9400
2010 Focus SES, SEL: $10,000 – $11,200
2011 Focus S, SE: $9800 – $11,000
2011 Focus SES, SEL: $11,800 – $13,000
2012 Focus S, SE: $11,200 – $13,000
2012 Focus Titanium: $15,500 – $16,500
2012 Focus SEL: $13,200 – $14,300
2012 Focus Electric: $17,300 – $18,800
2013 Focus S, SE: $12,800 – $15,000
2013 Focus Titanium: $17,500 – $18,700
2013 Focus ST, Electric: $18,500 – $20,000

Chevrolet Cobalt/Cruze

Description: Compact front-wheel-drive four-door sedan. Three Cruze trim levels have been offered: LS, LT, and LTZ. Eco edition also available, promising greater gas mileage. Cobalts came in coupe and sedan form. Cobalt XFE editions of 2009-2010 were modified for greater fuel economy.

History: Cruze was introduced for 2011 as a replacement for the Cobalt, which had debuted as a 2005 model. A diesel-engine option was added for the 2014 model year.

Powertrain(s): Cruze has a standard 1.8-liter four-cylinder engine, developing 138 horsepower and 125 pound-feet of torque. Six-speed manual or six-speed automatic transmission. Optional is a 1.4-liter turbocharged engine, rated 138 horsepower and 148 pound-feet. Cobalts used a 148-horsepower, 2.2-liter engine; the Cobalt Sport held a 171-horsepower, 2.4-liter four-cylinder.

Specifications: Cruze is 181 inches long, on a 105.7-inch wheelbase; 70.7 inches wide and 58.1 inches high. Curb weight, about 3093 pounds. EPA fuel-economy estimate (2012): 25-mpg city/36-mpg highway with manual; 22/35 mpg with automatic. Turbo, 26/38 mpg with either manual or automatic. Eco edition estimated at 28/42 mpg with manual shift, or 26/39 mpg with automatic.

Cobalt sedan is 180.5 inches long, on a 103.3-inch wheelbase; 67.9 inches wide and 57.1 inches high. Curb weight, about 2780 pounds. EPA fuel-economy estimate (2008): 24-mpg city/33-mpg highway with manual; 21/33 mpg with automatic. Cobalt Sport estimated at 22/32 mpg with manual shift; 22/31 mpg with automatic.

Recall Note: Early in 2014, General Motors issued a highly publicized, long-delayed recall of a large number of Cobalts and related models, because the ignition switch could fail and shut off the ignition abruptly, causing the engine to stop, power steering to become inoperative, and airbags to fail to deploy in an accident.

Driving Impressions: [2009 Cobalt] Regular Cobalts combine reasonably brisk performance with ride comfort that's better than expected. This suspension soaks up more bumps than some compacts, making only rougher patches troublesome. Exhaust noise is an issue, but the well-behaved automatic transmission responds nicely. While accelerating, the Cobalt can sound almost like a mini-foghorn, though road noise is minimal. Confident steering feel is accompanied by an appealing level of agility for a modest compact. Cobalts are stable on the road, though staying on course can require some attention. Not many everyday drivers need to consider an SS coupe or sedan, unless they simply cannot resist the urge to experience stomp-from-a-stoplight thrills. Seating positions are a bit higher than typical, for good views ahead, but seats aren't the most comfortable. Backseat legroom is seriously cramped, and headroom wins no prizes.

Note: In the wake of the early 2014 recall for a risky ignition switch, reports began to surface about various trouble spots on Cobalts through the model's life span.

[2011 Cruze Turbo] Cruze handling and roadholding score well. The turbo LT sedan is pleasantly confident and reasonably agile (though short of athletic). Ride quality is less appealing. You feel nearly everything, including rumbles over pavement separators. Real bumps and holes produce quite a jarring impact. Acceleration is okay from a standstill, though automatic-transmission shifts are felt. Passing response is distressingly leisurely, especially for a turbo. Expect a fair amount of engine noise, but not so much action. Front seat feels and looks spacious, but visibility is impaired over left shoulder by very wide B-pillar. Gauges would be good if better illuminated.

Made in: (Cobalt) Ohio, USA; (Cruze) Ohio, USA

Average Retail Value
2007 Cobalt: $5000 – $6000
2007 Cobalt SS: $6500 – $8000
2008 Cobalt LS, LT: $5600 – $6600
2008 Cobalt Sport: $7000 – $7900
2008 Cobalt SS: $9000 – $10,000
2009 Cobalt XFE: $6200 – $7400
2009 Cobalt LS, LT: $7300 – $8300
2009 Cobalt SS: $10,500 – $11,700
2010 Cobalt XFE: $7000 – $9000
2010 Cobalt LS, LT: $7800 – $9500
2010 Cobalt SS: $12,500 – $13,800
2011 Cruze LS, LT: $11,800 – $12,800
2011 Cruze LTZ, Eco: $13,000 – $14,200
2012 Cruze LS: $12,800 – $13,800
2012 Cruze LT, Eco: $13,700 – $14,700
2012 Cruze LTZ: $15,700 – $17,000
2013 Cruze LS, LT: $14,000 – $15,000
2013 Cruze Eco, LTZ: $16,000 – $18,000

Honda Civic

Description: Compact front-wheel-drive four-door sedan or two-door coupe. In addition to regular gasoline-engine models, Civic Hybrid sedan has been offered since 2003.

History: First introduced for 1975, Civic has gone through a series of generations and was most recently redesigned for 2012.

Powertrain(s): 1.8-liter four-cylinder engine, developing 140 horsepower and 128 pound-feet of torque. Five-speed manual or five-speed automatic transmission. The sporty Civic Si holds a 2.4-liter four-cylinder rated at 201 horsepower and 170 pound-feet, with a six-speed manual transmission. Honda also offers a natural-gas version of the Civic sedan (sold mainly in California), as well as Civic Hybrid with a battery/gasoline powertrain and continuously variable transmission (CVT).

Specifications: [2012 sedan] 177.3 inches long, on a 105.1-inch wheelbase; 69 inches wide and 56.5 inches high. Curb weight, about 2608 pounds. Coupe is 175.5 inches long, on a 103.2-inch wheelbase. EPA fuel-economy estimate (2012): 28-mpg city/36-mpg highway with manual; 28/39 mpg with automatic. Civic Si, 22/31 mpg. Civic Hybrid, 44-mpg for both city and highway driving.

Driving Impressions: Ever since they first appeared in the 1970s, Civics have stressed practical virtues and reliability. When Honda introduced a redesigned Civic for 2012, many reviewers gave it poor marks. We did not concur. While the latest Civic isn't the most stimulating car on the market, and certainly falls short of sporty, no one should expect it to meet such criteria. Though not a vast improvement over the previous generation, the 2012-up Civic is a capable and satisfying common-sense automobile. Yes, the ride can be a little stiffer than some compacts, on certain road surfaces. But steering is sufficiently responsive and accurate, in keeping with its class. Brakes perform adequately. Acceleration is wholly appropriate, with nicely-behaved automatic-transmission shifts. Most of the time, the ride is just fine. Construction appears solid. Though hardly a "fun" car, the Civic is surprisingly enjoyable to drive.

Gauges are excellent. A big, bright, easy-to-read digital speedometer sits high up. Farther down, closer to the driver, is a comparable tachometer. Unlike some manual seat-height adjusters, the one in the Civic could hardly be easier to operate. Front-seat space is ample, though headroom could be a tad limited for tall folks. Seats are ordinary, but comfortable enough. The rear seat is cramped, especially if the front seat has been moved rearward. Legroom in that case is scant, and headroom ranks as marginal. Forget the center rear position, which is a flaw on nearly every recent model.

Made in: USA or Ontario, Canada

Average Retail Value
2007 Civic: $6500 – $8800
2007 Civic Hybrid: $7500 – $8500
2008 Civic DX: $7700 – $8500
2008 Civic LX, EX: $9400 – $11,400
2008 Civic Hybrid: $8700 – $9700
2009 Civic DX, VP: $8600 – $10,000
2009 Civic LX, EX: $10,500 – $12,300
2009 Civic Hybrid: $10,000 – $11,000
2010 Civic DX, VP: $9700 – $11,000
2010 Civic LX, EX: $11,700 – $13,600
2010 Civic Hybrid: $11,800 – $12,900
2011 Civic DX, VP: $10,900 – $12,500
2011 Civic LX, EX: $12,900 – $15,000
2011 Civic Hybrid: $13,700 – $15,000
2012 Civic DX: $12,200 – $13,200
2012 Civic HF, LX, EX: $13,700 – $16,800
2012 Civic Hybrid: $15,500 – $17,000
2013 Civic LX, HF: $15,400 – $16,500
2013 Civic EX: $17,200 – $18,500
2013 Civic Hybrid: $18,000 – $19,500

Toyota Corolla

Description: Compact front-wheel-drive four-door sedan. Three trim levels have been offered: base L, midlevel LE, and sportier S.

History: Among the oldest nameplates in the U.S. market, Corolla dates back to 1969. Introduced in its latest form for 2014, Corolla had last been redesigned for 2009.

Powertrain(s): 1.8-liter four-cylinder engine, developing 132 horsepower and 128 pound-feet of torque. Five-speed manual or four-speed automatic transmission.

Specifications: 180 inches long, on a 102.4-inch wheelbase; 69.4 inches wide and 57.7 inches high. Curb weight, about 2734 pounds. EPA fuel-economy estimate (2012): 27-mpg city/34-mpg highway with manual; 26/34 mpg with automatic.

Driving Impressions: Toyota's long-lived compact qualifies as good in nearly every area, though it cannot achieve greatness in any of them. Performance is capable, and the ride generally satisfies, though some rough spots transmit a bit of trouble. Automatic-transmission operation is barely noticed. Easy enough to drive, the Corolla stays on course. Still, it doesn't feel quite as centered as some rivals, demanding a bit more attention than expected.

Nicely quiet, the Corolla emits no engine buzz, like some other small cars. Illuminated gauges are very easy to read, on a sensible dashboard layout. Front-seat comfort scores as good, as does space and support. The back seat also is comfortable, and even the center spot is more tolerable than most. Leg and head space are acceptable, if hardly bountiful. Visibility is fine all around. All told, Corolla is a sensible smaller-car choice, as it's been for decades; it just doesn't stand apart from others in this class.

Made in: Canada, Japan, or (recent models) Mississippi, USA

Average Retail Value
2007 Corolla: $6800 – $8000
2008 Corolla: $7800 – $8800
2009 Corolla: $9000 – $9900
2009 Corolla XRS, XLE: $11,500 – $12,700
2010 Corolla: $10,300 – $11,200
2010 Corolla XRS, XLE: $12,500 – $13,800
2011 Corolla: $11,700 – $12,700
2011 Corolla S: $13,000 – $14,000
2012 Corolla: $13,100 – $14,100
2012 Corolla S: $14,300 – $15,500
2013 Corolla: $14,500 – $15,500
2013 Corolla S: $16,000 – $17,200

Nissan Sentra

Description: Compact front-wheel-drive four-door sedan. Available in six trim levels: 2.0, 2.0 S, 2.0 SR, 2.0 SL, sporty SE-R, and sportier-yet SE-R Spec V.

History: Introduced for 1982, as the company's original Datsun name gave way to Nissan, the Sentra was last redesigned for 2013.

Powertrain(s): 2.0-liter four-cylinder engine, developing 140 horsepower and 147 pound-feet of torque. Six-speed manual transmission or continuously variable transmission (CVT). SE-R models contain a 2.5-liter engine rated 177 or 200 horsepower.

Specifications: 179.8 inches long, on a 105.7-inch wheelbase; 70.5 inches wide and 59.5 inches high. Curb weight, about 2930 pounds. EPA fuel-economy estimate (2012): 24-mpg city/31-mpg highway with manual; 24/30 mpg with CVT. SE-R estimate is 21/28 with manual; 26/34 mpg with CVT.

Driving Impressions: Latest (seventh-generation) Sentra borrowed styling cues from bigger Altima, delivers wholly satisfying road experience. Impressive ride quality: not cushiony soft, but nicely absorbent through all but harsh pavement imperfections. No handling complaints: dealt effectively with repeated back-and-forth curves on winding two-lane roads. Steering feel satisfying, though hardly sporty. Acceleration is fully adequate. Engine noise due to CVT isn't a problem, but even on modest inclines, you must push harder on gas, yielding more noise than pickup. Plenty of headroom and legroom; driver's elbow space more restricted. Seat bottoms aren't especially long, but cushioned well, so thigh support helpful. Gauges are simply great: large and lit. Navigation screen is small and rather low.

Made in: Mexico or (2013-on) Mississippi, USA

Average Retail Value
2007 Sentra: $6700 – $7400
2007 Sentra SE-R: $8000 – $9000
2008 Sentra, S: $7700 – $8500
2008 Sentra SL: $8500 – $9400
2008 Sentra SE-R: $9000 – $10,000

2009 Sentra: $8800 – $9700
2009 Sentra SL: $9700 – $10,700
2009 Sentra SE-R: $10,300 – $11,500
2010 Sentra: $10,000 – $11,000
2010 Sentra SL, SE-R: $11,500 – $12,700
2011 Sentra: $11,300 – $12,300
2011 Sentra SL, SE-R: $12,800 – $14,000
2012 Sentra: $12,700 – $13,700
2012 Sentra SL, SE-R: $14,500 – $16,000
2013 Sentra: $14,300 – $15,300
2013 Sentra SR, SL: $15,800 – $17,000

(Mazda) Mazda3

Description: Compact front-wheel-drive four-door sedan or four-door hatchback. Available in four trim levels (SV, Sport, Touring, Grand Touring), with a choice of three engines. Performance-oriented Mazdaspeed3 model contains a turbocharged engine. Skyactiv engines were introduced as an option for 2012.

History: Introduced for 2004, the Mazda3 was redesigned for 2010, and again for 2014.

Powertrain(s): In 3i models, a 2.0-liter four-cylinder engine develops 148 horsepower and 135 pound-feet of torque. In 3s models, a 2.5-liter four-cylinder makes 167 horsepower and 168 pound-feet. Skyactiv 2.0-liter engine develops 155 horsepower and 148 pound-feet. Turbo 2.3-liter in Mazdaspeed generates 263 horsepower and 280 pound-feet. Mazda3i uses five-speed manual or five-speed automatic transmission; 3s gets six-speed manual or five-speed automatic; Skyactiv uses six-speed manual or six-speed automatic; Mazdaspeed is six-speed manual only.

Specifications: [sedan] 180.9 inches long, on a 103.9-inch wheelbase; 69.1 inches wide and 57.9 inches high. Curb weight, about 2780 pounds. Hatchback is 177.4 inches long. EPA fuel-economy estimate (2012 Mazda3i): 25-mpg city/33-mpg highway with manual; 24/33 mpg with automatic. Mazda3s: 20/28 mpg with manual; 22/29 mpg with automatic. Skyactiv: 27/39 mpg with manual; 28/40 mpg with automatic. Mazdaspeed estimated at 18-mpg city/25-mpg highway.

Driving Impressions: As reworked for 2010, Mazda's compact hit the mark in handling, but the high-revving engine in the 3s model can be either invigorating or irritating. All along, Mazda has promoted the Mazda3 as affordable sportiness, promising the "soul of a sports car." Inside and out, the 2010-generation Mazda3 flaunts a sporty look and feel. Mazda's high-revving 3s engine translates to brisk takeoffs and easy merging/passing, even if you're off by one gear. For a sporty hatchback, the Mazda3s hatchback delivers a surprising easygoing ride. Handling is where this hatchback shines brightest. Few cars in this price class behave so nimbly, whipping through corners and curves with excitement that can satisfy even the less-enthusiastic driver, and delight lovers of spirited motoring.

Our biggest complaint was that the engine revved so high, so rapidly, that it was hard to control when starting off from a standstill. That may be good for spirited driving, but annoying in ordinary use. On the other hand, the manual gearbox is among the slickest and easiest to use, requiring minimal effort to flick between ratios. Engine noise is appropriate for the vehicle, with a high whine as rpms rise but quiet enough while cruising. Orange-lit gauges are easy to read, despite being set deep into nacelles. Below, however, is a mysterious amalgamation of knobs and buttons for audio functions, many of them utterly cryptic.

Made in: Japan or USA; or (starting 2014) Mexico

Average Retail Value
2007 Mazda3 i: $6400 – $7100
2007 Mazda3 s: $7700 – $8700
2007 MazdaSpeed3: $9000 – $10,500
2008 Mazda3 i: $7300 – $8200
2008 Mazda3 s: $9200 – $11,200
2008 MazdaSpeed3: $10,700 – $12,200
2009 Mazda3 i: $8300 – $9500
2009 Mazda3 s: $10,800 – $12,800
2009 MazdaSpeed3: $12,500 – $14,000
2010 Mazda3 i: $9400 – $11,200
2010 Mazda3 s: $12,500 – $14,000
2010 MazdaSpeed3: $14,500 – $16,000
2011 Mazda3 i: $10,500 – $13,000

2011 Mazda3 s: $14,200 – $16,200
2011 MazdaSpeed3: $16,200 – $17,700
2012 Mazda3 i: $11,700 – $16,500
2012 Mazda3 s: $15,900 – $18,500
2012 MazdaSpeed3: $17,800 – $19,300
2013 Mazda3 i: $14,000 – $18,500
2013 Mazda3 i SV: $13,000 – $14,000
2013 Mazda3 s: $18,000 – $20,500
2013 MazdaSpeed3: $20,500 – $22,000

Dodge Caliber/Dart

Description: Compact front-wheel-drive four-door sedan. Five trim levels were offered on 2013 Dart: SE, SXT, Rallye, Limited, and R/T, with three powertrain choices. Aero (fuel-efficient) and GT editions also are available. Caliber came with as many as four engine choices, including a 285-horsepower Turbo in SRT4 edition.

History: Reviving a model name from the company's past (1963-76), Dart was introduced for 2013 as a replacement for the Caliber, which had debuted as a 2007 model. Dart was the first Chrysler Group vehicle to be built on Fiat Group architecture.

Powertrain(s): [Dart] 2.0-liter four-cylinder engine, developing 160 horsepower and 148 pound-feet of torque; 1.4-liter MultiAir turbo, making 160 horsepower and 184 pound-feet; or 2.4-liter four-cylinder in, producing 184 horsepower and 174 pound-feet. Six-speed manual, six-speed automatic, or six-speed dual dry clutch transmission. [2012 Caliber] 2.0-liter four-cylinder engine, developing 158 horsepower and 141 pound-feet of torque. Five-speed manual or continuously variable transmission (CVT). Pre-2012 Caliber could have 148-horsepower, 1.8-liter four-cylinder or 172-horsepower, 2.4-liter four-cylinder. Caliber SRT4 held 2.4-liter engine, making 285 horsepower.

Specifications: [Dart] 183.9 inches long, on a 106.4-inch wheelbase; 72 inches wide and 57.7 inches high. Curb weight, about 3186 pounds. [Caliber] 173.8 inches long, on a 103.7-inch wheelbase; 68.8 inches wide and 60.4 inches high. Curb weight, about 2940 pounds. EPA fuel-economy estimate (2012 Caliber): 24-mpg city/32-mpg highway with manual; 23/27 mpg with CVT. (2013 Dart): 25/36 mpg with manual; 24/34 mpg with automatic. Dart 1.4-liter: 27/39 mpg with manual; 27/37 mpg with dual clutch transmission. Dart Aero 1.4-liter: 28/41 mpg with manual; 28/40 mpg with dual clutch unit. Dart 2.4-liter: 23/33 mpg with manual; 21/30 mpg with automatic.

Driving Impressions: Caliber was intended to be a low-budget compact, and it showed. The turbo model, in particular, exhibited the Caliber's marginal construction quality.

[2007 Caliber] Acceleration is sluggish with the 1.8-liter engine and manual shift. Too often, that engine felt like it was straining, not eager to get to speed. On the plus side, the gearbox shifts quite well and the clutch is reasonably well-behaved (though care is needed to get smooth takeoffs). Overall, the base Caliber yields a pleasant experience, but more power would be welcome. You get considerably more get-up-and-go with the 2.0-liter engine and CVT, even though the power differential isn't great. This shiftless transmission works effectively, though when you push hard on the gas, the engine snaps into high rpm and it takes a while for the car to catch up. Few mature drivers should feel a compelling need for the stronger 2.4-liter engine in the R/T.

Caliber yields only occasionally notable jarring, but road noise can be considerable on coarser surfaces. Manual-shift Calibers emit a struggling sound while accelerating. Even with the base model, handling is at least semi-sporty in nature, inspiring more confidence than expected. Front seat bottoms aren't long, but offer good thigh support. Side bolstering is moderate and back support adequate. Front leg space is long, but the driver's knee might touch the console. Front headroom is quite good, as is elbow space. Rear headroom is okay, but the roof is lower at the outside positions. Rear legroom dips to marginal. Visibility is unobstructed, but rear quarter windows are worthless.

[2013 Dart] Clearly a sizable step ahead of Caliber, the modern-day Dart isn't perfect by any means. On two-lane roads, a Dart SXT with the Multi Air 1.4-liter engine delivered a generally excellent ride, but hit some pavement separators quite hard. Easy to drive, that Dart stays on course reasonably well, and its relatively light feel is appropriate. Manual shift is a drawback. The gearshift lever has a nice big knob and operates with long throws, but shifting between first and second gears could get balky. Gauges in the turbo Dart are a bit too stylized for easy reading. Front-seat space is very good. Rear occupants get ample space at the sides. The center rear position for a fifth passenger is high, with little or no head clearance. A non-turbo Dart Limited with automatic proved much more appealing. It's no powerhouse, but that version delivers civilized powertrain behavior with clean, crisp transmission shifts. Performance, though relatively tame, is appropriate for this class. Ride comfort is satisfying; handling unexceptional but pleasing.

Made in: Illinois, USA

Average Retail Value
2007 Caliber: $5500 – $6300
2007 Caliber R/T: $7000 – $8000
2008 Caliber: $6200 – $7000
2008 Caliber R/T: $8000 – $9000
2008 Caliber SRT4: $10,000 – $11,000
2009 Caliber: $7100 – $8200
2009 Caliber R/T: $9800 – $11,000
2009 Caliber SRT4: $11,500 – $12,700
2010 Caliber Express: $8400 – $9400
2010 Caliber Main, SE, Heat, SXT: $9000 – $10,500
2010 Caliber Rush, Uptown, R/T: $11,500 – $12,700
2011 Caliber Express: $9800 – $10,800
2011 Caliber Main, Heat: $11,800 – $13,000
2011 Caliber Rush, Uptown: $13,200 – $14,500
2012 Caliber: $11,500 – $13,000
2013 Dart: $13,200 – $16,000
2013 Dart GT: $17,500 – $18,800

Hyundai Elantra

Description: Compact sedan and Touring hatchback, positioned above the subcompact Accent. Touring models offered in GLS and SE trim, with larger engine.

History: First introduced for 1992, the Elantra was redesigned for

1996, and again for 2001 and 2007. Most recently, the Elantra was last redesigned for the 2011 model year.

Powertrain(s): (sedan) 1.8-liter four-cylinder engine, developing 148 horsepower and 131 pound-feet of torque. Six-speed manual or six-speed automatic transmission. Touring wagon holds 2.0-liter engine, rated 138 horsepower and 136 pound-feet, driving five-speed manual or four-speed automatic transmission.

Specifications: (sedan) 178.3 inches long, on a 106.3-inch wheelbase; 69.9 inches wide and 56.5 inches high. Curb weight, about 2661 pounds. Initial EPA fuel-economy estimate (2012): 29-mpg city/40-mpg highway with either transmission. (wagon) 176.2 inches long, 69.5 inches wide and 59.8 inches high; about 2937 pounds. EPA estimate: 23/31 mpg with five-speed manual transmission; 23/30 mpg with four-speed automatic.

EPA Note: Late in 2012, Hyundai adjusted many of its fuel-economy estimates downward, reducing the Elantra sedan's estimate to 28-mpg city/38-mpg highway, with either transmission.

Driving Impressions: Manual-shift Elantras have had a problem with matching of the gearbox and clutch, but automatic-transmission models function better. Like other Hyundai models, the Elantra has improved considerably in recent years. Ride comfort is okay on smooth roads, but an Elantra coupe can bounce harshly when the surface turns rougher. Handling is easy and pleasant, but short of sporty. Yes, the coupe's stylish shape conveys sporty suggestions; but underneath, it's a small car that happens to have two doors and a curvy profile. Acceleration is appropriate: wholly adequate, and actually rather spirited from a standstill or when hitting the gas pedal at 40 mpg. Automatic-transmission shifts are often felt, but not annoyingly so, and the Elantra's engine is pleasantly quiet-running.

Head-ducking may be needed to enter the coupe, but it's comfortable and supportive once you're in the driver's seat. In fact, it's way less cramped in the front seat than the coupe's exterior profile suggests, with plenty of toe, elbow, and leg room. Older or non-agile folks aren't likely to attempt the back seat, despite slide-forward access. Don't expect much rear headroom, thanks to the two-door's low, sloping roofline. Shoppers who need more backseat space, or easier access, would be better off with a four-door Elantra.

Made in: South Korea

Average Retail Value
2007 Elantra: $5900 – $6700
2008 Elantra: $6900 – $7700
2009 Elantra GLS, SE: $8000 – $9000
2009 Elantra Touring Wagon: $9800 – $11,000
2010 Elantra sedan: $9400 – $11,200
2010 Elantra Touring Wagon: $11,000 – $12,800
2011 Elantra: $11,000 – $13,000
2012 Elantra: $13,000 – $15,000
2012 Elantra Limited sedan: $15,500 – $16,800
2013 Elantra: $14,600 – $17,200
2013 Elantra Limited: $17,500 – $18,800

Additional Compact Cars

Kia Forte (introduced for 2010); Mitsubishi Lancer; Subaru Impreza (standard all-wheel drive); Buick Verano; Fiat 500L (extended-length, launched for 2014); Volkswagen Golf (hatchback) and Jetta (sedan).

MIDSIZE CARS

Honda Accord

Description: Midsize front-wheel-drive four-door sedan or two-door coupe. Offered in a variety of trim levels, including LX, SE, EX, and EX-L, with a four-cylinder or V-6 engine.

History: With ancestry dating all the way back to 1975, the latest, redesigned Accord was introduced for 2013, with a newly available Lane Departure Warning system.

Powertrain(s): 2.4-liter four-cylinder engine, developing 177 horsepower and 161 pound-feet of torque; 190-horsepower version standard in EX models. EX V6 models contain a 3.5-liter V6 engine, rated 271 horsepower and 254 pound-feet. Five-speed manual or five-speed automatic transmission.

Specifications: [sedan] 194.1 inches long, on a 110.2-inch wheelbase; 72.7 inches wide and 58.1 inches high. Curb weight, about 3204 pounds. EPA fuel-economy estimate (2012): four-cylinder, 22-mpg city/31-mpg highway with manual shift; 23/34 mpg with automatic. Estimate for V6: 19-mpg city/30-mpg highway.

Driving Impressions: [2008 Accord] Honda's 190-horsepower four-cylinder engine, as tested in an EX sedan, produced more than adequate performance, with moderate engine blare on hard acceleration. Handling is nothing special, but an Accord imparts confidence with good steering feel. Harsh responses seldom occur, as the Accord delivers a well-controlled ride. Response is unquestionably stronger and more effortless with the V-6 and automatic. Front and rear passengers get ample space, but tilt-ahead headrests could annoy some occupants. In a V-6 coupe, the six-speed manual transmission shifted easily enough, but not quite precisely. Neither is the clutch quite as easy to control as some. You get loads of power to accelerate, but pay for that performance with a snug cockpit and forget-it back seat.

Surprisingly, the 177-horsepower LX with automatic could be the most enjoyable of all the powertrain combinations. Performance is clearly sufficient: milder-mannered, but essentially satisfying. The LX interior is more basic, too. Yet, the 177-hp engine is quieter than a lot of four-cylinders, yielding only slight blare on acceleration. Oddly, it feels more easygoing than the 190-hp version, which feels like it's trying too hard. The LX's four-speed automatic transmission managed to shift more crisply and easily than the six-speed in upper models. Gear changes are noticeable, but not obtrusive at all. This is the sensible version, with most of the important Accord features. With a four-speed manual gearbox, on the other hand, the LX engine likes to stay revved when letting up on gas, which can annoy.

[2013 Accord] As redesigned for 2013, Accord exudes overall excellence even more than its excellent predecessor. Smooth, refined ride; suspension works expertly to ease the road experience. Handling is impressive for a family sedan, helped by excellent steering feel and feedback, and augmented by enthusiastic V-6 performance. Plenty of passenger space, plus ample trunk. However, center rear position is no pleasure. Satisfying driver's seat contains long-enough bottom and offers good support. Some controls are fine; others awful. Like so many automakers, Honda packs way too many entertainment and convenience features into Accord. Button for Lane Departure Warning, adding as a 2013 option, can be overzealous at times.

Made in: Most have been made in USA; some in Japan

Average Retail Value
2007 Accord VP, LX, SE: $8000 – $10,000
2007 Accord EX: $9500 – $11,700
2007 Accord Hybrid: $13,000 – $14,200
2008 Accord LX: $9200 – $10,500
2008 Accord EX: $10,700 – $13,000
2009 Accord LX: $10,500 – $12,000
2009 Accord SE, EX: $13,000 – $16,000
2010 Accord LX: $12,000 – $13,200
2010 Accord EX: $13,500 – $16,200
2011 Accord LX: $13,700 – $15,000
2011 Accord SE, EX: $15,000 – $18,000
2012 Accord LX: $15,500 – $16,800

2012 Accord SE, SX: $16,800 – $19,800
2013 Accord LX: $18,500 – $20,000
2013 Accord Sport, EX: $20,000 – $24,000
2013 Accord Touring: $27,000 – $29,000

Toyota Camry

Description: Midsize front-wheel-drive four-door sedan with four-cylinder or V-6 power. L, LX, SE, and XLE trim levels were offered in 2012. Hybrid version has been available since 2007.

History: Toyota first launched the Camry in 1983. In its current guise, the Camry was redesigned for 2012.

Powertrain(s): 2.5-liter four-cylinder engine, developing 178 horsepower and 170 pound-feet of torque. Optional 3.5-liter V6 engine rated 268 horsepower and 248 pound-feet. Hybrid uses 2.4-liter four-cylinder, developing 200 horsepower, coupled to electric motor and battery pack. All models have six-speed automatic transmission except for Hybrid, which uses a continuously variable transmission (CVT).

Specifications: 189.2 inches long, on a 109.3-inch wheelbase; 71.7 inches wide and 57.9 inches high. Curb weight, about 3190 pounds. EPA fuel-economy estimate (2012): 25-mpg city/35-mpg highway with four-cylinder; 21/30 mpg with V6; 43/39 mpg for Hybrid.

Driving Impressions: For years, critics have faulted each Camry generation, mostly scoffing at its alleged ho-hum styling. Well, a lot of customers don't seem bothered by the criticism, because they've kept Toyota's midsize sedan near the top of the popularity list for a long time. Roadgoing thrills aren't part of the package, but Camry delivers the goods in terms of ride comfort and roominess. Acceleration sets no records either, but performance is wholly appropriate for this sedan's category. No one has to worry about keeping up with traffic, even with the four-cylinder engines that have become popular lately as an alternative to less-thrifty V-6s; Handling is admittedly ordinary, but that's true of most of the midsize competitors, too.

As redesigned for 2012, the Camry approaches exceptional in most every area, including handling. Satisfying steering feel and sense of control almost border on semi-sporty, which was hardly the case before. Four-cylinder performance seems almost effortless, helped by the well-behaved automatic transmission. Visibility could hardly be better, and the ride is easygoing, as the compliant suspension absorbs most commotion without fuss. Backseat headroom is limited for all passengers, though the center seat isn't hard as in many recent sedans. Front seats aren't big on head space, either.

Made in: Japan or USA

Average Retail Value
2007 Camry CE, LE: $9000 – $10,200
2007 Camry SE, XLE: $11,000 – $13,000
2007 Camry Hybrid: $10,000 – $11,200
2008 Camry, LE: $10,000 – $11,300
2008 Camry SE, XLE: $12,200 – $14,000
2008 Camry Hybrid: $11,800 – $13,000
2009 Camry, LE: $11,200 – $12,500
2009 Camry SE, XLE: $13,500 – $15,500
2009 Camry Hybrid: $13,800 – $15,000
2010 Camry, LE: $12,500 – $13,800
2010 Camry SE, XLE: $14,700 – $16,600
2010 Camry Hybrid: $15,800 – $17,000
2011 Camry, LE: $13,800 – $15,100
2011 Camry SE, XLE: $16,000 – $18,100
2011 Camry Hybrid: $17,500 – $18,800
2012 Camry L, LE: $15,500 – $16,500
2012 Camry SE, XLE: $17,500 – $20,000
2012 Camry Hybrid: $19,500 – $21,000
2013 Camry L, LE: $17,300 – $18,500
2013 Camry SE, XLE: $19,200 – $22,800
2013 Camry Hybrid: $21,500 – $23,000

Ford Fusion

Description: Midsize front-wheel-drive four-door sedan, with four-cylinder or V-6 engine. Hybrid (battery/gasoline) version also available, since 2010. Five trim levels were offered in 2012: S, SE, SEL (V6), Sport (V6), and Hybrid.

History: Introduced for 2006, Fusion was redesigned for the 2010 model year. Also that year, the Fusion Hybrid debuted. As part of the subsequent 2013 redesign, a plug-in hybrid version, called the Fusion Energi, was introduced.

Powertrain(s): 2.5-liter four-cylinder engine, developing 175 horsepower and 172 pound-feet of torque. Optional 3.0-liter V-6 rated 240 horsepower and 223 pound-feet; 3.5-liter V-6 in Sport model rated 263 horsepower and 249 pound-feet. Fusion Hybrid uses 191-horsepower four-cylinder engine, coupled to electric motor and battery pack. Six-speed manual or six-speed automatic transmission.

Specifications: 190.6 inches long, on a 107.4-inch wheelbase; 72.2 inches wide and 56.8 inches high. Curb weight, about 3285 pounds. EPA fuel-economy estimate (2012): 22-mpg city/29-mpg highway with manual shift; 23/33 mpg with automatic. Optional 3.0-liter V6 gets estimate of 20/28 mpg (automatic only); 3.5-liter V-6 rated at 18/27 mpg. Fusion Hybrid gets EPA estimate of 41-mpg in city driving and 36-mpg on the highway.

Driving Impressions: [2010 Fusion Hybrid] For a Hybrid, the Fusion delivers surprisingly spirited acceleration. Naturally, it's totally smooth and ultra-quiet. This Fusion also handles and steers quite well: at least as nicely as a typical midsize family sedan. Ride comfort also compares to a conventional sedan, as the suspension seldom transmits much nastiness to occupants. Fusion is one of the most transparent hybrids. It's difficult to tell when the gasoline engine is running, without studying the panel display. Engine shutoffs are barely noticed. Start-up after a stop is detectable, but barely so.

Our 2010 Fusion had a driver ergonomics issue, with the bottom of the dashboard positioned way too close to the brake pedal. Visibility is excellent all around, but front headroom is marginal. Front seats are nicely supportive for thighs and back, and abundantly cushioned. Backseat space is so-so, and the center spot is simply awful: a hard seat that positions the occupant's head perilously close to the overhead light. On the unusual instrument-panel layout, all-electronic gauges are quite helpful, once you're accustomed to them. The information display is diverse, but it demands some study. Trunk space is constricted somewhat by the hybrid components, but the glovebox is sizable. The available navigation system includes a big, clear screen, but it sits rather low.

Made in: Mexico

Average Retail Value
2007 Fusion S, SE: $6500 – $8200
2007 Fusion SEL: $7500 – $9200
2008 Fusion SE: $7500 – $8500
2008 Fusion SE, SEL: $8500 – $10,500
2009 Fusion S: $8700 – $9600
2009 Fusion SE, SEL: $9700 – $12,500
2010 Fusion S, SE: $10,000 – $12,000
2010 Fusion SEL, Sport: $12,000 – $15,500
2010 Fusion Hybrid: $14,000 – $15,500
2011 Fusion S, SE: $11,500 – $14,500
2011 Fusion SEL, Sport: $13,500 – $16,800
2011 Fusion Hybrid: $15,500 – $17,000
2012 Fusion S, SE: $13,500 – $16,500
2012 Fusion SEL, Sport: $15,500 – $18,700
2012 Fusion Hybrid: $17,500 – $19,000
2013 Fusion S, SE: $16,200 – $18,800
2013 Fusion Titanium: $20,000 – $22,000
2013 Fusion Hybrid: $19,500 – $21,200
2013 Fusion Energi: $26,500 – $28,500

Nissan Altima

Description: Midsize front-wheel-drive four-door sedan or two-door coupe. Four-cylinder (2.5) models come in base or S trim; V-6 version comes in SR trim level. Nissan also has offered an Altima Hybrid.

History: Originally introduced for 1993, the Altima was reworked for 2007, and most recently redesigned for 2013.

Powertrain(s): 2.5-liter four-cylinder engine, developing 175 horsepower and 180 pound-feet of torque; 3.5-liter V-6 produces 270 horsepower and 258 pound-feet. Altima Hybrid contains 198-horsepower four-cylinder engine, coupled to electric motor and battery pack. Six-speed manual gearbox or continuously variable transmission

(CVT).

Specifications: [sedan] 189.8 inches long, on a 109.3-inch wheelbase; 70.7 inches wide and 57.9 inches high. Curb weight, about 3145 pounds. Coupe is 182.5 inches long on a 105.3-inch wheelbase, and 55.3 inches tall. EPA fuel-economy estimate (2012): 23-mpg city/32-mpg highway with manual shift, 23/31 mpg with CVT. Estimate for V-6 engine is 18/27 mpg with manual, or 20/27 mpg with CVT. Hybrid (CVT only) gets an estimate of 35 mpg in city driving and 33 mpg on the highway.

Driving Impressions: [2007 sedan] Phenomenal handling on twisty two-lane roads is the byword for a V-6 Altima. With manual shift, this is a truly enjoyable automobile to toss around a bit, in the low gears. A beautifully-behaved clutch adds to the pleasure, but the shifter is a tiny bit clanky. Sometimes, too, it seems like you're in 5th or 6th gear when you're actually in 3rd or 4th. Overall, Altima is a seriously substantial car, providing plenty of room up front. Super visibility is due to plentiful glass. With its taut suspension and close-to-sporty behavior, as well as excellent steering feel, the V-6 Altima offers fine road feel and connection to the pavement. Drivers enjoy a high confidence level, and the low cowl produces a good view ahead. Although the taut suspension results in greater body motion on imperfect surfaces, it's not really uncomfortable.

A four-cylinder stick-shift sedan also yielded fine ride quality, along with adept handling. You hardly notice lesser bumps, and the Altima makes quick work of deeper ones. Even the four-cylinder delivers plenty of exuberant energy with only moderate engine noise. Nissan took the lead with continuously variable transmissions (CVTs). In this installation, the CVT performs with satisfying smoothness (as expected), without excessive engine noise when accelerating. Long seat bottoms offer good thigh support. The higher back also is satisfying, but back support isn't quite up to par. Especially with leather upholstery, you may sometimes feel as if you're about to slide downward. Gauges are basic, but easy to read.

Made in: Mississippi or Tennessee, USA

Average Retail Value
2007 Altima 2.5: $8000 – $9400
2007 Altima 3.5: $11,000 – $13,500
2007 Altima Hybrid: $9200 – $10,500
2008 Altima 2.5: $9100 – $12,000
2008 Altima 3.5: $12,300 – $15,000
2008 Altima Hybrid: $11,000 – $12,300
2009 Altima 2.5: $10,300 – $13,300
2009 Altima 3.5: $13,700 – $15,800
2009 Altima Hybrid: $12,700 – $14,000
2010 Altima 2.5: $11,700 – $15,200
2010 Altima 3.5: $15,500 – $17,500
2010 Altima Hybrid: $14,200 – $15,500
2011 Altima 2.5: $13,200 – $16,800
2011 Altima 3.5: $17,200 – $19,000
2011 Altima Hybrid: $16,000 – $17,500
2012 Altima 2.5: $14,800 – $18,000
2012 Altima 3.5: $19,000 – $21,000
2013 Altima 2.5: $16,500 – $19,000
2013 Altima 2.5 SL: $21,500 – $22,700
2013 Altima 3.5: $20,700 – $23,800

Hyundai Sonata

Description: Midsize front-wheel-drive four-door sedan, with four-cylinder or V-6 engine. Three trim levels offered: base GLS, sporty SE, and top-end Limited, as well as Sonata Hybrid (battery/gasoline) that uses conventional automatic transmission. Sonata is loosely related to the Kia Optima.

History: Introduced for 1989, the Sonata was last redesigned for the 2011 model year. Earlier Sonatas had a choice of four-cylinder or V-6 engine, but only four-cylinders have been offered in recent models.

Powertrain(s): 2.4-liter four-cylinder engine, developing 198 or 200 horsepower and 184 or 186 pound-feet of torque. Available Turbocharged 2.0-liter four-cylinder, available in SE and Limited, produces 274 horsepower and 269 pound-feet. Sonata Hybrid uses 209-horsepower, 2.4-liter engine coupled to electric motor and battery pack. Six-speed manual or six-speed automatic transmission.

Specifications: 189.8 inches long, on a 110-inch wheelbase; 72.2 inches wide and 57.9 inches high. Curb weight, about 3199 pounds. EPA fuel-economy estimate (2012): 24-mpg city/35-mpg highway with either transmission. Turbocharged engine got estimate of 22/34 mpg. Hybrid's estimate is 35 mpg in city driving and 40 mpg on the highway.

Note: Late in 2012, Hyundai revised some of its fuel-economy estimates downward, citing errors in initial testing. Only the hybrid version of the Sonata was affected, dropping by 1 mpg: from 35/40 mpg (city/highway) to 34/39 mpg.

Driving Impressions: [2009 Sonata] In its 2009 form, the Sonata exhibits a surprising level of all-around excellence. The smooth V-6 engine provides plenty of punch. This sedan is barely bothered by most bumps, practically brushing aside the majority of trouble spots. Even the SE edition, with its tauter suspension, delivers a serene and easygoing ride over most surfaces. There's little discernible loss of ride comfort in exchange for the SE's tautness. Steering is tight and controlled, and Sonata tracks neatly, requiring little correction on straightaways. Hyundai's automatic transmission delivers quick and sure response from the V-6 engine. Acceleration in a four-cylinder PZEV model is markedly less swift, but nearly as refined.

Visibility is trouble-free, and front-seat occupants enjoy plenty of space. On the down side, the blue-lit odometer and trip odometer are difficult to read, due to lack of contrast. Gauges are easier to read, though not quite the best of the lot. The available navigation system generally works well, but occasionally gave an imperfect response. Its electronic voice, too, sometimes mispronounced street names dramatically. Rear leg room and toe space are fine, but seats are a bit on the hard side. The center spot is hard and short on headroom.

Made in: Alabama, USA

Average Retail Value
2007 Sonata GLS: $6100 – $7000
2007 Sonata SE: $7000 – $8000
2007 Sonata Limited: $8000 – $9000
2008 Sonata GLS: $7100 – $8000

2008 Sonata SE: $8000 – $9000
2008 Sonata Limited: $9200 – $10,200
2009 Sonata GLS: $8300 – $9300
2009 Sonata SE: $9400 – $10,400
2009 Sonata Limited: $11,000 – $12,000
2010 Sonata GLS: $9700 – $10,800
2010 Sonata SE: $11,200 – $12,700
2010 Sonata Limited: $13,000 – $14,000
2011 Sonata GLS: $12,500 – $13,700
2011 Sonata SE, Limited: $14,000 – $17,000
2011 Sonata Hybrid: $15,800 – $17,000
2012 Sonata GLS: $14,000 – $15,000
2012 Sonata SE, Limited: $15,500 – $19,500
2012 Sonata Hybrid: $16,800 – $18,500
2013 Sonata GLS: $15,700 – $16,700
2013 Sonata SE: $17,500 – $19,300
2013 Sonata Limited: $19,500 – $21,700
2013 Sonata Hybrid: $18,000 – $22,000

Kia Optima

Description: Midsize front-wheel-drive four-door sedan. Trim levels include base LX, step-up EX, and sporty SX. Kia also has offered an Optima Hybrid with a four-cylinder gasoline engine, electric motor, and battery pack. Earlier Optimas were available with a four-cylinder or V-6 engine, but recent examples have been four-cylinder only. Optima is loosely related to the Hyundai Sonata.

History: Introduced for 2001, the Optima was last redesigned for the 2011 model year.

Powertrain(s): 2.4-liter four-cylinder engine, developing 200 horsepower and 186 pound-feet of torque. Available Turbocharged 2.0-liter four-cylinder generates 274 horsepower and 269 pound-feet. Hybrid uses 206-horsepower four-cylinder engine, coupled to electric motor and battery pack. Six-speed manual or six-speed automatic transmission. Hybrid is automatic-only.

Specifications: 190.7 inches long, on a 110-inch wheelbase; 72.1 inches wide and 57.3 inches high. Curb weight, about 3206 pounds.

EPA fuel-economy estimate (2012): 24-mpg city/35-mpg highway with either transmission. Turbo gets estimate of 22/34 mpg. Optima Hybrid is rated at 34/39 mpg.

Note: Like Hyundai, its corporate parent, Kia revised some of its fuel-economy estimates downward during 2013, due to errors in the initial testing process. Only the hybrid version of the Optima was affected, dropping by 1 mpg: from 35/40 mpg (city/highway) to 34/39 mpg.

Driving Impressions: Although the 2011 Optima doesn't quite measure up to Kia's ambitious promise, it ranked as a giant step ahead in the segment. The prior Optima was an appealing, high-value sedan; but the latest one is a superior road car that handles with utter certainty and behaves in an assured manner. Few significant drawbacks are evident, apart from thick B-pillars that impede over-shoulder views. While quiet generally, the base engine (with automatic) can definitely be heard when headed uphill, as it begins to strain a bit. Only then can you tell it's a four-cylinder, not a V-6. The LX suspension is on the taut side, to maintain handling skills; but ride quality remains good. Still, lumpy pavement can induce substantial body motion, though it recovers quickly and smartly from each reaction. Base-engine performance is wholly adequate, as long as drivers don't have excessive expectations. Acceleration from a standstill is on the moderate side. Passing power (the important trait) is more satisfying. Front seats are wide and quite comfortable, with support ranking as average or slightly above. Occupants get plenty of room all-around. Large white-on-black gauges are deep-set but easy enough to read.

Made in: South Korea or (2012-up) Georgia, USA

Average Retail Value
2007 Optima LX: $5700 – $6500
2007 Optima EX: $6400 – $7300
2008 Optima LX: $6700 – $7500
2008 Optima EX: $7500 – $8500
2009 Optima LX: $8100 – $9000
2009 Optima EX, SX: $9500 – $12,000
2010 Optima LX: $9800 – $10,700
2010 Optima EX, SX: $12,000 – $14,000
2011 Optima LX: $13,500 – $14,500

2011 Optima EX: $15,500 – $17,500
2011 Optima SX: $17,800 – $19,300
2012 Optima LX: $14,800 – $15,800
2012 Optima EX: $16,700 – $18,800
2012 Optima SX: $20,000 – $21,500
2012 Optima Hybrid: $16,000 – $17,200
2013 Optima LX: $16,500 – $17,700
2013 Optima EX: $18,800 – $20,000
2013 Optima Hybrid: $17,500 – $19,000
2013 Optima EX Hybrid: $24,500 – $26,500
2013 Optima Turbo: $23,500 – $26,000

Additional Midsize Cars

Mazda6; Subaru Legacy and Outback (all-wheel drive); Nissan Maxima; Hyundai Azera; Buick Regal; Chrysler 200; Dodge Avenger; Volkswagen CC and Passat; Chevrolet Malibu.

FULL-SIZE CARS

Ford Taurus

Description: Full-size front-wheel-drive or all-wheel-drive four-door sedan with V-6 engine. Offered in SE, SEL, and top Limited trim levels. Ford also offers a high-performance SHO, taking its model designation for a model offered in the 1990s.

History: Part of Ford's midsize lineup since 1986, Taurus faded away after 2006, then reappeared a year later, transformed into a full-size sedan that edged aside the Five Hundred nameplate. A substantially revised Taurus debuted for 2010, again as a full-size model.

Powertrain(s): 3.5-liter V-6 engine, developing 263 horsepower and 249 pound-feet of torque. Taurus SHO contains turbocharged 3.5-liter V-6, generating 365 horsepower and 350 pound-feet. All Taurus sedans have a six-speed automatic transmission.

Specifications: 202.9 inches long, on a 112.9-inch wheelbase; 76.2 inches wide and 60.7 inches high. Curb weight, about 4015 pounds. EPA fuel-economy estimate (2012): 18-mpg city/26-mpg highway (17/25 mpg with all-wheel drive). Taurus SHO's estimate is 17-mpg city/25-mpg highway.

Driving Impressions: [2010 Taurus] Ride comfort is the foremost bonus, as the Taurus seldom encounters a troublesome road imperfection. Now and then, however, an exception to that rule may occur. Driving a front-drive Taurus through some painful pavement, the ride turned surprisingly stiff, almost jolting. As the highway improved, the ride smoothed out nicely again. Ford's V-6 delivers plenty of energy to pass/merge from lower speeds. From 55 mph or more, response is refined and steady but somewhat tame. Some downshifts are a bit hesitant and uncertain, at least for a moment. Gear changes can even be somewhat abrupt, and almost curt, though not an annoyance. Overall automatic-transmission performance isn't quite as smooth and immediately responsive as some six-speed units.

Seats are firm and highly supportive, amply cushioned for long-term comfort. There's a definite cockpit feel to the interior, with a console that firmly separates front occupants. Blue-lit gauges are exceptionally easy to read, despite sitting in deep nacelles. Ford developed some of the most pleasantly cushioned headrests for front occupants. Out back is a huge (20 cubic foot) trunk. Although Taurus is mostly quiet-running, passengers can hear engine when it's pushing hard.

[2013 Taurus] After only a few moments in a Taurus Limited, it was clear that this sedan had advanced from mostly excellent to better yet, with one notable exception: a snarly (though subdued) engine sound during acceleration. Rather exuberant from a standstill, the V-6 is less assertive at highway speeds, though clearly more than adequate. Very good ride comfort is accompanied by a touch of road noise. Shifts are crisp but not instantaneous. Taurus is a big car, though it doesn't really feel too excessive from behind the wheel. Front occupants get loads of space.

As before, the high-performance SHO sedan comes across as more compelling than a regular Taurus. Among other differences, the SHO lacks the engine snarl of the less-potent V-6. Overall, the powertrain feels smoother, as well as markedly stronger. Ford promotes the SHO's "linear power delivery," which is exactly what you get – and plenty of it. Any difference in the SHO's taut suspension is noticed only on imperfect pavement. Otherwise, the SHO rides quite well on smooth surfaces. Excellent steering feel is tauter than on a regular Taurus, but this performance sedan is especially easy to drive. The nicely-textured fabric steering-wheel cover is a seldom-seen feature.

Made in: Illinois, USA

Average Retail Value
2010 Taurus SE, SEL, Ltd.: $13,700 – $16,000
2010 Taurus AWD: $16,000 – $17,500
2010 Taurus SHO: $18,500 – $20,000
2011 Taurus SE, SEL, Ltd.: $14,800 – $17,200
2011 Taurus AWD: $17,200 – $18,700
2011 Taurus SHO: $20,000 – $21,500
2012 Taurus SE, SEL, Ltd.: $16,000 – $18,500
2012 Taurus AWD: $18,500 – $20,000

2012 Taurus SHO: $22,800 – $24,500
2013 Taurus SE, SEL, Ltd.: $17,500 – $19,700
2013 Taurus AWD: $20,000 – $22,000
2013 Taurus SHO: $26,000 – $28,000

Chevrolet Impala

Description: Full-size (or large midsize) front-wheel-drive four-door sedan with V-6 engine. LS, LT, LTZ.

History: Impala is an old nameplate, dating back to 1958. The current version was introduced for 2000, and reworked for 2006; the 3.6-liter V-6 debuted for 2012. High-performance SS model has emerged for the 2014 model year.

Powertrain(s): 3.6-liter V-6 engine, developing 303 horsepower and 264 pound-feet of torque. All Impalas have six-speed automatic transmission.

Specifications: 200.4 inches long, on a 110.5-inch wheelbase; 72.9 inches wide and 58.7 inches high. Curb weight, about 3555 pounds. EPA fuel-economy estimate (2012): 18-mpg city/30-mpg highway.

Driving Impressions: Bearing one of the longest-lived nameplates in the industry, Chevrolet's Impala is among the few remaining full-size sedans, and has been the top seller in that league. Like other models from the "Detroit 3," the Impala has improved considerably over the years, edging ever closer to import-brand quality. Though it still falls a bit short of that level, Chevrolet's largest sedan delivers a generally satisfying, if not fully refined, experience. Lack of a four-cylinder option translates to fuel economy that could be better in city driving, but is surprisingly thrifty on the highway for a relatively large automobile. Some shoppers might be more content with a midsize Chevrolet Malibu, which does come with a four-cylinder engine, though its EPA fuel-economy estimate with V-6 power is actually lower than the Impala's. Oddly, though the Malibu is considerably shorter than an Impala, its wheelbase is actually a bit longer.

Made in: USA or Canada

Average Retail Value
2007 Impala LS, LT: $7000 – $8000
2007 Impala LTZ: $8500 – $9500
2007 Impala SS: $9500 – $10,700
2008 Impala LS, LT: $7900 – $9200
2008 Impala LTZ: $9800 – $10,800
2008 Impala SS: $10,800 – $12,200
2009 Impala LS, LT: $9000 – $10,000
2009 Impala LTZ: $11,000 – $12,000
2009 Impala SS: $12,500 – $14,000
2010 Impala LS, LT: $10,200 – $11,400
2010 Impala LTZ: $12,200 – $13,500
2011 Impala LS, LT: $11,500 – $12,700
2011 Impala LTZ: $13,500 – $14,800
2012 Impala LS, LT: $13,000 – $14,200
2012 Impala LTZ: $15,500 – $17,000
2013 Impala LS, LT: $14,700 – $15,900
2013 Impala LTZ: $18,000 – $20,000

Chrysler 300

Description: Full-size rear-wheel or all-wheel-drive four-door sedan with V-6 or V-8 engine. Base, Limited, 300S, and 300C trim levels have been offered. So has a high-performance SRT8 edition with a 470-horsepower engine.

History: Chrysler first marketed a 300 model in 1955. Known as the "letter-series 300," that sport-luxury coupe and convertible stayed in the lineup for a decade. The modern-day 300 debuted for 2005, sharing its structure with the Dodge Charger.

Powertrain(s): 3.6-liter V-6 engine, developing 292 horsepower and 260 pound-feet of torque; or 5.7-liter Hemi V-8, producing 363 horsepower and 394 pound-feet. A 6.4-liter V-8 in the SRT8 model generates 470 horsepower and 470 pound-feet. The V-6 is available with either a five-speed or six-speed automatic transmission, but V-8 models come only with a six-speed automatic.

Specifications: 198.6 inches long, on a 120.2-inch wheelbase; 75

inches wide and 58.4 inches high. Curb weight, about 3961 pounds. EPA fuel-economy estimate (2012): 18-mpg city and 27-mpg highway with V-6 and five-speed automatic, or 19/31 mpg with the six-speed automatic. The 5.7-liter V-8 gets an estimate of 16/25 mpg, and the SRT8 rates a less-thrifty 14/23 mpg. All-wheel-drive models get slightly lower fuel-economy estimates.

Driving Impressions: [2008 Chrysler 300C] Totally smooth throughout, the 300C benefits from exuberant throttle response with its Hemi V-8, but those performance characteristics don't interfere with full refinement. Very slight, subdued snarl is evident during hard acceleration, but otherwise this sedan is supremely quiet. Only the most ardent performance buffs need to consider the SRT8 edition. Balanced steering feel helps this large sedan maneuver easily, but pushing a 300C hard in curves can produce tire squeal. Since this is Chrysler's flagship model, the smooth ride is exactly what prospective customers might expect. Nautical-style gauges enhance the classy interior. All Chrysler 300 models offer abundant passenger space. Rear-seat leg room is simply enormous in the Walter P. Chrysler Executive Series sedan, including footrests on each side. Built on a wheelbase six inches longer than usual, the Executive Series includes a uniquely calibrated rendition of Chrysler's Electronic Stability Program.

Made in: Canada

Average Retail Value
2007 Chrysler 300: $8000 – $8900
2007 300 Touring, Ltd.: $9000 – $11,000
2007 Chrysler 300C: $11,000 – $13,000
2007 Chrysler 300 SRT8: $14,000 – $15,500
2008 Chrysler 300: $9500 – $10,500
2008 300 Touring, Ltd.: $10,700 – $12,700
2008 Chrysler 300C: $13,000 – $14,500
2008 Chrysler 300 SRT8: $17,000 – $18,500
2009 300 LX, Touring: $11,200 – $13,000
2009 Chrysler 300 Ltd.: $12,500 – $14,200
2009 Chrysler 300C: $15,200 – $17,500
2009 Chrysler 300 SRT8: $20,200 – $22,000
2010 Chrysler 300 Touring: $13,500 – $16,000

2010 Chrysler 300 Ltd.: $15,500 – $18,000
2010 Chrysler 300C: $17,300 – $19,000
2010 Chrysler 300 SRT8: $23,700 – $25,500
2011 Chrysler 300, Ltd.: $16,000 – $17,800
2011 Chrysler 300C: $19,500 – $21,000
2012 Chrysler 300: $19,000 – $21,500
2012 Chrysler 300S: $23,000 – $26,000
2012 Chrysler 300C: $22,000 – $26,000
2012 Chrysler 300 SRT8: $29,500 – $32,000
2013 Chrysler 300: $22,200 – $24,500
2013 Chrysler 300S: $25,200 – $29,000
2013 Chrysler 300C: $24,500 – $31,000
2013 Chrysler 300 SRT8: $31,500 – $35,500

Buick LaCrosse

Description: Full-size front-wheel-drive (or all-wheel-drive) four-door sedan with four-cylinder or V-6 engine. Base, Convenience, Leather, and Premium trim levels have been offered.

History: Introduced for 2005, the LaCrosse was redesigned for 2010 with new engine choices.

Powertrain(s): 2.4-liter four-cylinder engine develops 197 horsepower and 172 pound-feet of torque. Optional 3.6-liter V-6 (available for top Premium models) produces 303 horsepower and 264 pound-feet. All LaCrosse sedans have six-speed automatic transmission. Earlier models (circa 2008) could have 200-horsepower, 3.0-liter V-6; 240-horsepower, 3.6-liter V-6; or 5.3-liter V-8 rated at 300 horsepower.

Specifications: 197 inches long, on a 111.7-inch wheelbase; 73.1 inches wide and 59.2 inches high. Curb weight, about 3835 pounds. EPA fuel-economy estimate (2012): 25-mpg city/36-mpg highway with four-cylinder; or a far less frugal 17/27 mpg with V-6.

Driving Impressions: [2010] LaCrosse is clearly one of General Motors' better efforts, at a time when such achievements are critical. While not perfect, it ranked as a big step ahead and a substantial improvement over the first-generation model. The 2010 sedan felt solid all around. Though rather long, it has a slim appearance and drives as if it were a relatively narrow, modestly-weighty sedan. Acceleration is smooth and effortless with the CXS's 3.6-liter V-6 engine. The 3.0-liter engine offers ample energy, though the transmission sometimes delayed downshifts when needed most.

On the CXS, Buick's suspension soaks up any bumps and holes with ease, seldom transmitting notable nastiness to occupants. Through rougher spots, the CXL edition wasn't quite gentle, but otherwise yielded a pleasant, Buick-like ride. Easy to drive and steer, this Buick won't fool anyone into thinking it has sporty aspirations, but it handles adeptly for its class. In fact, it maneuvers crisply, not at all like Buicks of the more distant past. Gauges, though stylish, are not the easiest to read and can be confusing at a glance. Otherwise, the driver faces logically-placed controls. The driver's seat is comfortable, with good support. Except for a very light whoosh when accelerating with some vigor, the LaCrosse is exceptionally quiet-running. Execution of several details could be better, such as inside front-door handles that are hard to find by touch.

Made in: USA

Average Retail Value
2007 LaCrosse CX, CXL: $6500 – $7700
2007 LaCrosse CXS: $7700 – $8700
2008 LaCrosse CX, CXL: $7900 – $9400
2008 LaCrosse CXS: $10,500 – $11,800
2008 LaCrosse Super: $12,500 – $14,000
2009 LaCrosse CX: $9700 – $11,000
2009 LaCrosse CXL, Super: $12,000 – $14,500
2010 LaCrosse CX, CXL: $12,000 – $16,000
2010 LaCrosse CXS: $17,500 – $19,000
2011 LaCrosse CX, CXL: $14,500 – $18,000
2011 LaCrosse CXS: $19,500 – $21,000
2012 LaCrosse: $17,300 – $21,000
2012 LaCrosse Premium: $19,000 – $23,000
2012 LaCrosse Touring: $23,000 – $24,700
2013 LaCrosse: $20,500 – $24,000
2013 LaCrosse Premium: $22,700 – $25,500
2013 LaCrosse Touring: $26,000 – $28,000

Toyota Avalon

Description: Full-size front-wheel-drive four-door sedan with V-6 engine, offered in base or Limited trim.

History: Toyota's largest sedan was redesigned for 2011. Mildly reworked for 2013, Avalon has served as Toyota's flagship sedan since 1995. New hybrid model made its initial appearance for the 2013 model year.

Powertrain(s): 3.5-liter V-6 engine, developing 268 horsepower and 248 pound-feet of torque. All Avalons have a six-speed automatic transmission.

Specifications: 197.6 inches long, on a 111-inch wheelbase; 72.8 inches wide and 58.5 inches high. Curb weight, about 3572 pounds. EPA fuel-economy estimate (2012): 20-mpg city/29-mpg highway.

Driving Impressions: Avalon is a surprisingly appealing family sedan, with far more merits than drawbacks. Not much to complain about, apart from two irritants: 1. Consulting the owner's manual is mandatory, in order to do much of anything with the navigation system. 2. Seems to be too much space between brake and gas pedals. Also, a few minor issues such as hard-to-see fuel and temperature gauges. In contrast, the speedometer and tach have large, easy-to-read markings and numerals.

Even in Eco mode, performance is satisfying and smooth. Avalon breezes along in near-silence, emitting just enough sound to let you know you're cruising. Automatic-transmission response is prompt and quite smooth, though not indiscernible. Ride comfort is another plus: not many pavement flaws transmit more than moderate harshness, though an occasional bump can hit rather hard. Just-right steering feel, with fine feedback. Visibility mostly trouble-free, though headrests impede a bit. Front-seat comfort appealing, though some head-ducking might be needed to enter. Once there, space is abundant, though heads of tall folks might approach roof. Rear side occupants get satisfactory space and comfort, but center rider endures hard (if wide) perch; still, that center position is better than in most cars.

Made in: Japan or Kentucky, USA

Average Retail Value
2007 Avalon XL, Touring: $9500 – $10,500
2007 Avalon XLS, Ltd.: $11,000 – $12,500
2008 Avalon XL, Touring: $11,000 – $12,000
2008 Avalon XLS, Ltd.: $12,500 – $14,000
2009 Avalon XL: $12,700 – $13,700
2009 Avalon XLS, Ltd.: $14,700 – $16,200
2010 Avalon XL: $15,000 – $16,000
2010 Avalon XLS, Ltd.: $17,800 – $18,800
2011 Avalon: $20,000 – $21,500
2012 Avalon: $22,000 – $24,000
2013 Avalon XLE: $24,500 – $27,000
2013 Avalon Limited: $27,800 – $29,500
2013 Avalon Hybrid: $29,500 – $34,000

Additional Full-size Cars

Dodge Charger; Ford Crown Victoria (discontinued after 2008); Kia Cadenza (launched for 2014); Hyundai Genesis falls into near-luxury class.

MINIVANS

Dodge Grand Caravan

Description: Similar to the more luxurious Chrysler Town & Country, Dodge's long-lived minivan is the last mainstream model built by a domestic automaker. Both models were introduced way back in 1984, as the first of their kind, finding favor in suburban families. Later, as those suburbanites started to switch to SUVs and crossover models, minivans in general fell out of favor. Grand Caravans received a freshening for the 2011 model year.

History: Introduced for 1984, Dodge's minivan was redesigned for 1991 and 1996, then for 2001 and 2008.

Powertrain(s): 3.6-liter V-6 engine, developing 283 horsepower and 260 pound-feet of torque. Six-speed automatic transmission.

Specifications: 202.5 inches long, on a relatively long 121.2-inch wheelbase; 76.9 inches wide and 68.9 inches high. Curb weight, about 4321 pounds. EPA fuel-economy estimate (2012): 17-mpg city/25-mpg highway.

Driving Impressions: More than any minivan on the market, the Grand Caravan (and its upscale Town & Country cousin) are reminiscent of minivans from the past, though updated with some recent technology.

Made in: Ontario, Canada

Average Retail Value
2007 Caravan (short-wheelbase): $4800 – $5800
2007 Grand Caravan: $5500 – $7500
2008 Grand Caravan: $8000 – $10,000
2009 Grand Caravan: $9400 – $11,800
2010 Grand Caravan: $11,000 – $13,500
2011 Grand Caravan: $12,700 – $15,000
2011 Grand Caravan R/T: $15,700 – $17,200

2012 Grand Caravan: $14,600 – $17,700
2012 Grand Caravan R/T: $18,200 – $20,000
2013 Grand Caravan: $16,500 – $20,500
2013 Grand Caravan R/T: $21,500 – $23,500

Honda Odyssey

Description: From the start, Honda's minivan competed strongly against those from the "Detroit 3," but only one of those competitors (Chrysler/Dodge) continues to offer this body style. Ford dropped its minivan after 2007; Chevrolet did so after 2008. Contemporary rivals include the Toyota Sienna, Nissan Quest, and Kia Sedona. For 2012, the Odyssey came in five trim levels: LX, EX, EX-L (leather), Touring, and Touring Elite.

History: First introduced for 1995, with swing-out doors, the Odyssey evolved into a conventional minivan for 1999; then redesigned for 2005 and again for the 2011 model year. An Odyssey may be configured to hold as many as eight occupants.

Powertrain(s): 3.5-liter V-6 engine, developing 248 horsepower and 250 pound-feet of torque, driving a five-speed automatic transmission (six-speed on recent Touring models).

Specifications: 202.9 inches long, on a 118.1-inch wheelbase; 79.2 inches wide and 68.4 inches high. Curb weight, about 4337 pounds. EPA fuel-economy estimate (2012): 18-mpg city/27-mpg highway (Touring: 19/28 mpg).

Driving Impressions: [2011 model] Handling is the Number One trait of the Odyssey, measured against its minivan rivals. Roadholding is hard to beat; in fact, most minivans don't come close. Steering feel, especially on later models, is just as appealing as claimed by Honda: heavy enough to produce a high confidence level, but light enough for comfort. An Odyssey can whip through curves handily. The ride isn't as glassy-smooth as in some minivans, with some body motion transmitted to occupants; but there's nary a hint of harshness on any normal pavement. On smooth surfaces, the ride is quite lovely; even moderate imperfections aren't troubling at all.

Acceleration isn't quite stunning, but almost vigorous. There's no shortage of power under any reasonable condition, delivered smoothly and confidently. Only the slightest snarl is heard when pushed, and the Odyssey is exceptionally quiet overall. Seats are effectively bolstered, well-cushioned, and helpfully supportive. Unusually wide door sills could make it difficult for some passengers to get inside, though reaching the third-row seat isn't as tough as expected.

Made in: Alabama, USA

Average Retail Value
2007 Odyssey LX, EX: $8300 – $9800
2007 Odyssey Touring: $13,000 – $14,500
2008 Odyssey LX, EX: $9800 – $11,900
2008 Odyssey Touring: $15,500 – $17,000
2009 Odyssey LX, EX: $11,700 – $13,800
2009 Odyssey Touring: $18,000 – $19,800
2010 Odyssey LX, EX: $13,800 – $15,800
2010 Odyssey EX-L, Touring: $19,000 – $22,200
2011 Odyssey LX, EX: $17,500 – $22,000
2011 Odyssey Touring: $26,000 – $28,500
2012 Odyssey LX, EX: $19,700 – $25,000
2012 Odyssey Touring: $28,500 – $31,500
2013 Odyssey LX, EX: $22,200 – $28,000
2013 Odyssey Touring: $31,500 – $34,800

Toyota Sienna

Description: Family minivan with sliding side doors and seven or eight-passenger capacity. Trim levels offered in 2012 included a base model, LE, SE, XLE, and Limited. All-wheel drive has been an option.

History: Introduced for 1998. Toyota's minivan was redesigned for 2004, and again for 2011.

Powertrain(s): Base and LE models held a 2.7-liter four-cylinder engine, rated at 187 horsepower and 186 pound-feet of torque. Upper models got a 3.5-liter V-6 engine, developing 266 horsepower and 245 pound-feet of torque. All 2012 models had a six-speed automatic transmission.

Specifications: 200.2 inches long, on a 119.3-inch wheelbase; 78.1 inches wide and 68.9 inches high. Curb weight, about 4275 pounds. EPA fuel-economy estimate (2012): 19-mpg city/24-mpg highway with four-cylinder engine; 18/25 mpg with V-6 (17/23 mpg with all-wheel drive).

Driving Impressions: Like most other Toyota products, the Sienna is known for sensible, reliable operation. Along with Honda's Odyssey, the Toyota Sienna is also among the most refined members of the minivan group. Therefore, you can expect a satisfying ride and quiet operation, even if handling qualities aren't quite as stimulating as those of the Odyssey or, say, a Nissan Quest.

Made in: Indiana, USA

Average Retail Value
2007 Sienna CE, LE: $8600 – $9600
2007 Sienna XLE: $12,500 – $15,000
2008 Sienna CE, LE: $10,100 – $11,500
2008 Sienna XLE: $14,500 – $17,500
2009 Sienna CE, LE: $12,000 – $13,500
2009 Sienna XLE: $17,000 – $20,000
2010 Sienna CE, LE: $14,500 – $16,000
2010 Sienna XLE: $20,000 – $23,000
2011 Sienna CE, LE: $17,000 – $19,500
2011 Sienna SE, XLE, Ltd.: $23,000 – $27,500
2012 Sienna, LE: $19,200 – $21,200
2012 Sienna SE, XLE, Ltd.: $26,000 – $29,700
2013 Sienna: $21,700 – $24,000
2013 Sienna SE, XLE, Ltd.: $28,500 – $32,500

Nissan Quest

Description: Family minivan with sliding side doors and seven-passenger capacity. Four trim levels were offered for 2012: S, SV, SL, and top-of-the-line LE

History: First introduced for 1993 (similar to Mercury Villager), the Quest was redesigned for 1999 and for 2004. The latest redesign was for the 2011 model year, following a one-season absence from

Nissan's lineup.

Powertrain(s): 3.5-liter V-6 engine, developing 260 horsepower and 240 pound-feet of torque. Continuously variable, gearless transmission (CVT).

Specifications: 200.8 inches long, on a 118.1-inch wheelbase; 77.6 inches wide and 71.5 inches high (73 inches with roof rack). Curb weight, about 4371 pounds (S model). EPA fuel-economy estimate (2012): 19-mpg city/24-mpg highway.

Driving Impressions: [2011 model] Like Honda's Odyssey, the Quest has been known for semi-sporty handling, compared to its other minivan rivals. In fact, some observers consider it the sportiest of the minivan lot, though Odyssey shines about as brightly in road behavior. Whichever model ranks Number One, Nissan's Quest promises an even more carlike driving experience than usual for this vehicle category. More sure-footed than the minivan norm, Quest holds the road smartly and behaves confidently, doing just about everything right. Tromping on the gas pedal does produce a momentary delay, but it's followed by smoothly eager response. There's plenty of energy for smooth takeoffs and easy merging onto Interstates. Ride comfort as satisfying as any rival's. Though you may feel road-surface changes, few are bothersome. Steering is on the moderately heavy side, but the Quest is easy to maneuver, and twisting the wheel doesn't really take much effort. Seats are almost sublimely comfortable: snug yet loose-feeling.

Made in: Japan

Average Retail Value
2007 Quest, S: $7200 – $8000
2008 Quest SL, SE: $8000 – $9300
2009 Quest, S: $8700 – $10,000
2010 Quest SL, SE: $10,000 – $11,800
2009 Quest, S: $10,800 – $12,200
2009 Quest SL, SE: $12,800 – $14,800
2010 Quest: No 2010 model was marketed.
2011 Quest S, SV: $15,200 – $17,000
2011 Quest SL, LE: $19,500 – $22,000
2012 Quest S, SV: $17,000 – $19,000

2012 Quest SL, LE: $22,000 – $24,500
2013 Quest S, SV: $21,000 – $23,500
2013 Quest SL, LE: $26,000 – $28,800

Kia Sedona

Description: Family minivan with sliding side doors and seven-passenger capacity. For 2012, two trim levels were offered: LX and step-up EX

History: First introduced for 2002, Kia's minivan was redesigned for the 2006 model year and remained on sale through the 2012 model year. No 2013 or 2014 models were marketed, but an all-new Sedona minivan goes on sale in late 2014, as a 2015 model.

Powertrain(s): 3.5-liter V-6 engine, developing 271 horsepower and 248 pound-feet of torque. Six-speed automatic transmission.

Specifications: 202 inches long, on a 118.9-inch wheelbase; 78.1 inches wide and 69.3 inches high. Curb weight, about 4374 pounds. EPA fuel-economy estimate (2012): 18-mpg city/25-mpg highway.

Driving Impressions: Initial examples of the Sedona were best known as the cheapest minivans on the market, though not the foremost in quality. They were also more prone to sucking up considerable fuel than the competition. Kia's minivan changed markedly in its second generation. Though not quite on a par with the Honda Odyssey and Toyota Sienna, the Kia Sedona has edged steadily closer to that level, roughly matching the domestic minivans, if not the best of the import brands.

Made in: South Korea

Average Retail Value
2007 Sedona LX: $5500 – $6500
2007 Sedona EX: $7000 – $8000
2008 Sedona LX: $6800 – $8000
2008 Sedona EX: $8500 – $9700
2009 Sedona LX: $8400 – $9700
2009 Sedona EX: $10,500 – $12,000

2010 Sedona LX: $10,400 – $11,800
2010 Sedona EX: $12,700 – $14,200
2011 Sedona LX: $12,800 – $14,200
2011 Sedona EX: $15,000 – $16,500
2012 Sedona LX: $15,300 – $16,800
2012 Sedona EX: $17,500 – $19,000

COMPACT CROSSOVERS/SUVs

Ford Escape

Description: Compact front-wheel-drive (or all-wheel-drive) four-door crossover/SUV wagon, with four-cylinder or V-6 engine. XLS, XLT, and Limited trim levels have been offered. Escape Hybrid, with battery-gasoline powertrain, has been available during most years.

History: Introduced for 2005, Ford's Escape has been redesigned for 2014.

Powertrain(s): 2.5-liter four-cylinder engine, developing 171 horsepower and 171 pound-feet of torque. Available 3.0-liter V-6 engine produces 240 horsepower and 223 pound-feet. Recent Hybrid uses 153-horsepower four-cylinder engine, coupled to electric motor and battery pack. Five-speed manual or six-speed automatic transmission, except Hybrid has continuously variable transmission (CVT).

Specifications: 174.7 inches long, on a 103.1-inch wheelbase; 71.1 inches wide and 67.8 inches high. Curb weight, about 3445 pounds. EPA fuel-economy estimate (2012): 22-mpg city/28-mpg highway with manual shift; 20/27 mpg with automatic. With V-6 engine and automatic, estimate is 18/23 mpg. Hybrid is rated 30-mpg city/27-mpg highway. All-wheel-drive versions have lower fuel-economy estimates.

Driving Impressions: [2008 Hybrid] Ford's smallest crossover SUV has always been a pleasant vehicle to drive. Capable and comfortable, too. That's also true of the Hybrid edition, which was part of the lineup through 2012. Although the hybrid powertrain we tested worked exactly as intended, a distinct "bump" was noticeable when the engine restarted at a stoplight – but not when that engine shut off. As promised, too, the Hybrid can run a short distance, at low speed, on battery power alone. Though small, the Charge/Assist gauge on the dashboard is easy to see.

Entry into the Escape is easy enough, except for a rather high sill to cross. Comfortable seats offer good support, but are just a little on the hard side. Ride quality is a tad harsher than some competitors on rougher pavement, but just fine on smoother surfaces. Acceleration won't excite anyone, but it's not meant to: performance is spot-on for a vehicle of this sort, and sure to satisfy most drivers. Easy maneuverability is helped by moderately light steering.

Made in: USA

Average Retail Value
2007 Escape XLS: $6200 – $7500
2007 Escape XLT: $7000 – $8500
2007 Escape Limited: $8500 – $9700
2007 Escape Hybrid: $7500 – $8800
2008 Escape XLS: $7700 – $9000
2008 Escape XLT: $8500 – $10,000
2008 Escape Limited: $10,500 – $12,300
2008 Escape Hybrid: $10,000 – $11,800
2009 Escape XLS: $9200 – $10,800
2009 Escape XLT, Ltd.: $10,200 – $13,500
2009 Escape Hybrid: $13,000 – $15,700
2010 Escape XLS: $11,000 – $12,500
2010 Escape XLT, Ltd.: $12,100 – $15,500
2010 Escape Hybrid: $16,000 – $18,700
2011 Escape XLS: $12,800 – $14,500
2011 Escape XLT, Ltd.: $14,000 – $17,500
2011 Escape Hybrid: $19,200 – $22,000
2012 Escape XLS: $14,800 – $16,500
2012 Escape XLT, Ltd.: $16,000 – $20,000
2012 Escape Hybrid: $21,500 – $24,500
2013 Escape S: $17,000 – $18,200
2013 Escape SE, SEL: $18,000 – $21,000
2013 Escape Titanium: $21,500 – $23,500

Mazda CX-5

Description: Compact front-wheel-drive (or all-wheel-drive) four-door crossover/SUV wagon with four-cylinder.

History: Introduced for 2013, CX-5 was Mazda's smallest crossover SUV.

Powertrain(s): 2.0-liter four-cylinder engine, developing 155 horsepower and 150 pound-feet of torque. Six-speed manual or six-speed automatic transmission. New Skyactiv 2.5-liter engine available for 2014, on upper models.

Specifications: 178.7 inches long, on a 106.3-inch wheelbase; 72.4 inches wide and 65.7 inches high. Curb weight, about 3208 pounds. EPA fuel-economy estimate (2013): 26-mpg city/35-mpg highway with manual shift; 26/32 mpg with automatic. All-wheel-drive versions, offered only with automatic, has lower fuel-economy estimate: 25-mpg city/31-mpg highway.

Driving Impressions: Only a few moments are needed behind the wheel to realize that CX-5 feels just like a top-rung sport machine should: tightly attached to the pavement and, even in ordinary driving, bringing a satisfied nod to the driver. Steering feel is the superlative high point. This little crossover stays beautifully on-track, building upon Mazda's long-standing focus on sporty handling. A comfortable ride complements top-notch handling, but the powertrain does not quite reach the same pinnacle. Automatic-transmission shifts are quiet and crisp, but too "busy" at times. Push hard on the gas pedal at lower speed, and a delay to downshift may be quite noticeable, followed by abrupt forward motion. All too often, the transmission reaches higher gears swiftly, which is good for gas mileage but not performance. Acceleration actually is most effective with a rather gentle push on the pedal. The engine buzzes while accelerating.

Front-compartment space is plentiful, but the driver's seat isn't so cushiony on the bottom. However, long seat bottoms are welcome. Rear seat is roomy, but also marred by hard seat bottoms. Oddly, the center position, despite a hard seatback, feels more cushiony than the sides.

Headroom is good in both front and rear, and the cargo hold is spacious. Gauges are gently lit and pleasantly easy to read, navigation screen is tiny, though easy enough to read.

Made in: Japan

Average Retail Value
2013 CX-5: $17,500 – $21,500
2013 CX-5 Grand Touring: $22,500 – $24,200

Toyota RAV4

Description: Compact front-wheel-drive (or all-wheel drive) four-door crossover/SUV wagon with four-cylinder or V-6 engine. Base, Sport, and Limited trim levels have been offered. A RAV4 Hybrid joined the lineup for 2012, with a battery/gasoline powertrain.

History: First introduced for 1996, Toyota's RAV4 was redesigned for 2006 and, most recently, as a 2012 model.

Powertrain(s): 2.5-liter four-cylinder engine, developing 179 horsepower and 172 pound-feet of torque. Optional 3.5-liter V-6 produces 269 horsepower and 246 pound-feet. Four-speed automatic with four-cylinder engine, or five-speed automatic transmission with V-6.

Specifications: 181.9 inches long, on a 104.7-inch wheelbase; 71.5 inches wide and 66.3 inches high. Curb weight, about 3494 pounds. EPA fuel-economy estimate (2012): 21-mpg city/27-mpg highway; V-6 models get estimate of 19/26 mpg. All-wheel-drive versions have lower fuel-economy estimates.

Driving Impressions: Not only did the RAV4 originally go on sale around the same time as Honda's CR-V, long before most competitors joined that fray, the two have been prime competitors ever since. They also tend to have more similarities than differences.

Toyota added some 14 inches to overall length of the RAV4 for 2006, to make room for available three-row seating, seating up to seven. Accommodating front seats are comfortable, with more side bolstering than expected. Second-row legroom is acceptable and headroom ample, but somewhat hard cushioning detracts from comfort. Getting into the third row is barely possible for grown-ups, demanding something of a crawl. The second row does slide forward a bit, for third-row access. Third-row seats fold flat, but not to floor level.

Despite having space for three rows, it doesn't feel all that big. Like others in this class, the RAV4 leans toward sportiness but never really approaches that level. A compliant suspension gives the easy-to-drive RAV4 a pleasing ride. Toyota beats the rival CR-V in performance, simply because of the RAV4's available V-6 engine. The four-cylinder is reasonably energetic and generally quiet, but not silent. Toyota's V-6 version practically leaps ahead, rather than easing up to speed. In terms of acceleration, it feels more like a dashing sport sedan than an SUV.

Made in: Japan or Canada

Average Retail Value
2007 RAV4: $9800 – $11,500
2007 RAV4 Sport, Ltd.: $11,000 – $13,200
2008 RAV4: $11,000 – $13,200
2008 RAV4 Sport, Ltd.: $12,100 – $15,500
2009 RAV4: $12,400 – $14,500
2009 RAV4 Sport, Ltd.: $13,700 – $17,000
2010 RAV4: $13,900 – $16,500
2010 RAV4 Sport, Ltd.: $15,200 – $19,000
2011 RAV4: $15,500 – $18,500
2011 RAV4 Sport, Ltd.: $16,800 – $21,000
2012 RAV4: $17,500 – $20,500
2012 RAV4 Sport, Ltd.: $19,000 – $23,500
2012 RAV4 EV: $31,000 – $33,000
2013 RAV4 LE, XLE: $20,000 – $23,000
2013 RAV4 Limited: $23,000 – $25,500
2013 RAV4 EV: $35,000 – $38,000

Honda CR-V

Description: Compact front-wheel-drive (or all-wheel drive) four-door crossover/SUV wagon with four-cylinder engine. LX, EX, and EX-L trim levels have been offered.

History: First introduced back in 1997, Honda's CR-V was last redesigned for 2012.

Powertrain(s): 2.4-liter four-cylinder engine, developing 185 horsepower and 163 pound-feet of torque. Five-speed automatic transmission.

Specifications: 178.5 inches long, on a 103.1-inch wheelbase; 71.6 inches wide and 65.1 inches high. Curb weight, about 3426 pounds. EPA fuel-economy estimate (2012): 23-mpg city/31-mpg highway (20/30 mpg with all-wheel drive).

Driving Impressions: [2010 CR-V] Only a few moments behind the wheel are needed to observe that the CR-V qualifies as excellent all around: solid, stable, well-made, easy to drive. Despite being priced toward the upper end of the compact crossover scale, it's easy to see why the CR-V continues to attract buyers, even amid all the competition. Add Honda's reputation for overall reliability, and the CR-V is a crossover that needs to be considered by all but the most budget-minded shoppers. Quiet? You bet. Smooth-running? Definitely. Only in acceleration does the CR-V lag behind some competitors, despite the power increase for 2010. Even if performance is on the mild side, it's wholly adequate for a crossover SUV. In mixed driving (largely urban), a CR-V delivered nearly 21 mpg.

[2012 CR-V] Easy to enter and easy to drive, the 2012 CR-V delivers a smooth ride. Bumps are noticed, but recovery is immediate and only occasionally bothersome. Ample acceleration awaits, and Honda's automatic transmission performs effectively with some low-range shifts felt and others not. Downshifts are gracious, appropriate, and prompt – hard to beat. Though the CR-V is very quiet running overall, some growliness may be heard while accelerating, which is a bit out of character. Pleasantly light steering feel is accompanied by very good control and confidence. In twisty maneuvers on rural roads, the CR-V proved to be well-behaved.

Front-seat comfort is fine, though bottoms could be longer. Side bolstering isn't snug, but adequate. Headroom, leg space, and elbow room score well for front occupants.

A large one-section glovebox sits low (it was two-section previously). The clear but small navigation screen sits in a good, almost protruding, position. An information screen above it is very deep-set, yet both can wash out in sunlight. The highly distinctive instrument-panel layout features a flowing curve at the bottom. The huge, white-on-black speedometer could hardly be easier to read. The back seat is roomy for three, with seats that are firmer than in front; even the center position is tolerable.

Compared to the latest version, the pre-2012 model isn't as refined or modern, and lacks the 2012's light touch; but it's an effective and satisfying vehicle. Despite a bit of an old-fashioned feel, the earlier CR-V remains appealing in its own way, and shouldn't be discounted.

Made in: Ohio, USA; Mexico; or Japan

Average Retail Value
2007 CR-V LX: $10,000 – $11,000
2007 CR-V EX: $11,500 – $13,000
2008 CR-V LX: $11,200 – $12,500
2008 CR-V EX: $13,000 – $14,500
2009 CR-V LX: $12,500 – $14,000
2009 CR-V EX: $14,000 – $16,200
2010 CR-V LX: $13,800 – $15,300
2010 CR-V EX: $15,300 – $17,000
2011 CR-V LX, SE, EX: $15,200 – $17,800
2011 CR-V EX-L: $17,500 – $19,500
2012 CR-V LX, EX: $17,000 – $20,500
2012 CR-V EX-L: $21,000 – $23,200
2013 CR-V LX, EX: $19,000 – $23,000
2013 CR-V EX-L: $23,000 – $25,500

Hyundai Tucson

Description: Compact front-wheel-drive (or all-wheel drive) four-door crossover/SUV wagon with choice of four-cylinder engines. Base GL, midrange GLS, and upper Limited trim levels have been offered.

History: Introduced for 2005, Tucson was last redesigned for 2010. Hyundai also offers two larger crossover SUVs: the Santa Fe, and Santa Fe Sport.

Powertrain(s): 2.0-liter four-cylinder engine, developing 165 horsepower and 146 pound-feet of torque. Optional for upper models, 2.4-liter engine produces 176 horsepower and 168 pound-feet. Five-speed manual or six-speed automatic transmission (V-6, automatic-only).

Specifications: 173.2 inches long, on a 103.9-inch wheelbase; 71.7 inches wide and 66.3 inches high. Curb weight, about 3366 pounds. EPA fuel-economy estimate (2012): 20-mpg city/27-mpg highway with manual shift; 23/31 mpg with automatic. Larger engine gets estimate of 22/32 mpg (21/28 mpg with all-wheel drive).

Driving Impressions: Sleek, inspired styling makes the Tucson stand apart from the small-crossover pack, though recent models (2010-up) come across as more ordinary than their 2007-09 predecessors. Those were pleasant vehicles with a bit of a distinctive feel. On-center steering didn't feel quite right on our test-drive of a 2010 model: not quite sure of itself, thus needing periodic correction to stay on course. A satisfying ride is welcome, though it's no better than several rivals. Performance is eager, too; but again, so are several competitors. Seats offer excellent support and firm comfort, with bottoms that are satisfyingly long. The driver gets plenty of head, elbow, and leg space. Though attractive, the interior has a bit of a plastic-like look, though upholstery on our test model had a rather interesting pattern.

Made in: South Korea

Average Retail Value
2007 Tucson GLS: $6500 – $7500
2007 Tucson Ltd., SE: $7500 – $9000
2008 Tucson GLS: $8000 – $9000
2008 Tucson Ltd., SE: $9200 – $11,000
2009 Tucson GLS: $9600 – $10,600
2009 Tucson Ltd., SE: $11,200 – $13,200
2010 Tucson: $11,200 – $15,000
2011 Tucson GL: $12,800 – $14,300
2011 Tucson GLS, Ltd.: $15,000 – $18,000
2012 Tucson GL: $14,500 – $16,000
2012 Tucson GLS, Ltd.: $16,000 – $20,000
2013 Tucson GL: $16,300 – $17,800
2013 Tucson GLS, Ltd.: $17,600 – $21,500

Kia Sportage

Description: Compact front-wheel-drive (or all-wheel drive) four-door crossover/SUV wagon with regular or turbocharged four-cylinder engine. Basic design is related to Hyundai Tucson. Base, LX, and EX trim levels have been offered, along with turbocharged SX.

History: With a history dating back to 1995, the modern-day Sportage was last redesigned for the 2011 model year.

Powertrain(s): 2.4-liter four-cylinder engine, developing 176 horsepower and 168 pound-feet of torque. Turbocharged 2.0-liter engine in SX model produces 256 horsepower and 264 pound-feet. Six-speed manual or six-speed automatic transmission.

Specifications: 174.8 inches long, on a 103.9-inch wheelbase; 73 inches wide and 64.4 inches high. Curb weight, about 3157 pounds. EPA fuel-economy estimate (2012): 21-mpg city/29-mpg highway with manual shift; 22/32 mpg with automatic (21/28 mpg with all-wheel drive). Turbocharged SX gets estimate of 22/29 mpg (21/26 mpg with AWD).

Driving Impressions: Anyone who happens to recall driving an early Kia Sportage, back in the 1990s, would be mighty surprised to observe the qualities of recent examples. Back in 1995, the first-generation Sportage exhibited all the questionable characteristics that critics often liked to apply to Korean-built vehicles. After taking a breather in 2003-04, Kia was back with a vastly different, far superior Sportage, ready to become a serious contender in the soon-to-develop compact crossover race. Driving characteristics are similar to the Hyundai Tucson (described above), which is built on the same foundation.

Made in: South Korea

Average Retail Value
2007 Sportage LX: $6400 – $7900
2007 Sportage EX: $7800 – $9000
2008 Sportage LX: $7500 – $9200
2008 Sportage EX: $9200 – $10,500
2009 Sportage LX: $9000 – $10,200
2009 Sportage EX: $11,200 – $12,500

2010 Sportage LX: $10,800 – $12,800
2010 Sportage EX: $13,000 – $14,500
2011 Sportage: $13,200 – $16,000
2011 Sportage SX: $18,500 – $20,500
2012 Sportage: $15,000 – $18,500
2012 Sportage SX: $20,000 – $22,300
2013 Sportage: $17,000 – $20,000
2013 Sportage SX: $21,700 – $24,000

Subaru Forester

Description: Compact all-wheel drive four-door crossover/SUV wagon with horizontally-opposed four-cylinder engine (regular or turbocharged). Foresters come in 2.5X or 2.5XT trim, with a variety of sub-trim levels offered.

History: First introduced for 1998, Forester was last redesigned for 2009.

Powertrain(s): 2.5-liter four-cylinder engine, developing 170 horsepower and 170 pound-feet of torque. Turbocharged 2.5-liter engine rated 224 horsepower and 226 pound-feet. Five-speed manual or four-speed automatic transmission (turbo, automatic-only).

Specifications: 179.5 inches long, on a 103-inch wheelbase; 70.1 inches wide and 65.9 inches high. Curb weight, about 3250 pounds. EPA fuel-economy estimate (2012): 21-mpg city/27-mpg highway with either manual or automatic transmission; turbocharged SX gets estimate of 19-mpg city/24-mpg highway,

Driving Impressions: [2009] An altogether enjoyable vehicle, the 2009 Forester delivers excellent ride quality in urban environments. The revised suspension is effectively compliant, absorbing nearly all surface commotion. Foresters are highly maneuverable, too. With the non-turbo engine a Forester X accelerates rather modestly. Actually, the turbo isn't exactly stirring either, and "turbo lag" is noticeable, though not necessarily troubling. Generally quiet, the Forester does suffer some engine noise, partly because the non-turbo four-cylinder revs to rather high speeds: most noticeable with manual shift. That gearbox isn't the greatest, but Subaru's automatic transmission behaves well.

Even in the most challenging spots, the all-wheel-drive Forester is totally capable off-road. On unpaved roads, it coped well with severe bumps, though an occasional nasty sound could be heard from down below, in seriously harsh areas. Visibility is superior. The large speedometer is easy enough to read, if a little "busy" in appearance. Front seats are comfortable, roomy, and inviting. Back seats have shockingly large leg and foot room, even with the front seat pushed fairly far rearward.

Made in: Japan

Average Retail Value
2007 Forester X: $8200 – $9300
2007 Forester XT, L.L. Bean: $12,500 – $13,700
2008 Forester X: $9700 – $11,000
2008 Forester XT, L.L. Bean: $14,000 – $15,500
2009 Forester X: $11,500 – $13,200
2009 Forester XT: $15,500 – $16,800
2010 Forester 2.5X: $13,500 – $15,800
2010 Forester 2.5XT: $17,000 – $18,500
2011 Forester 2.5X: $15,600 – $17,500
2011 Forester 2.5X Touring: $19,000 – $20,700
2011 Forester 2.5XT: $18,700 – $20,700
2011 Forester 2.5XT Touring: $21,500 – $23,000
2012 Forester 2.5X: $17,700 – $20,000
2012 Forester 2.5X Touring: $21,500 – $23,500
2012 Forester 2.5XT: $20,500 – $22,500
2012 Forester 2.5XT Touring: $23,800 – $25,800
2013 Forester 2.5X: $19,800 – $21,800
2013 Forester 2.5X Touring: $23,500 – $25,500
2013 Forester 2.5XT: $22,700 – $24,500
2013 Forester 2.5XT Touring: $26,000 – $28,000

Additional Compact Crossovers/SUVs

Buick Encore; Jeep Compass and Patriot; Jeep Wrangler (the traditional Jeep); Mitsubishi Outlander Sport; Nissan Juke; Volkswagen Tiguan.

MIDSIZE CROSSOVERS/SUVs

Toyota Highlander

Description: Midsize front-wheel-drive (or all-wheel drive) four-door crossover SUV with V-6 engine (or hybrid V-6). Four-cylinder engine option began in 2009.

History: Introduced for 2001, Highlander was redesigned for 2008.

Powertrain(s): 3.5-liter V-6 engine, developing 290 horsepower and 286 pound-feet of torque. Optional turbocharged 2.0-liter four-cylinder rated 240 horsepower and 270 pound-feet. Both engines mate with a five-speed automatic transmission.

Specifications: 188.4 inches long, on a 109.8-inch wheelbase; 75.2 inches wide and 68.1 inches high. Curb weight, about 4266 pounds. EPA fuel-economy estimate (2012): 17-mpg city/25-mpg highway.

Driving Impressions: [2008 Highlander] Acceleration in a gas-engine Highlander bears out Toyota's claim for more additional, useful power than before. Smooth response adds to the experience, and passing reactions are generally prompt. At times, though, the powertrain seems to hold the vehicle back a bit – an inconsistency that detracts from overall refinement. Satisfying ride comfort helps boost the attraction, though. Steering is relatively light, but handling ranks a cut above the midsize-SUV norm.

The Hybrid's EV button is appealing, but keeping the vehicle in electric mode wasn't easy. ECON mode, which promises greater gas mileage, holds you back significantly. Clearly, it's not the mode to be in if you expect to pass or merge anytime soon. Initial startup with the Hybrid is somewhat sluggish, but performance is good once the system catches hold and evens out. Ride comfort is hard to beat for an SUV of any stripe. Body lean is noticeable on expressway on-ramps, but not bad for an SUV. Front-seat occupants get plenty of space in any Highlander. Second-row side seats also have abundant room, but the skinny center position isn't inviting at all.

Midsize Crossovers/SUVs

Made in: Japan or (recent models) USA

Average Retail Value
2007 Highlander: $10,500 – $14,000
2007 Highlander Limited: $13,500 – $16,200
2007 Highlander Hybrid: $12,500 – $15,000
2008 Highlander: $12,500 – $16,000
2008 Highlander Limited: $16,000 – $19,000
2008 Highlander Hybrid: $14,500 – $17,000
2009 Highlander: $14,600 – $19,000
2009 Highlander Limited: $18,700 – $22,000
2009 Highlander Hybrid: $17,000 – $21,000
2010 Highlander: $16,700 – $21,500
2010 Highlander Limited: $21,000 – $24,500
2010 Highlander Hybrid: $20,000 – $24,500
2011 Highlander: $18,800 – $23,800
2011 Highlander Limited: $23,200 – $27,500
2011 Highlander Hybrid: $25,000 – $29,500
2012 Highlander: $21,100 – $26,000
2012 Highlander Limited: $25,500 – $29,000
2012 Highlander Hybrid: $28,000 – $32,000
2013 Highlander: $23,500 – $28,500
2013 Highlander Limited: $28,000 – $31,500
2013 Highlander Hybrid: $32,000 – $35,500

Ford Explorer

Description: Large midsize rear-wheel-drive (or all-wheel drive) four-door SUV with V-6 or V-8 engine; four-cylinder in recent years. Base, XLT, and Limited trim levels were offered in 2012.

History: Ford launched its first Explorer SUV for 1991, and it was last redesigned for 2011, transformed into car-bodied form, distinct from its previous truck foundation.

Powertrain(s): 3.5-liter V-6 engine, developing 290 horsepower and 286 pound-feet of torque. Available turbocharged 2.0-liter four-cylinder rated 240 horsepower and 270 pound-feet. Each engine mates with a six-speed automatic transmission. Earlier Explorers had a V-8 engine option, and a five-speed automatic for the V-6.

Specifications: 197.1 inches long, on a 112.6-inch wheelbase; 90.2 inches wide (82.5 inches with mirrors folded) and 71 inches high. Curb weight, about 4695 pounds. EPA fuel-economy estimate (2012): 20-mpg city/25-mpg highway with four-cylinder; 18-mpg city/24-mpg highway with V-6 (17/22 mpg with all-wheel drive). Hybrid gets an estimate of 28 mpg for both city and highway driving.

Driving Impressions: Behind the wheel, the redesigned 2011 Explorer has a lot going for it. Refined? Yes. Quiet? Very much so. Energetic? Definitely, and brisk from lower speeds. Carlike? For the most part, yes. In fact, you can check off most consideration factors as pluses. Yet, this Explorer generation lacks a certain amount of character, compared to earlier versions. Explorer used to be a bit special. Not so much anymore. If anything, it's become more of a cookie-cutter model, easily matching but not necessarily beating the competition.

On the plus end, the Explorer benefits from good steering feel: on the light side, but not inappropriate. Easy to maneuver, this midsize SUV rides smoothly, as its suspension appears ready to tackle and contain nearly all trouble spots. Views are okay except past the very wide C-pillars, especially on the right. On the other hand, the information-screen layout looks almost incoherent. For many shoppers nowadays, Ford's Sync system makes the difference: love it (younger shoppers) or hate it (many others). There's nothing to feel in terms of controls: just flat "buttons" on the panel, and odd virtual buttons on the screen, such as "Where Am I?" Using them also is accompanied by annoying chirps. The Explorer driver absolutely must study the owner's manual to use Sync properly. Front-seat space is ample (with mild bolstering), but the second row less so. Unless front seats are positioned well forward, second-row legroom is cramped. Headroom falls short of voluminous, too. But the center spot is better than most. As for the third row, you can hardly see the seats back there, much less get to them easily. Cargo space is passable with a shallow well, but most users are likely to fold down those limited-use third-row seats to get truly useful luggage room.

Made in: Illinois, USA

Average Retail Value
2007 Explorer: $7500 – $10,500
2007 Explorer Limited: $10,000 – $12,000
2008 Explorer: $9500 – $13,000
2008 Explorer Limited: $11,500 – $13,800
2009 Explorer: $11,700 – $15,200
2009 Explorer Limited: $14,000 – $16,000
2010 Explorer XLT: $14,500 – $17,500
2010 Explorer Eddie Bauer: $16,500 – $19,500
2010 Explorer Limited: $17,500 – $20,000
2011 Explorer: $19,000 – $21,500
2011 Explorer XLT: $21,300 – $24,500
2011 Explorer Limited: $23,500 – $26,500
2012 Explorer: $21,000 – $23,800
2012 Explorer XLT: $23,500 – $26,500
2012 Explorer Limited: $26,500 – $29,500
2013 Explorer: $23,200 – $26,500
2013 Explorer XLT, Ltd.: $25,500 – $31,000
2013 Explorer Sport: $32,500 – $36,500

Chevrolet Traverse

Description: Midsize front-wheel-drive (or all-wheel drive) four-door crossover/SUV wagon with V-6 engine; closely related to GMC Acadia and Buick Enclave. LS, 1LT, 2LT, and LTZ trim levels have been offered.

History: Introduced for 2009.

Powertrain(s): 3.6-liter V-6 engine, developing 281 or 288 horsepower and 266 or 270 pound-feet of torque, depending on model. Six-speed automatic transmission.

Specifications: 205 inches long, on a 118.9-inch wheelbase; 78.4 inches wide and 72.8 inches high. Curb weight, about 4925 pounds. EPA fuel-economy estimate (2012): 17-mpg city/24-mpg highway (16/23 mpg with all-wheel drive).

Driving Impressions: [2009] Apart from an occasional odd creaking around the steering column of the Traverse that was tested, this wagon operated quietly, behaved capably on the road, and delivered a generally enjoyable experience. Smooth engine response is a bit more energetic than some competitive crossovers, though short of startling, and the automatic transmission is especially well-behaved. Acceleration is assertive enough from a standstill, but less so at speed, though clearly acceptable for this class. Though easy to maneuver and to drive, the Traverse isn't as easy to judge as some rivals. Ride quality is satisfying most of the time, but harsh obstacles may produce some overreaction; even jolting and jarring. Steering feel is good, if on the light side. Though uninspiring, Traverse handles confidently enough, though it doesn't seem quite as sure-footed in curves as some vehicles in this class. Apart from the comparatively high driving position, there's no sense of truckiness.

Step-in is somewhat high, but front-seat space is abundant. Second-row legroom could be better, and cargo volume is fairly modest if the third-row seats are up. Green-lit gauges are excellent, though they dim somewhat at twilight when the headlights go on. Available blind-spot mirrors aren't especially helpful, due to their small size. The same is true of the rearview camera system that places the image in a corner of the inside mirror. More utilitarian than joyful, the Traverse lacks the polish of the closely-related Buick Enclave or GMC Acadia, and doesn't feel quite as refined overall.

Made in: USA

Average Retail Value
2009 Traverse LS: $14,000 – $15,800
2009 Traverse LT, LTZ: $15,700 – $20,000
2010 Traverse LS, LT: $15,700 – $18,000
2010 Traverse LTZ: $20,000 – $22,800
2011 Traverse LS, LT: $17,500 – $20,500
2011 Traverse LTZ: $21,500 – $24,500
2012 Traverse LS, LT: $19,500 – $22,700
2012 Traverse LTZ: $23,500 – $26,000
2013 Traverse LS, LT: $22,000 – $25,800
2013 Traverse LTZ: $27,500 – $30,500

Dodge Durango

Description: Midsize rear-wheel-drive (or all-wheel drive) four-door crossover/SUV wagon with V-6 engine or, on R/T edition, V-8 power.

History: First launched for 1998, the seven-passenger Durango disappeared after 2009, but then reemerged in revised form as a 2011 model.

Powertrain(s): 3.6-liter V-6 engine, developing 290 horsepower and 260 pound-feet of torque, mating with a five-speed automatic transmission. R/T model holds 5.7-liter V-8 that produces 360 horsepower and 390 pound-feet, driving a six-speed automatic.

Specifications: 199.8 inches long, on a 119.8-inch wheelbase; 75.8 inches wide and 71.6 inches high. Curb weight, about 4913 pounds. EPA fuel-economy estimate (2012): 16-mpg city/23-mpg highway. R/T edition gets an estimate of 14-mpg city/20-mpg highway (13/20 mpg with all-wheel drive).

Driving Impressions: In its post-bailout mode, Chrysler has been pushing hard to create the impression that its reworked products are dramatically better than ever. In reality, while each of them has improved to an extent, some moved a lot farther ahead than others. Durango clearly falls into the latter category, pushing well beyond its predecessor. In fact, the tongue-in-cheek claims made in one commercial (that Durango had been toning up in Europe, gone to school, etc.) almost seem true. Based upon its handling capabilities, ride comfort, and overall quality, the latest Durango has almost moved into a different league.

Made in: Delaware or Michigan, USA

Average Retail Value
2007 Durango: $7000 – $10,000
2007 Durango Limited: $8500 – $11,300
2008 Durango: $8200 – $12,500
2008 Durango Limited: $9800 – $13,000
2009 Durango SE: $10,000 – $13,500
2009 Durango SLT, Limited: $11,500 – $16,500
2010 Durango: No 2010 models built

2011 Durango: $18,000 – $23,500
2011 Durango Citadel, R/T: $22,200 – $26,000
2012 Durango: $20,500 – $25,700
2012 Durango Citadel, R/T: $24,500 – $28,700
2013 Durango: $23,500 – $28,000
2013 Durango Citadel, R/T: $27,500 – $31,500

Honda Pilot

Description: Midsize front-wheel-drive (or all-wheel drive) four-door crossover/SUV wagon with V-6 engine. LX, EX, and EX-L trim levels have been offered.

History: Introduced for 2003, the eight-passenger Pilot was last redesigned for 2009.

Powertrain(s): 3.5-liter V-6 engine, developing 250 horsepower and 250 pound-feet of torque, mating with five-speed automatic transmission.

Specifications: 190.9 inches long, on a 109.2-inch wheelbase; 78.5 inches wide and 71 inches high. Curb weight, about 4499 pounds. EPA fuel-economy estimate (2012): 18-mpg city/25-mpg highway (17/24 mpg with all-wheel drive).

Driving Impressions: Not as carlike or modern-feeling as some rivals, Honda's Pilot is solid and tight, capable and roomy. Performing well, it also rides comfortably enough; but underneath, occupants can detect a refined, yet moderately trucklike feel. Honda's V-6 emits subdued blare on acceleration, but it's no noisier than competitors. Automatic-transmission operation is more noticeable than in some other SUVs, but not troubling. Steering and handling are trouble-free, if unexceptional.

Climbing inside demands a step up. Once there, stylish gauges are reasonably easy to read, and the navigation screen (if installed) is big, high, and bright. Front-seat occupants get ample space and comfort, though the driving position may feel a trifle cramped. Seat bottoms could be longer, but thigh support is excellent, joined by surprisingly snug side bolstering. The second row is spacious, but seats feel almost as firm as an old-fashioned bench, and bottoms are somewhat short. The center position's seatback is even harder. Wide-opening back doors and a slide-forward second-row seat ease access to the third row. In short, Pilot does nearly everything quite well. You also get the benefit of Honda's long-lived reputation for reliability, and only a few rivals have offered Pilot's eight-row seating. Yet, this SUV doesn't quite stand out from the competition.

Made in: Alabama, USA

Average Retail Value
2007 Pilot: $9200 – $11,500
2007 Pilot EX: $11,200 – $12,800
2008 Pilot: $11,000 – $13,500
2008 Pilot SE, EX: $13,000 – $15,500
2009 Pilot: $13,200 – $16,200
2009 Pilot EX, Touring: $15,800 – $19,800
2010 Pilot: $15,700 – $19,300
2010 Pilot EX, Touring: $19,000 – $23,000
2011 Pilot: $18,500 – $22,000
2011 Pilot EX-L, Touring: $22,300 – $26,500
2012 Pilot: $21,500 – $24,500
2012 Pilot EX-L, Touring: $25,300 – $29,500
2013 Pilot: $23,500 – $27,500
2013 Pilot EX-L, Touring: $28,000 – $32,500

Hyundai Santa Fe

Description: Hyundai's larger sport-utility vehicle seats up to seven occupants, but is smaller than the Veracruz wagon. Santa Fe competes against such models as the Chevrolet Equinox, Ford Edge, and Nissan Murano. Four-cylinder and V-6 engines have been offered, with two-wheel or all-wheel drive. For 2012, four trim levels were available: GLS and Limited (with standard four-cylinder power) and SE (with standard V-6).

History: Introduced for 2001, the Santa Fe was redesigned for 2007 and 2010, and again for the 2013 model year. Hyundai also launched a smaller Santa Fe Sport with a four-cylinder engine for 2013, but the regular Santa Fe remained, powered only by the V-6.

Powertrain(s): Hyundai's 2.4-liter four-cylinder engine makes 175 horsepower and 169 pound-feet of torque, versus 276 horsepower and 248 pound-feet for the 3.5-liter V-6. Both engines mate with a six-speed automatic transmission.

Specifications: 184.1 inches long, on a 106.3-inch wheelbase; 74.4 inches wide and 67.9 inches high. Curb weight, about 3875 pounds. EPA fuel-economy estimate (2012): 20-mpg city/28-mpg highway with four-cylinder and two-wheel drive; 20/25 mpg with four-cylinder and all-wheel drive; 20/26 mpg with V-6 engine.

Driving Impressions: [2008] Warming up to the larger Santa Fe isn't quite as easy as taking to the more compact Santa Fe Sport. Still, the bigger Santa Fe's engine delivers good punch, helped by a smooth automatic transmission. Ride comfort is about average for this class; a Santa Fe deals effectively with bumps, but doesn't lose its trucky feel. On the road, it's quiet but not silent, with a touch of engine sound inevitably discernible. Easy to maneuver, with a comparatively tight turning radius for its size, Hyundai's larger SUV has somewhat light steering, but not excessively so. Gauges are basic but easy to read, and visibility is excellent all-around.

Made in: Alabama or Georgia, USA

Average Retail Value
2007 Santa Fe: $8000 – $11,000
2008 Santa Fe GLS, SE: $9300 – $11,500
2008 Santa Fe Limited: $11,500 – $13,000
2009 Santa Fe GLS, SE: $10,700 – $13,500
2009 Santa Fe Limited: $13,500 – $15,000
2010 Santa Fe GLS, SE: $12,200 – $15,000
2010 Santa Fe Limited: $14,700 – $16,500
2011 Santa Fe GLS, SE: $14,000 – $17,000
2011 Santa Fe Limited: $16,800 – $19,000
2012 Santa Fe GLS, SE: $16,000 – $19,200
2012 Santa Fe Limited: $19,000 – $21,500
2013 Santa Fe GLS: $22,500 – $24,500
2013 Santa Fe Limited: $26,000 – $28,000

Kia Sorento

Description: Positioned above the Sportage and similar to Hyundai's Santa Fe, Kia's Sorento seats up to seven occupants and has come with either a four-cylinder engine or a V-6. Two-wheel and all-wheel drive versions have been available. The 2012 lineup included base, LX, EX GDI, and SX models, the latter with a standard V-6.

History: Introduced for 2003, the Sorento was last redesigned for the 2011 model year. A new base trim level debuted, along with a more powerful four-cylinder engine.

Powertrain(s): Base and LX models in 2012 held a 2.4-liter four-cylinder engine, rated at 175 horsepower and 169 pound-feet of torque. Standard in the EX GDI was a new 2.4-liter four-cylinder, making 191 horsepower and 181 pound-feet. SX models got a standard 3.5-liter V-6 engine, developing 276 horsepower and 248 pound-feet of torque. Most models used a six-speed automatic transmission, but a six-speed manual gearbox was available with the 175-hp engine.

Specifications: 183.9 inches long, on a 106.3-inch wheelbase; 74.2 inches wide and 67.3 inches high. Curb weight, about 3737 pounds. EPA fuel-economy estimate (2012): 21-mpg city/28-mpg highway with 175-hp engine and manual shift; 21/27 mpg with automatic; and 21/29 mpg with two-wheel drive rather than all-wheel drive. With the new GDI engine, the initial estimate was 21/28 mpg (22/32 mpg with two-wheel drive). Choosing a V-6 dropped the estimate to 19/25 mpg (20/26 mpg with two-wheel drive).

EPA Note: Late in 2012, Kia revised fuel-economy estimates of certain models, including the Sorento with the new GDI engine, due to an error in the original result. The revised estimate was 20/26 mpg (city/highway) with all-wheel drive, and 21/30 mpg with two-wheel drive.

Driving Impressions: [2011] Like compact crossovers, the midsize crossover/SUV field is a crowded place. Kia's Sorento hasn't been a member that stands well above the pack, but it deserves a place at the table, especially after losing its old truck-type platform as part of the 2011 redesign. A fully solid feel suggests excellent build quality, and the Sorento delivers a satisfying, seldom-tarnished ride. Even when the surfaces gets lumpy, little nastiness is transmitted to occupants. Acceleration is generally good, but the four-cylinder engine can lag just when swift pickup is most needed, even when the terrain is flat. Handling is somewhat ho-hum, but the Sorento is easy to drive and maneuver. Gauges are easy to read. Even with seat moved all the way down, though, the driver might feel somewhat high; that seat is firm, yet comfortable.

Made in: (early models) South Korea; (recent models) Alabama, USA

Average Retail Value
2007 Sorento: $6600 – $9000
2008 Sorento: $7800 – $9000
2008 Sorento EX: $9500 – $11,000
2009 Sorento: $9700 – $11,000
2009 Sorento EX: $12,000 – $13,800
2010 Sorento: No 2010 models were marketed.
2011 Sorento, LX: $14,700 – $16,800
2011 Sorento EX, SX: $17,000 – $20,000
2012 Sorento, LX: $16,200 – $18,700
2012 Sorento EX, SX: $19,000 – $23,000
2013 Sorento LX, EX: $18,200 – $22,000
2013 Sorento SX: $22,000 – $24,500

Jeep Grand Cherokee

Description: Midsize sport-utility vehicle is the largest Jeep model. Competing against such models as the Nissan Pathfinder and Toyota 4Runner, the Grand Cherokee came with a choice of three engines, topped by the high-performance 465-horsepower SRT8 edition. Chrysler's Jeep division also offers smaller Patriot, Compass, and Wrangler models.

History: First introduced for 1993, the Grand Cherokee was last redesigned for 2011. The SRT8 edition has been available for most years.

Powertrain(s): Standard engine in 2012 was a 3.6-liter V-6, making

290 horsepower and 264 pound-feet of torque, driving a five-speed automatic transmission. Optional was a 5.7-liter Hemi V-8, developing 360 horsepower and 390 pound-feet, mating with a six-speed automatic. The SRT8 edition held a 6.4-liter V-8 that generated 465 horsepower and 465 pound-feet of torque, working with a five-speed automatic.

Specifications: 189.8 inches long, on a rather long 114.8-inch wheelbase; 76.3 inches wide and 69.4 inches high. Curb weight, about 4660 pounds. EPA fuel-economy estimate (2012): 16-mpg city/22-mpg highway with V-6 and four-wheel drive (16/23 mpg with 2WD); 13/20 mpg with 5.7-liter V-8 and four-wheel drive (14/20 mpg with 2WD). SRT8 edition got a less-frugal estimate of 13/18 mpg (city/highway).

Driving Impressions: Topping the Jeep lineup in size, Grand Cherokee also stands at the pinnacle in terms of posh amenities. Those extras cost plenty when the Grand Cherokee was new, and they add quite a bit to its price on the used-car market, too. This isn't a Jeep for truly serious off-road trekking, by any means; but with four-wheel drive, it can handle moderately rough terrain, and do so without significant discomfort to the occupants. On the pavement, a Grand Cherokee rides with reasonable comfort, comparable to the competition. Performance depends upon the engine choice, but very few shoppers are likely to be in real need of the high-performance SRT editions. A V-6 will do the job well enough to suit most everyone, while consuming significantly less fuel than any of the V-8s, though none of them rank as thrifty in urban driving.

Made in: Michigan, USA

Average Retail Value
2007 Grand Cherokee Laredo: $9000 – $10,700
2007 Grand Cherokee Ltd., Overland: $11,500 – $14,500
2007 Grand Cherokee SRT8: $20,500 – $22,000
2008 Grand Cherokee Laredo: $10,500 – $12,500
2008 Grand Cherokee Ltd., Overland: $13,300 – $15,300
2008 Grand Cherokee SRT8: $23,500 – $25,500
2009 Grand Cherokee Laredo: $12,200 – $14,500
2009 Grand Cherokee Ltd., Overland: $16,000 – $19,000

2009 Grand Cherokee SRT8: $27,000 – $29,500
2010 Grand Cherokee Laredo: $14,500 – $17,200
2010 Grand Cherokee Limited: $19,000 – $22,000
2010 Grand Cherokee SRT8: $31,000 – $33,500
2010 Grand Cherokee Laredo: $19,000 – $22,000
2011 Grand Cherokee Ltd., Overland: $24,000 – $28,500
2012 Grand Cherokee Laredo: $21,200 – $24,200
2012 Grand Cherokee Ltd., Overland: $26,500 – $30,800
2012 Grand Cherokee SRT8: $42,000 – $45,000
2013 Grand Cherokee: $23,500 – $28,500
2013 Grand Cherokee Overland: $30,000 – $34,000
2013 Grand Cherokee SRT8: $46,000 – $49,000

Additional Midsize SUVs

Chevrolet Equinox; Dodge Journey; Ford Edge; Mazda CX-9; Nissan Rogue and Murano; Nissan Pathfinder and Xterra; Toyota Venza; Volkswagen Touareg.

FULL-SIZE SUVs

Chevrolet Tahoe/GMC Yukon

Description: Full-size rear-wheel-drive (or four-wheel-drive) four-door SUV with V-8 engine. Seating up to nine, Tahoe and Yukon are similar in structure and powertrains. Hybrid version has been available, too.

History: GM's large SUVs (including the larger Suburbans) have a long history, and were last redesigned for 2007. All-new versions have been introduced for the 2015 model year.

Powertrain(s): 5.3-liter four-cylinder engine, developing 320 horsepower and 335 pound-feet of torque, mates with six-speed automatic transmission. Hybrid model contains 332-horsepower, 6.0-liter V-8 and continuously variable transmission (CVT).

Specifications: 202 inches long, on a 116-inch wheelbase; 79 inches wide and 77 inches high. Curb weight, about 5524 pounds. EPA fuel-economy estimate (2012): 15-mpg city/21-mpg highway. Hybrid gets estimate of 20-mpg city/23-mpg highway.

Driving Impressions: [2008 Yukon Hybrid] Like other hybrid vehicles, this Yukon did exactly what was claimed by GMC, and did it adeptly. Apart from the auto-stop action, the Hybrid drives just like any Yukon – or similar Chevrolet Tahoe – as redesigned for the 2007 model year. More refined than its predecessors, the 2007-up Yukon yields a satisfying ride for a big SUV. As with other hybrid models, the Yukon's V-8 engine shuts off automatically as you ease to a stop, and starts up again as soon as you touch the gas pedal. Driving on battery alone is possible. However, it takes a terribly gentle foot on the accelerator pedal to keep the system in battery operation as you start off. Operation is fully automatic and largely seamless, but you can usually feel the gasoline engine come into play, working along with the electric motor. You can watch a diagram on the display screen, which shows the power source(s) currently in use.

Made in: Texas or (pre-2009) Wisconsin, USA

Pricing Note: Valuations of GMC Yukon are similar to figures shown for Chevrolet Tahoe.

Average Retail Value
2007 Tahoe LS: $14,500 – $17,000
2007 Tahoe LT, LTZ : $17,000 – $20,000
2008 Tahoe LS, LT: $16,700 – $20,000
2008 Tahoe LTZ, Hybrid: $20,000 – $23,200
2009 Tahoe LS, LT: $19,000 – $23,000
2009 Tahoe LTZ, Hybrid: $23,500 – $28,000
2010 Tahoe LS, LT: $21,500 – $26,000
2010 Tahoe LTZ, Hybrid: $27,000 – $31,500
2011 Tahoe LS, LT: $24,000 – $29,000
2011 Tahoe LTZ, Hybrid: $30,500 – $35,000
2012 Tahoe LS, LT: $26,700 – $31,200
2012 Tahoe LTZ, Hybrid: $33,700 – $39,000
2013 Tahoe LS, LT: $29,500 – $34,000
2013 Tahoe LTZ, Hybrid: $37,000 – $42,000

Toyota Sequoia

Description: Full-size rear-wheel-drive (or four-wheel-drive) four-door SUV with V-8 engine. Base SR5, midlevel Limited, and top Platinum trim levels have been offered.

History: Introduced for 2001, Sequoia was redesigned for 2008.

Powertrain(s): 4.6-liter V-8 engine, developing 310 horsepower and 327 pound-feet of torque. Limited and Platinum models hold 5.7-liter V-8, producing 381 horsepower and 401 pound-feet. All Sequoias have a six-speed automatic transmission.

Specifications: 205.1 inches long, on a 122-inch wheelbase; 79.9 inches wide and 74.6 inches high. Curb weight, about 5970 pounds. EPA fuel-economy estimate (2012): 14-mpg city/20-mpg highway (13/18 mpg with all-wheel drive). Larger V-8 gets estimate of 13-mpg city/18-mpg highway (13/17 mpg with all-wheel drive).

Driving Impressions: No doubt about it, this is one big (and heavy)

SUV. That's hardly a surprise, since it's built on the same chassis as Toyota's sizable Tundra pickup truck. If you really must have a full-size SUV, and can pay the price, Toyota's version has a lot to recommend it. Sequoia merits start with the company's well-known reputation for reliability, along with a level of refinement that places this big SUV near the head of its class. That's something of a surprise, since it's built on the same foundation as Toyota's Tundra full-size pickup truck. Then again, even the Tundra yields a ride that's far less trucklike than pickups of the recent past. Despite the Sequoia's heft, too, the sizable V-8 delivers sufficient strength to satisfy any reasonable owner. Of course, shoppers who crave the biggest Toyota of them all could opt instead for a Land Cruiser.

Made in: Indiana, USA

Average Retail Value
2007 Sequoia SR5: $13,500 – $15,000
2007 Sequoia Limited: $16,000 – $17,700
2008 Sequoia SR5: $17,000 – $18,800
2008 Sequoia Ltd., Platinum: $21,000 – $26,800
2009 Sequoia SR5: $20,000 – $22,000
2009 Sequoia Ltd., Platinum: $24,500 – $31,500
2010 Sequoia SR5: $23,000 – $25,000
2010 Sequoia Ltd., Platinum: $28,000 – $34,500
2011 Sequoia SR5: $26,000 – $28,000
2011 Sequoia Ltd., Platinum: $31,500 – $37,500
2012 Sequoia SR5: $29,200 – $31,500
2012 Sequoia Ltd., Platinum: $35,500 – $42,000
2013 Sequoia SR5: $33,000 – $35,500
2013 Sequoia Ltd., Platinum: $39,500 – $46,000

Additional Full-size SUVs

Buick Enclave; Ford Flex; Nissan Armada.

PICKUP TRUCKS

(Dodge) Ram 1500

Description: Full-size rear-wheel-drive (or four-wheel-drive), two or four-door pickup truck, with V-6 or V-8 engine.

History: Dodge used the Ram model designation on its large pickup trucks for decades, until Ram became a separate brand for the 2010 model year. Full-size trucks were redesigned for 2006 and again for 2009.

Powertrain(s): 3.7-liter V-6 engine, developing 215 horsepower and 235 pound-feet of torque. Available 4.7-liter V-8 produces 310 horsepower and 330 pound-feet. Optional 5.7-liter Hemi V-8 generates 390 horsepower and 407 pound-feet. A four-speed automatic transmission mates with the V-6 engine; or six-speed automatic with either V-8. Earlier models also were offered with a manual gearbox.

Specifications: Regular-cab short-bed is 209 inches long, on a 120.5-inch wheelbase; 79.4 inches wide and 74.6 inches high. Crew Cab is 229 inches long, on a 140.5-inch wheelbase. Curb weight, regular-cab short-bed, is about 4518 pounds. Earlier Ram models came in regular-cab, Quad Cab, and Mega Cab body styles. EPA fuel-economy estimate (2012): 14-mpg city/20-mpg highway with rear-wheel drive and any engine.

Driving Impressions: [2009] Stepping into a Ram 1500 Laramie 4x4 without running boards is the first hurdle. Frankly, it's quite a climb. In addition to newfound refinement, the 2009 Ram with a Hemi V-8 engine delivered plenty of energy. Even so, it didn't feel quite scintillating, held back a bit by the truck's weight. Still, there's certainly no shortage of helpful power. Behind the wheel, it's almost possible to forget you're in a full-size truck, lulled by its reasonably quiet, easygoing stride. Some trucklike sounds are detectable, but not much. A four-wheel-drive Ram is simply terrific on snow-covered pavement. On any surface type, the ride does get jittery when imperfections crop up, which could make a long trek somewhat taxing.

Compared to earlier Ram ride quality, however, this one is a pleasure on the road. Although the steering feel is comfortable and confident, this Ram still feels like a truck when rolling through curves and corners. That's as it should be. Good-size mirrors help visibility, though the over-left-shoulder view is impaired.

Made in: USA

Pricing Note: Because full-size pickups come in a bewildering array of trim levels, engine types, bed lengths, drive systems, etc., the range of valuations is immense. Therefore, we are providing only the minimum value: the lowest figure in each range. That low-end model is typically a no-frills Work Truck with a V-6 engine.

Average Retail Value
2007 Ram 1500 Regular Cab: $7000 up
2007 Ram 1500 Quad Cab: $9500 up
2007 Ram 1500 Mega Cab: $13,000 up
2008 Ram 1500 Regular Cab: $7900 up
2008 Ram 1500 Quad Cab: $11,000 up
2008 Ram 1500 Mega Cab: $14,000 up
2009 Ram 1500 Regular Cab: $9000 up
2009 Ram 1500 Quad Cab: $12,500 up
2009 Ram 1500 Crew Cab: $15,200 up
2010 Ram 1500 Regular Cab: $10,200 up
2010 Ram 1500 Quad Cab: $14,000 up
2010 Ram 1500 Crew Cab: $16,300 up
2011 Ram 1500 Regular Cab: $11,800 up
2011 Ram 1500 Quad Cab: $15,700 up
2011 Ram 1500 Crew Cab: $18,000 up
2012 Ram 1500 Regular Cab: $13,800 up
2012 Ram 1500 Quad Cab: $17,500 up
2012 Ram 1500 Crew Cab: $20,000 up
2013 Ram 1500 Regular Cab: $16,000 up
2013 Ram 1500 Quad Cab: $19,500 up
2013 Ram 1500 Crew Cab: $22,000 up

Ford F-150

Description: Full-size rear-wheel-drive (or four-wheel-drive), two- or four-door pickup truck, with V-6, turbocharged V-6, or V-8 engine.

History: For decades, Ford's F-150 has been the top-selling truck – and the top-selling vehicle – in the U.S. Introduced way back in 1953 as the F-100. Launched for 1984, its F-150 successor was last redesigned for the 2009 model year.

Powertrain(s): 3.7-liter V-6 engine, developing 302 horsepower and 278 pound-feet of torque. Available 5.0-liter V-8 produces 360 horsepower and 380 pound-feet. Optional 6.2-liter V-8, available in top models, generates 411 horsepower and 432 pound-feet. Six-speed automatic transmission. In 2010, a V-8 engine was standard, while 2011 models came with a choice of two V-6s or a reworked V-8.

Specifications: Regular-cab short-bed, 213.1 inches long, on a 126-inch wheelbase; 78.9 inches wide and 74.6 inches high. Curb weight, about 4743 pounds. EPA fuel-economy estimate (2012): 17-mpg city/23-mpg highway with V-6 engine and rear-drive (16/21 mpg with four-wheel drive); 16/22 mpg with turbo V-6 and rear-drive (15/21 mpg with 4WD); 15/21 mpg with 5.0-liter V-8 and rear-drive (14/19 mpg with 4WD); 13/18 mpg with 6.2-liter V-8 and rear-drive (12/16 mpg with 4WD).

Driving Impressions: [2011 F-150] In just about every way, the F-150 stands tall: performance, powertrain refinement, handling qualities, capacity, passenger space. Sure, it's on the noisy side, but so are the other full-size pickups. Yes, the ride can get lumpy and bouncy; but again, that's the price one pays for the benefits of a big truck. Trouble is, each of Ford's competitors keeps improving as well. In fact, the "best" truck may be the one that was redesigned most recently, simply because that's the one that leapfrogged a bit ahead of its rivals, at least temporarily. None of this matters to big-pickup enthusiasts, however. Nearly all of them have a favorite brand, and are unlikely to have much good to say about the competition.

Made in: USA

Pricing Note: Because full-size pickups come in a bewildering array of trim levels, engine types, bed lengths, drive systems, etc., the range of valuations is immense. Therefore, we are providing only the minimum value: the lowest figure in each range. That low-end model is typically a no-frills Work Truck with a V-6 engine.

2007 F-150 Regular Cab: $6000 up
2007 F-150 Super Cab: $8000 up
2007 F-150 Super Crew: $11,000 up
2008 F-150 Regular Cab: $7000 up
2008 F-150 Super Cab: $9500 up
2008 F-150 Super Crew: $12,500 up
2009 F-150 Regular Cab: $8200 up
2009 F-150 Super Cab: $11,000 up
2009 F-150 Super Crew: $14,000 up
2010 F-150 Regular Cab: $9800 up
2010 F-150 Super Cab: $13,000 up
2010 F-150 Super Crew: $15,800 up
2011 F-150 Regular Cab: $11,500 up
2011 F-150 Super Cab: $15,000 up
2011 F-150 Super Crew: $17,800 up
2012 F-150 Regular Cab: $13,200 up
2012 F-150 Super Cab: $17,200 up
2012 F-150 Super Crew: $19,800 up
2013 F-150 Regular Cab: $15,000 up
2013 F-150 Super Cab: $19,500 up
2013 F-150 Super Crew: $22,000 up

Chevrolet Silverado 1500

Description: Full-size rear-wheel-drive (or four-wheel-drive) two- or four-door pickup truck, with V-6 or V-8 engine. Silverado Hybrid has 332-horsepower, 6.0-liter V-8.

History: Introduced for 1999 to replace C/K series, the Silverado was last redesigned for 2007.

Powertrain(s): 4.3-liter V-6 engine, developing 195 horsepower and 260 pound-feet of torque. Available 4.8-liter V-8 produces 302 horsepower and 305 pound-feet. Optional 5.3-liter V-8 generates 315 horsepower and 338 pound-feet. Ford's 6.2-liter V-8 generates 403 horsepower and 407 pound-feet. The F-150 Hybrid uses a 6.0-liter V-8, rated at 332 horsepower. Four-speed or six-speed (5.3- and 6.2-liter) automatic transmission.

Specifications: Regular-cab short-bed is 205.6 inches long, on a 119-inch wheelbase; 79.9 inches wide and 73.8 inches high. Curb weight, about 4633 pounds. EPA fuel-economy estimate (2012): 15-mpg city/20-mpg highway with V-6 and rear-drive (14/18 mpg with four-wheel drive); 14/19 mpg with 4.8-liter V-8 and rear-drive (13/18 mpg with 4WD); 15/22 mpg with 5.3-liter V-8 and rear-drive (15/21 mpg with 4WD); 13/18 mpg with 6.2-liter V-8 and rear-drive (12/18 mpg with 4WD). Hybrid estimate is 20-mpg city/23-mpg highway.

Driving Impressions: [2009 Silverado XFE – fuel-efficient model] Driving and handling qualities of the XFE differ little from a standard Silverado with a comparable engine. Powertrain response is satisfactory and familiar for a pickup, if nothing to exclaim about. Though the six-speed automatic transmission helps deliver the fuel-economy improvement, it doesn't always behave properly. Downshifts can be jerky at times, and tepid response occurs some of the time.

Ride comfort hardly ranks as gentle, but the Silverado XFE is well-snubbed, without suffering overreactions from its suspension. Inside, the chrome-surrounded, deep-set gauges seem somewhat old-fashioned.

Made in: Mexico or USA

Pricing Note: Because full-size pickups come in a bewildering array of trim levels, engine types, bed lengths, drive systems, etc., the range of valuations is immense. Therefore, we are providing only the minimum value: the lowest figure in each range. That low-end model is typically a no-frills Work Truck with a V-6 engine.

Average Retail Value
2007 Silverado Regular Cab: $7000 up
2007 Silverado Extended Cab: $10,000 up
2007 Silverado Crew Cab: $11,500 up
2008 Silverado Regular Cab: $8200 up
2008 Silverado Extended Cab: $11,300 up
2008 Silverado Crew Cab: $13,300 up
2009 Silverado Regular Cab: $9500 up
2009 Silverado Extended Cab: $12,800 up
2009 Silverado Crew Cab: $15,000 up
2010 Silverado Regular Cab: $11,000 up

2010 Silverado Extended Cab: $14,500 up
2010 Silverado Crew Cab: $17,500 up
2011 Silverado Regular Cab: $12,500 up
2011 Silverado Extended Cab: $15,700 up
2011 Silverado Crew Cab: $18,700 up
2012 Silverado Regular Cab: $14,200 up
2012 Silverado Extended Cab: $17,500 up
2012 Silverado Crew Cab: $20,500 up
2013 Silverado Regular Cab: $16,500 up
2013 Silverado Extended Cab: $19,500 up
2013 Silverado Crew Cab: $22,500 up

Additional Pickup Trucks

Honda Ridgeline; Nissan Titan; Toyota Tundra. Compact pickup trucks have been offered by Toyota (Tacoma), Chevrolet (Colorado), Dodge (Dakota), and Nissan (Frontier).

SPORTY CARS

Ford Mustang

Description: Rear-wheel-drive two-door coupe and convertible, available with V-6 or V-8 engine.

History: First launched as a 1964 model, the Mustang has been part of Ford's lineup ever since. Mustang was last redesigned for the 2013 model year.

Powertrain(s): 3.7-liter V-6 engine, developing 305 horsepower and 280 pound-feet of torque. Available 5.0-liter V-8 engine, installed in GT models, produces 412 horsepower and 390 pound-feet. Six-speed manual or six-speed automatic transmission. Recent Boss 302 model contains 5.0-liter V-8 that generates 444 horsepower and 380 pound-feet of torque. Ford also offers a Shelby GT500 with a supercharged 5.4-liter V-8, cranking out 550 horsepower and 510 pound-feet.

Specifications: 188.1 inches long, on a 107.1-inch wheelbase; 73.9 inches wide and 55.6 inches high. Curb weight, about 3750 pounds. EPA fuel-economy estimate (2012): V-6 model, 19-mpg city/29-mpg highway with manual shift, or 19/21 mpg with automatic. GT V-8 estimated at 17/26 mpg with manual shift, or 18/25 mpg with automatic.

Driving Impressions: Mustangs tend to elicit opposing views. Fans of Ford's ponycar absolutely love them. Yet, some car enthusiasts can't stand them. More than most modern vehicles, despite technological improvements, Mustang is nearly as reminiscent of the past as the present, much less the future.

[2013 Mustang V-6 automatic] Mustang fans are sure to love it. Others, maybe not so much. Despite plenty of technical advances over the years, Mustang retains traditional American-sport feel. Not just the rear-drive, but raucous sound (highly subdued with V-6), jumpy/bouncy ride on imperfect pavement, highly competent handling (in any form), and energetic performance. Expect a brief delay when hitting the gas hard, but then a rather vigorous burst. The dashboard retains a traditional look, too: stylized gauges, but not too bad to read. A head-duck may be needed to get inside, but seats are quite comfortable, with helpful support. Rear legroom is meager for two; not much space for heads, either. Engine vibration is more of an issue than noise. Visibility is poor, with small rear quarter windows and headrests blocking the rear view. Good-size trunk, but high loading liftover.

[2013 Mustang GT] Ford's Mustang GT is almost like a completely different vehicle from the V-6, qualifying as full-bore history. Unsubtle exhaust, heavy steering and shifter (short throws; not always easy to tell where you are), and overall weighty feel aren't so different from V-8 Mustangs of the past. A heavy clutch, too; which takes effort and attention. Exuberant energy awaits, but delivered the old-fashioned way: loudly and more than a bit harshly, so as to be noticed. Sure, this will be heresy to Mustang fans, but the GT belongs to an era that's largely gone.

Made in: USA

Average Retail Value
2007 Mustang V-6 coupe: $8800 – $10,000
2007 Mustang V-6 conv.: $9800 – $10,800
2007 Mustang GT coupe: $11,500 – $12,700
2007 Mustang GT conv.: $13,200 – $14,200
2007 Shelby GT500 coupe: $18,500 – $20,000
2007 Shelby GT500 conv.: $21,500 – $23,000
2008 Mustang V-6 coupe: $10,000 – $11,200
2008 Mustang V-6 conv.: $11,000 – $12,000
2008 Mustang GT coupe: $13,300 – $14,700
2008 Mustang GT conv.: $15,000 – $16,500
2008 Shelby GT500 coupe: $21,000 – $22,500
2008 Shelby GT500 conv.: $24,000 – $25,500
2009 Mustang V-6 coupe: $11,500 – $13,000
2009 Mustang V-6 conv.: $12,700 – $14,000
2009 Mustang GT coupe: $15,200 – $16,700
2009 Mustang GT conv.: $17,200 – $18,700
2009 Shelby GT500 coupe: $24,000 – $25,500
2009 Shelby GT500 conv.: $27,000 – $28,700
2010 Mustang V-6 coupe: $13,300 – $14,800
2010 Mustang V-6 conv.: $14,500 – $15,800

2010 Mustang GT coupe: $17,800 – $19,500
2010 Mustang GT conv.: $20,000 – $21,500
2010 Shelby GT500 coupe: $28,000 – $29,700
2010 Shelby GT500 conv.: $31,000 – $33,000
2011 Mustang V-6 coupe: $15,200 – $16,500
2011 Mustang V-6 conv.: $16,500 – $18,000
2011 Mustang GT coupe: $20,000 – $22,000
2011 Mustang GT conv.: $22,500 – $24,000
2011 Shelby GT500 coupe: $33,000 – $34,500
2011 Shelby GT500 conv.: $36,000 – $38,000
2012 Mustang V-6 coupe: $17,200 – $18,500
2012 Mustang V-6 conv.: $18,300 – $19,800
2012 Mustang GT coupe: $22,300 – $23,800
2012 Mustang GT conv.: $25,000 – $26,500
2012 Mustang Boss 302 cpe: $31,500 – $33,000
2012 Shelby GT500 coupe: $37,500 – $39,000
2012 Shelby GT500 conv.: $40,500 – $42,500
2013 Mustang V-6 coupe: $19,200 – $21,000
2013 Mustang V-6 conv.: $20,200 – $21,800
2013 Mustang GT coupe: $24,500 – $26,700
2013 Mustang GT conv.: $27,000 – $29,000
2013 Mustang Boss 302 cpe: $35,000 – $37,000
2013 Shelby GT500 coupe: $47,000 – $50,000
2013 Shelby GT500 conv.: $50,000 – $52,500

Chevrolet Camaro

Description: Rear-wheel-drive two-door coupe and convertible, available with V-6 or V-8 engine.

History: The first-generation Camaro debuted back in 1967, and lasted into 2002. For 2010, Chevrolet revived the Camaro model designation on a modern version, with styling touches reminiscent of the past. A convertible joined the initial coupe for 2011, and a 580-horsepower ZL1 became available a year later.

Powertrain(s): 3.6-liter V-6 engine, developing 323 horsepower and 278 pound-feet of torque. Optional 6.2-liter V-8 engine, installed in SS models, produces 426 horsepower and 400 pound-feet (400 horsepower and 410 pound-feet with automatic). Supercharged 6.2-

liter V-8 in ZL1 makes 580 horsepower and 556 pound-feet. Six-speed manual or six-speed automatic transmission.

Specifications: 190.4 inches long, on a 112.3-inch wheelbase; 75.5 inches wide and 54.2 inches high. Curb weight, about 3750 pounds. EPA fuel-economy estimate (2012 Camaro V-6): 17-mpg city/28-mpg highway with manual shift; 18/29 or 19/30 mpg with automatic. Camaro SS V-8: 16/24 mpg with manual; 15/24 mpg with automatic. Camaro ZL1: 14/19 mpg with manual; 12/18 mpg with automatic.

Driving Impressions: [2010 Camaro] More than some retro cars, the Camaro retains a substantial amount of its ancestor's character. You can expect plenty of attention from passersby who fondly recall the original generations. Huge exhaust outlet enclosures at the rear help capture yearning glances. Even with the V-6 engine, the exhaust delivers a loud, whoop-like sound when accelerating relatively hard. Otherwise, it's reasonably quiet. Road noise is more restrained than expected, especially with such big tires. The V-6 engine yields bountiful energy at start-up, and to pass or merge. Thus, there's not much need for a V-8. Despite moving out assertively, the V-6 Camaro feels heavy overall – again, like the original. Accelerating from 35-40 mph, response may be markedly less than vigorous if a downshift doesn't take place.

Gauges are distinctive and deep-set, but relatively easy to read. So are the available auxiliary gauges, but they're positioned so low (just above the console) that you can easily forget their presence. Over-the-shoulder visibility is nearly non-existent, making outside mirror use mandatory. Tiny rear quarter panes help little (the left one not at all). Both the windshield and back window are quite squat, though views directly to the rear aren't bad. Handling excels, as expected – quite reminiscent of the original. But this Camaro isn't quick-steering sporty in character. Despite a taut suspension, the ride is reasonably smooth most of the time. In fact, you can eventually forget what kind of car you're in.

Getting inside isn't so difficult, and the Camaro's front seat is seriously comfortable. Don't even think about the back seat unless you're young and agile. A high-liftover trunk lid opens to reveal drop-down loading into a small space. Hugely long doors can be a problem when parking. Most notably, the modern Camaro feels far better-built than the original, which was distressingly rickety.

Enthusiasts who recall original Camaros almost invariably are thinking of the hot V-8 versions. Chevrolet followed through with a V8-powered SS coupe. More than V-6 Camaro, the SS comes across as a "toy car," packed with unnecessary power. It's essentially a fantasy machine for aging baby boomers. Built-in engine shake is coupled with a burbling exhaust note, clearly intended to titillate. But for most drivers, those sensations seem quaintly out of place in today's world. Expect quite a lot of bouncing around in an SS. Jolting and jarring can be harsh on rough spots, though the ride is reasonably smooth on fine pavement. Clutch action with the manual gearbox is excellent, and the six-speed shifts positively, demanding moderate effort.

Made in: Canada

Average Retail Value
2010 Camaro V-6 coupe: $16,000 – $18,000
2010 Camaro SS coupe: $21,500 – $23,200
2011 Camaro V-6 coupe: $17,100 – $19,300
2011 Camaro V-6 conv.: $21,000 – $22,500
2011 Camaro SS coupe: $23,500 – $25,300
2011 Camaro SS conv.: $25,500 – $27,500
2012 Camaro V-6 coupe: $18,300 – $20,500
2012 Camaro V-6 conv.: $22,800 – $24,800
2012 Camaro SS coupe: $26,000 – $27,800
2012 Camaro SS conv.: $28,000 – $30,000
2012 Camaro ZL1 coupe: $39,500 – $41,500
2013 Camaro V-6 coupe: $19,700 – $22,500
2013 Camaro V-6 conv.: $25,000 – $27,000
2013 Camaro SS coupe: $28,700 – $30,500
2013 Camaro SS conv.: $31,000 – $33,000
2013 Camaro ZL1 coupe: $42,000 – $44,000
2013 Camaro ZL1 conv.: $46,500 – $49,000

Mazda MX-5 (Miata)

Description: Rear-wheel-drive two-door, two-passenger roadster.

Retractable hardtop available, in lieu of fabric roof.

History: First introduced for 1990 as the Miata, Mazda's sports car later adopted the MX-5 designation. Mazda doesn't often make major changes. The MX-5 was last redesigned for 2006, though an all-new model is expected for 2016.

Powertrain(s): 2.0-liter four-cylinder engine, developing 167 horsepower and 140 pound-feet of torque with manual shift (158 horsepower and 148 pound-feet with automatic). Five- or six-speed (on Touring model) manual gearbox or six-speed automatic transmission.

Specifications: 157.3 inches long, on a 91.7-inch wheelbase; 67.7 inches wide and 49 inches high. Curb weight, about 2445 pounds. EPA fuel-economy estimate (2012): 22-mpg city/28-mpg highway with five-speed manual; 21/28 mpg with six-speed manual; 21/28 mpg with six-speed automatic.

Driving Impressions: [2009 MX-5] Some manufacturers fall short on a given model's most notable characteristic, but that's hardly the case with Mazda. The original Miata was sheer fun to drive, and so is its recent successor. This is one car that hasn't lost any of its charm. Acceleration won't set hearts thumping, unless you really push hard on the gas – which means the engine starts to sound a bit strained. Mazda's gearbox is a joy to manipulate: not quite the slickest, but highly inviting to use. Just-right clutch operation permits quite easy takeoffs, yet the clutch stands ready to absorb all the engine delivers, without balking.

Handling is the MX-5's Number One attribute, including a beautiful quick-steering feel. Steering is not light, but doesn't demand great muscle, either. The ride is surprisingly comfortable for a sports car. Only really harsh bumps produce nasty reactions. Getting in and out is easier than some might think, but occupants do drop down into the seat, then swing their legs around. Trunk space is more substantial than expected. A deep well holds a roller suitcase with space to spare. Traditional white-on-black gauges are easy enough to read. Noise is definitely an issue. Some drivers welcome the sounds, but others might deem them a constant annoyance. With the top up, visibility is somewhat restricted toward the rear corners.

[2013 MX-5 with stick shift and hardtop] In its latest iteration, Mazda's roadster is closer than nearly all rivals to sports cars of the distant past. Noise and vibration? Sure. Snug quarters? Absolutely. In exchange, hard to beat handling, like sports cars of old, with only hints of the modern configuration below. An MX-5 can be spirited, but feels as if it's working, not loafing along. Headroom is so-so; left elbow space tiny; legs snug. It's still an experience, but takes significant effort to steer and shift. Thus, not for the puny.

Made in: Japan

Pricing Note: Models with hardtop, rather than fabric top, cost more than figures shown.

Average Retail Value
2007 MX-5: $7800 – $9500
2008 MX-5: $9000 – $11,000
2008 MX-5 Special Ed.: $12,000 – $13,000
2009 MX-5: $10,500 – $12,700
2010 MX-5: $12,200 – $14,300
2011 MX-5: $14,000 – $16,000
2011 MX-5 Special Ed.: $17,500 – $19,000
2012 MX-5: $16,200 – $18,500
2012 MX-5 Special Ed.: $21,000 – $23,000
2013 MX-5: $18,500 – $20,500

Mini Cooper

Description: Rear-wheel-drive two-door coupe and convertible, available with regular or turbocharged (Cooper S) four-cylinder engine. John Cooper Works editions have a more powerful turbocharged engine.

History: Under BMW stewardship, the modern-day Mini debuted for 2002. For 2008, a longer, five-passenger Clubman joined the original coupe. An all-wheel-drive Countryman debuted for 2012, along with a distinctively-styled two-door coupe. A two-door Paceman sport variant of the Countryman emerged for 2013.

Powertrain(s): Regular Cooper models hold a 1.6-liter four-cylinder engine, developing 121 horsepower and 114 pound-feet of torque. A turbocharged 1.6-liter four-cylinder in the Cooper S produces 181 horsepower and 177 pound-feet. John Cooper Works editions are rated 208 horsepower and 192 pound-feet. Six-speed manual or six-speed automatic transmission.

Specifications: 146.6 inches long, on a 97.1-inch wheelbase; 66.3 inches wide and 55.4 inches high. Curb weight, about 2535 pounds. Clubman is 155.9 inches long, on a 100.3-inch wheelbase. EPA fuel-economy estimate (2012): 29-mpg city/37-mpg highway with manual shift; 28/36 mpg with automatic. Cooper S: 27/35 mpg with manual; 26/34 mpg with automatic. John Cooper Works (manual only): 25-mpg city/33-mpg highway.

Driving Impressions: [2009 Cooper S] Few cars exceed the soft-top Cooper's "fun" quotient, though it's only a joy for two occupants. Apart from lack of backseat space, there's not much to complain about when behind the wheel of a Cooper S. Noisy? Absolutely. Rough riding? Sure thing. Yet, even what would ordinarily appear to be drawbacks are almost positive selling points when you're talking about Minis. Few cars are as much fun to drive, or as satisfying. BMW's claim of "go-kart" handling for its smallest model is substantially accurate. Though a Mini stays firmly on course on straightaways, a slight tug on the steering wheel heads it into a new direction, instantly.

On the other hand, a large penalty in ride comfort must be paid for such tenacious control and rewarding handling. Mini drivers must slow down appreciably for potholes and pavement flaws, as this little car can hit them terrifyingly hard. Overall, ride quality is harsh indeed. Even over rough bumps, though, the Mini demonstrates particularly solid build quality. In the Cooper S, the turbo engine delivers pulling power that's gratifying even to drivers who don't care all that much about ardent acceleration. The gearbox is one of the best: enjoyable to manipulate, readily changing gears with a true flick of the wrist; and the clutch is beautifully matched to deliver the goods in performance and easy takeoffs.

Front-seat space is abundant enough, but the rear is laughable. If the front seat is positioned relatively rearward, back leg space may disappear completely. Cargo space is even more minuscule. Those front seats are beautifully supportive and serious, yet generally comfortable – though not everyone may be equally ecstatic. Visibility is rather good, despite thick fabric roof pillars. Regular use of mirrors is essential, though. Huge center speedometer is great. The convertible top goes up/down without a bit of fuss, though blocking a bit of the rearward view when down.

Made in: England

Average Retail Value
2007 Mini Cooper coupe: $7000 – $7800
2007 Mini Cooper conv.: $8100 – $9000
2007 Mini Cooper S coupe: $7900 – $8700
2007 Mini Cooper S conv.: $9500 – $10,500
2008 Mini Cooper coupe: $8200 – $9200
2008 Mini Cooper conv.: $9200 – $10,200
2008 Mini Cooper S coupe: $9500 – $10,500
2008 Mini Cooper S conv.: $11,200 – $12,300
2008 Mini Clubman: $9200 – $10,200
2008 Mini Clubman S: $10,200 – $11,200
2009 Mini Cooper coupe: $9500 – $10,500
2009 Mini Cooper conv.: $11,000 – $12,000
2009 Mini Cooper S coupe: $10,800 – $11,800
2009 Mini Cooper S conv.: $12,800 – $13,800
2009 Mini Clubman: $10,500 – $11,500
2009 Mini Clubman S: $11,800 – $12,800
2010 Mini Cooper coupe: $11,000 – $12,000
2010 Mini Cooper conv.: $12,700 – $13,800
2010 Mini Cooper S coupe: $12,800 – $13,900
2010 Mini Cooper S conv.: $15,500 – $16,800
2010 Mini Clubman: $11,700 – $12,700
2010 Mini Clubman S: $14,000 – $15,000
2011 Mini Cooper coupe: $13,000 – $14,200
2011 Mini Cooper conv.: $15,000 – $16,200
2011 Mini Cooper S coupe: $15,000 – $16,100
2011 Mini Cooper S conv.: $18,000 – $19,500
2011 Mini Clubman: $13,000 – $14,000
2011 Mini Clubman S: $16,000 – $17,200
2011 Mini Countryman: $16,200 – $17,500
2011 Mini Countryman S: $18,500 – $20,000
2012 Mini Cooper coupe: $14,500 – $15,800

2012 Mini Cooper conv.: $17,500 – $18,700
2012 Mini Cooper S coupe: $17,700 – $19,000
2012 Mini Cooper S conv.: $20,700 – $22,000
2012 Mini Roadster: $17,000 – $18,000
2012 Mini Roadster S: $20,500 – $21,700
2012 Mini Clubman: $15,000 – $16,200
2012 Mini Clubman S: $18,000 – $19,200
2012 Mini Countryman: $17,500 – $18,800
2012 Mini Countryman S: $20,000 – $21,500
2013 Mini Cooper coupe: $16,500 – $17,800
2013 Mini Cooper conv.: $19,500 – $21,000
2013 Mini Cooper S coupe: $19,700 – $21,200
2013 Mini Cooper S conv.: $23,500 – $25,000
2013 Mini Clubman: $17,000 – $18,200
2013 Mini Clubman S: $21,000 – $22,500
2013 Mini Countryman: $20,000 – $21,200
2013 Mini Countryman S: $22,300 – $23,700
2013 Mini Paceman: $20,000 – $21,300
2013 Mini Paceman S: $24,000 – $25,500
2013 Countryman ALL4 AWD: $24,000 – $25,300
2013 Paceman ALL4 AWD: $21,500 – $29,000

Fiat 500

Description: Compact front-wheel-drive two-door coupe or sliding-roof Cabrio (convertible) with four-cylinder engine. Marketed by Chrysler, which is corporately connected to Fiat in Europe.

History: Introduced for 2012, the Fiat 500 resembled the Italian car of the same model that was highly popular in Europe during the 1950s and 1960s. A small number of early Fiat 500s reached the U.S. as well. For 2013, Fiat introduced a higher-powered Turbo, along with an even more potent Abarth coupe, followed by an Abarth convertible. An electric Fiat 500e debuted during 2013, along with a longer, four-door 500L; but both were 2014 models.

Powertrain(s): 1.4-liter four-cylinder engine, developing 101 horsepower and 98 pound-feet of torque. Five-speed manual transmission or six-speed automatic transmission. The Fiat 500 Turbo engine is rated 135 horsepower and 150 pound-feet. Fiat Abarth models hold a turbocharged 1.4-liter engine, rated at 160 horsepower and 170 pound-feet (manual shift only).

Specifications: 139.6 inches long, on a 90.6-inch wheelbase; 64.1 inches wide and 59.8 inches high. Curb weight, about 2363 pounds. EPA fuel-economy estimate (2012): 30-mpg city/38-mpg highway with manual; 27/34 mpg with automatic. Fiat Turbo and Abarth: 28-mpg city/34-mpg highway.

Driving Impressions: [Fiat 500 Cabrio] This is one frisky, friendly, fun-filled little machine. Harking back to the overall character and feel of European imports of the Sixties, but up-to-date technically, the Cabrio maneuvers neatly, feels sure of itself, and handles much like a more costly Euro-model than a typical subcompact. Even with the well-behaved six-speed automatic transmission, Fiat 500 Cabrio delivers eager performance. On even a modest upgrade, however, the engine starts to struggle, and downshifts are the rule from the excellent automatic transmission. Though not entirely gentle, the ride is hardly harsh. Steering feels light, yet tempting; in addition to being supremely agile, the Fiat 500 is an easy car to drive.

Huge concentric-circle gauges are not all easy to read, but the forward view is superior. Over-the-shoulder visibility is simply awful, so regular use of outside mirrors is mandatory. Cabrio's off-white plastic dashboard may be off-putting, but it does add a touch of extra character. Innovative fabric sliding roof on Cabrio can stay up, slide down part way (with the back window remaining in its regular position), or ease back all the way. For those who savor what we view as the ultimate in microcar driving, there's nothing like the Fiat 500 on the American road. Oddly, the four-door 500L has a completely different feel, as if barely related to the saucy two-door.

Made in: Toluca, Mexico

Average Retail Value
2012 Fiat 500 coupe: $10,000 – $12,500
2012 Fiat 500C conv.: $11,500 – $13,000
2012 Fiat 500 Abarth coupe: $13,700 – $15,000
2013 Fiat 500 coupe: $11,500 – $13,800
2013 Fiat 500C conv.: $13,000 – $16,000
2013 Fiat 500 Turbo coupe: $13,000 – $14,500

2013 Fiat 500 Abarth coupe: $15,500 – $17,000
2013 Fiat 500 Abarth conv.: $17,500 – $19,000

Volkswagen Beetle

Description: Front-wheel-drive two-door coupe and convertible, with regular or turbocharged four-cylinder engine. TDI (diesel) version also available, starting with 2013 model year.

History: Volkswagen revived the Beetle for the 1998 model year, giving it a bubble-top profile. Redesigning for 2012 lowered the roofline, causing the Beetle to more closely resemble historic models. Convertibles have been offered since 2005; the soft-top adopted the new profile for the 2013 model year.

Powertrain(s): 2.5-liter four-cylinder engine, developing 170 horsepower and 177 pound-feet of torque. Turbocharged 2.0-liter engine produces 200 horsepower and 207 pound-feet. Optional 2.0-liter diesel (TDI) four-cylinder makes 140 horsepower and 236 pound-feet. Five- or six-speed manual, six-speed automatic, or Direct Shift Gearbox (DSG, automated manual).

Specifications: 168.4 inches long, on a 99.9-inch wheelbase; 71.2 inches wide and 58.5 inches high. Curb weight, about 2939 pounds. EPA fuel-economy estimate (2012): 20-mpg city/28-mpg highway with manual shift; 20/29 mpg with automatic. Turbo: 20/28 mpg with manual; 22/30 mpg with DSG. Turbodiesel: 28/41 mpg with manual; 29/39 mpg with DSG.

Driving Impressions: [2013 Convertible] Magnificent ride comfort ranks as the foremost attribute of the base-model convertible, in its latest iteration. Nicely-controlled handling offers fine steering feel and feedback. The end result is close to sporty in nature. In ordinary driving, at least, there's no shortage of performance. Automatic-transmission shifts are barely noticed. With its top down, the Beetle Convertible is surprisingly quiet. Front-seat occupants can easily converse at highway speed. Seats are particularly comfortable, with good support and rather snug bolstering. Most gauges are easy to read, though the trip odometer is rather low in the instrument cluster.

Auxiliary gauges (if installed) sit atop the dashboard, quite easy to see at a glance.

No diesel sound is discernible at all in a Beetle Convertible with the TDI engine and Direct Shift Gearbox. Turbo torque comes into play potently when pushing on the pedal, though you may wait a bit for a downshift to match. No penalties are paid in performance for the diesel, and Direct Shift Gearbox (DSG) operation is masterful. So are its manual-shifting buttons, yielding virtually instant, unfettered response. Although Volkswagen's manual gearshift is especially easy to manipulate, the stick-shift TDI convertible isn't quite as pleasing to drive. Sometimes, throttle response isn't quite appropriate; and on hilly terrain, considerable shifting is needed. Manual shift feels more satisfying when coupled to the 200-horsepower Beetle Turbo. That engine clearly does enhance the Beetle's sporty disposition. A little wind noise was evident with the top raised. The top isn't really flat when stowed; rather, it sits beneath a moderate bulge behind the back seats.

Made in: Puebla, Mexico

Average Retail Value
2007 Beetle coupe: $6200 – $7000
2007 Beetle conv.: $7200 – $8200
2008 Beetle coupe: $7500 – $8800
2008 Beetle conv.: $9000 – $10,200
2009 Beetle coupe: $8800 – $10,000
2009 Beetle conv.: $11,500 – $13,000
2010 Beetle coupe: $10,200 – $11,500
2010 Beetle conv.: $14,000 – $15,500
2012 Beetle coupe: $13,500 – $16,500
2013 Beetle coupe: $16,200 – $18,000
2013 Beetle conv.: $19,500 – $23,500
2013 Beetle Turbo coupe: $18,200 – $20,000
2013 Beetle R-Line coupe: $21,000 – $22,500

Additional Sporty Cars

Hyundai Veloster (3-door coupe); Dodge Challenger (large coupe).

HYBRID CARS

Model Note: Prius and Insight are "dedicated" hybrids, offered only with a battery/gasoline powertrain. Most other hybrid models are variants of a vehicle that also comes with a conventional gasoline engine.

Toyota Prius

Description: Midsize front-wheel-drive, four-door "dedicated" hybrid (gasoline/electric) hatchback. Also available as Prius v wagon, Prius Plug-in Hybrid, and smaller Prius c hatchback.

History: Introduced for 2001 as a sedan, Prius was redesigned for 2004 as a hatchback, and redesigned again for the 2010 model year.

Powertrain(s): 1.8-liter four-cylinder engine, developing 134 horsepower and 105 pound-feet of torque, working with an electric motor. Continuously variable transmission (CVT).

Specifications: [Prius hatchback] 176.4 inches long, on a 106.3-inch wheelbase; 68.7 inches wide and 58.7 inches high. Curb weight, about 3042 pounds. EPA fuel-economy estimate (2012): 51-mpg city/48-mpg highway.

Driving Impressions: [2010] Slipping behind the wheel and starting off in the 2010 Prius was an utterly familiar experience to anyone who'd been in the prior-generation model. Plenty of details changed, but this Prius looks and feels much like its predecessor. Although the 2010 Prius handled better than before, a bit of deadness in the steering was noticeable in turns. On the expressway, a tiny touch of wander may occur, but otherwise the Prius maintains control easily. Ride comfort is appealing, though the Prius isn't especially cushiony and has a light overall feel. Acceleration is at least as satisfactory as expected, so the driver never needs to feel overwhelmed by traffic. Also as expected, the Prius is extra-quiet.

Front-seat occupants get plenty of space. Backseat riders also have sufficient room, though head space could be better and the center rear position falls short on comfort. Visibility is clear enough, except for that bar across the rear window. Windshield pillars are somewhat thick, too.

Made in: Japan

Average Retail Value
2007 Prius: $8400 – $9400
2007 Prius Touring: $10,000 – $11,000
2008 Prius: $9500 – $10,500
2008 Prius Touring: $11,200 – $12,200
2009 Prius: $10,900 – $12,000
2009 Prius Touring: $13,000 – $14,000
2010 Prius I, II, III: $12,500 – $13,800
2010 Prius IV, V: $15,000 – $17,000
2011 Prius I, II, III: $14,400 – $16,200
2011 Prius IV, V: $17,500 – $19,000
2012 Prius I, II, III: $16,400 – $18,000
2012 Prius IV, V: $19,500 – $21,600
2012 Prius plug-in: $18,500 – $24,000
2012 Prius v wagon: $18,500 – $20,200
2013 Prius I, II, III: $18,500 – $20,000
2013 Prius IV, V: $21,500 – $23,500
2013 Prius plug-in: $21,500 – $26,500
2013 Prius v wagon: $20,500 – $22,300
2013 Prius c: $15,500 – $18,500

Honda Insight

Description: Compact front-wheel-drive, four-door hybrid (gasoline/electric) hatchback. Base, LX, and EX trim levels.

History: Introduced for 2000 as a lightweight subcompact coupe, Insight disappeared after 2006, but then re-emerged for 2010 in a completely different, larger form.

Powertrain(s): 1.3-liter four-cylinder engine, developing 98 horsepower and 123 pound-feet of torque, working with electric motor and battery pack. Continuously variable transmission (CVT).

Specifications: 172.3 inches long, on a 100.4-inch wheelbase; 66.7 inches wide and 56.2 inches high. Curb weight, about 2717 pounds. EPA fuel-economy estimate (2012): 40-mpg city/43-mpg highway.

Driving Impressions: [2010 Insight] Compact Hondas aren't necessarily known for nimbleness, but the Insight handles with a fair degree of agility. Steering isn't quite instant-responding and doesn't always feel totally connected. While the hatchback rides comfortably on smooth pavement, occasional bumps hit harder. Even though the suspension seems more active than some, virtually all reactions are handily snubbed. While not qualifying as gentle, the Insight's ride ranks as well-controlled. Performance is enthusiastic enough for this class, scoring a bit higher than the hybrid-car average. Acceleration from a standstill is a little stronger than the response for passing or merging. Only a little engine sound occurs while accelerating, and it's refined in nature. Noise has long been an issue with CVT-equipped cars, which tend to keep the engine running at higher-than-normal speed while the car accelerates. But Honda's hybrid system keeps that sound to a minimum. Paddle shifters can provide the promised selection of simulated "gears," and the difference in performance is easily noted.

Indicators alongside the high-mounted digital speedometer change from blue to green, to reveal how efficiently the Insight is being driven. They can be difficult to see, but an easy-to-read needle-type Charge/Assist gauge also displays powertrain efficiency. Honda's idle-stop feature shuts off the engine as the car eases to a halt. In normal driving, it restarts as soon as you start to release the brake pedal. Front occupants get sufficient space, but those in the rear are more cramped. Rear headroom is skimpy. Toe space is acceptable but legroom isn't enticing, and short seat bottoms don't help. Comfortable front seats include helpful side bolstering. Getting into the backseat likely requires a body twist and ducking of one's head, but front riders face no such issues. Good visibility is aided by long back-door windows, but Insight shares one obstacle with Toyota's Prius: a horizontal bar across the back window.

Made in: Japan

Average Retail Value
2010 Insight: $10,200 – $12,000
2011 Insight, LX: $11,200 – $12,500
2011 Insight EX: $12,700 – $14,000
2012 Insight, LX: $12,500 – $13,800
2012 Insight EX: $14,000 – $15,300
2013 Insight, LX: $13,900 – $15,400
2013 Insight EX: $16,500 – $18,000

Ford C-Max Hybrid and Energi

Description: Midsize front-wheel-drive, four-door hybrid (gasoline/electric) hatchback. Tall-body wagon resembles Mazda5 wagon, comes in two forms: as C-Max Hybrid (battery/gasoline), and the C-Max Energi (plug-in hybrid). Combined output from 2.0-liter four-cylinder gasoline engine and battery-driven electric motor is 188 horsepower. SE and SEL editions offered.

History: Introduced to U.S. for 2013, after gaining popularity in Europe–but with a gasoline engine, not a hybrid or electric powertrain. Few are available on the used-car market as yet, but the C-Max is listed here because it's one of the few "dedicated" hybrids on sale.

Powertrain(s): 2.0-liter four-cylinder (Atkinson cycle) gasoline engine, developing 141 horsepower and 129 pound-feet of torque, coupled to 118-horsepower electric motor/generator and battery pack. Hybrid powersplit continuously variable transmission (eCVT). Plug-in hybrid can be plugged into electric outlet for recharging, but operates just like a regular hybrid on the road.

Specifications: 173.6 inches long, on a 104.3-inch wheelbase; 72 inches wide and 63.9 inches high. Curb weight, about 3640 pounds (Energi, 3899 pounds). EPA fuel-economy estimate: Initially stated as 47-mpg city/47-mpg highway. During 2013, Ford had to reduce the initial fuel-economy estimate of the C-Max to 45-mpg city/40-mpg highway, issuing rebates to early C-Max Hybrid buyers.

Driving Impressions: Confident and sure-footed, exuding quiet efficiency, C-Max has an enjoyable European feel overall: light to the touch, but not excessively so. Excellent ride complements the satisfying handling. Pavement separators may be felt, but only momentarily. Transition between battery-only operation and gasoline engine kicking in is barely discernible. Headroom is simply huge, augmented by ample elbow room. Front occupants sit in compartmentalized layout, but there's no space problem. Little to fault in the C-Max, which would be a pleasure to drive even if it didn't yield superior fuel economy.

Made in: Michigan, USA

Average Retail Value
2013 C-Max Hybrid: $18,000 – $20,000
2013 C-Max Energi: $20,500 – $22,500

ELECTRIC CARS

Nissan Leaf

Description: Compact front-wheel-drive pure-electric four-door hatchback.

History: Introduced for 2011, as the first strictly battery-powered car to expect substantial sales in the U.S. market.

Powertrain(s): Electric motor, developing 107 horsepower and 206 pound-feet of torque. Single-speed transmission.

Specifications: 175 inches long, on a 106.3-inch wheelbase; 69.7 inches wide and 61 inches high. Curb weight, about 3366 pounds. EPA fuel-economy estimate (2012): 106 city/92 highway equivalent miles per gallon (energy consumption estimated at 32/37 mpg).

Driving Impressions: [2011] Apart from its battery-powered status, the Leaf is an appealing little car: one with few frills, but down-to-business style. On relatively smooth roads, at least, the ride is easygoing and appealing. Handling is fairly typical compact-car, if a trifle woozy through some curves on two-lane roads. It's as if the car isn't totally in concert with the pavement, but you soon get used to its distinctive feel. Acceleration is so smooth on takeoff that the Leaf is moving more swiftly than it seems; but pickup lags at higher speeds. At low speeds, it responds quite nicely to the pedal, so keeping up with traffic and merging are essentially trouble-free. Two driving modes are available, and there's a noticeable difference between D and Eco mode. You can feel it change, if you're rolling at the time. The difference isn't huge, and there's not much reason to stay in other than Eco. Quiet? Definitely so, but a very slight whine is discernible when accelerating at low speeds.

The instrument panel has a lot of items to consider, but not all need to be checked regularly. Some are harder to see, including the odometer/trip meter, because they're low and unlit. Others are nicely illuminated. Visibility is excellent all-around. Front seats are exceptional: snugly bolstered and nicely supportive, but also amply cushioned for comfort. Front occupants get plenty of space, too. For rear passengers, toe space is not great, but legroom and headroom are good. The center rear occupant sits on a rather hard perch, but headroom is okay, unlike that position in many cars. Overall, the Leaf not only meets expectations, it exceeds them.

Made in: Japan or (2013-up) Tennessee, USA

Average Retail Value
2011 Leaf: $11,500 – $12,700
2012 Leaf: $14,000 – $15,500
2013 Leaf: $16,700 – $18,500

Chevrolet Volt

Description: Midsize front-wheel-drive, four-door hatchback with extended-range, plug-in powertrain.

History: Introduced for 2011, significantly changed in appearance from the original concept revealed at Detroit's North American International Auto Show.

Powertrain(s): 1.4-liter four-cylinder gasoline engine, developing 84 horsepower. Electric motor rated 149 horsepower and 273 pound-feet of torque. Single-speed transmission.

Specifications: 177.1 inches long, on a 105.7-inch wheelbase; 70.4 inches wide and 56.3 inches high. Curb weight, about 3781 pounds. EPA fuel-economy estimate (2012): 35-mpg city/40-mpg highway running on gasoline engine; 95/90 mpg running on electricity alone.

Driving Impressions: [2011] Driving a Volt differs little from being behind the wheel of a conventional midsize sedan. Solid and satisfying on the road, Volt has largely familiar feel. Acceleration to 60 mph takes less than 9 seconds, according to Chevrolet. That figure sounds about right, based on our test-drive. Acceleration feels brisk from a standstill, but often tepid from 35-45 mph (with some delay before the Volt reacts to a push on the pedal). Handling is nothing special, with no sense of sportiness. Volt yields a familiar compact/midsize sedan feel, and not much more. The ride is generally good on smooth surfaces; nearly flawless, in fact. On rougher stuff, you're likely to hear more than you feel. Visibility is fine all-around. Quiet-running is the rule. You can't hear much of anything until the gas engine turns on, which emits a fair amount of vibration at least initially. Once it's running for a while, the gas engine is sometimes barely discernible. Other times, it's quite noticeable.

There's a lot to see and consider on the dashboard, but it's nearly all optional. Drivers who want to get the most out of the car may want to scrutinize the displays regularly; for others, an occasional look will suffice. When the battery is about to run out of energy, a dashboard display indicates that zero miles are left. Shortly thereafter, the display changes to show the gas engine rather than the battery in operation. It's difficult to tell when the gas engine actually starts. Charging the battery at 110 volts is simple: just plug it in and watch for the green light atop the dashboard to illuminate. Depending on the orientation of our electrical outlet, the three-prong plug at the end of the charging cord can be a problem. Don't expect any kind of haste. Charging for two hours produced only 8 miles of driving.

Front-seat space is roomy and comfortable, with good support. Rear space for two is more snug but acceptable, though some heads may be close to the roof. The long hatch lid goes over a fair-size, uncovered cargo space. To some eyes, the off-white center console faceplate on our test Volt looked a little tacky and out of place; but an alternate color has been available.

Made in: USA

Average Retail Value
2011 Volt: $18,000 – $19,200
2012 Volt: $19,500 – $20,800
2013 Volt: $21,500 – $23,000

Additional Electric Cars

Mitsubishi i (i-MiEV) is the only other moderately-priced battery-powered model. High-end electric cars have been offered recently by such manufacturers as BMW and Tesla.

Addendum

A Closer Look at Today's Used Car Market

Trends and Practices

The Used Car Market in 2014

Many shoppers like to know what's happening in the used-car marketplace before they get too far into the shopping process. For that reason, we're including this final section. Featuring details of current trends and near-future predictions from experts, it's loaded with facts and figures.

Dealers, who buy and sell continuously, rely on such information to keep their businesses afloat, but it definitely doesn't appeal to everyone. Most of us buy a car only occasionally – every few years, at most. Thus, our interest may be strictly limited to how it affects us, personally. Not every used-car shopper is intrigued by the workings of the business as a whole; they just want to make a good buying decision, pay the price, and move on.

If you're not among those who savor such information, there's no penalty for skipping this chapter – or merely glancing through it in a hurry – concentrating on more practical matters.

Because of recent market conditions, used cars typically have cost more than might be expected. In the years immediately following the financial turmoil of 2008-09, when new-car sales shrunk sharply, late-model vehicles saw high demand and limited supply. Thus, prices stayed high. That's good news if you're selling your old car (or a dealer selling at retail), but not if you're buying a used model.

As a result of the scarcity of late-models, we even heard tales of car dealers paying so much for a prime example that making a profit turned out to be impossible. Some dealers reportedly were even paying more than *retail* price for extra-clean cars, when buying them *wholesale*, at one of the auctions. Clearly, no one can stay in business for long, if following the principle of "buy high, sell low."

Late in 2013, the tables turned somewhat. Used-car prices, which had been on the high side through much of the year, began to sink. During 2013, the average used vehicle was selling for $18,111 at a franchised dealership ($9,104 from an independent dealer). Pricing continued at high levels through the spring of 2014, but was expected to ease. "We expect a steady decline in used-vehicle prices," said ALG president Larry Dominique.

Supply and demand

We've seen the "beginnings of a rebound in used car supply," said Tom Kontos, executive vice-president of analytical services for ADESA (a major wholesale auction chain). "New car sales began to rise 3 or 4 years ago," and we're seeing a "reflection of that now" in used cars. "The supply situation is sort of universally affecting" the business, Kontos added, though not particularly differentiated by make or model.

Supply and demand work hand in hand to impact prices. High supply leads to lower prices; shortage of supply generally translates to higher prices. Already, declared Jonathan Banks, executive auto analyst for NADA Used Car Guides, "our market is completely different than it's ever been before." Specifically, the "quantity of demand is going to increase."

What about that "pent-up demand" that analysts have referred to in the past few years? It's definitely real, though Eric Lyman, vice-president of editorial for ALG (Automotive Lease Guide) believes it won't be satisfied before late 2017.

Used car prices in general "softened somewhat in 2013," ADESA's Kontos said in a phone interview early in 2014. Softening of used-car prices (meaning decline) continued in January, though mildly, compared to a year earlier. Wholesale volume growth, especially from off-lease, "continues to put downward pressure on prices," Kontos advised. The January wholesale prices showed a typical seasonal uptick.

Getting specific, Kontos noted that the average *wholesale* price in January was $9,983 (down 0.5 percent from a year before). Among the gainers in values: SUVs, full-size pickups, and vans. Most car and crossover segments saw price declines compared to the prior year. By

June, that average *wholesale* price for a used vehicle edged past $10,000, which was 4.7 percent higher than the average figure from June 2013.

Over the next few years, Raj Sundaram, group vice-president of dealer solutions for Dealertrack Technologies, advised during Used Car Week in November 2013, used-car prices should decline as supply rises significantly. Whether they're rising or falling, used-car prices remain a lot lower than the cost of an average new automobile. According to Alec Gutierrez, senior market analyst at Kelley Blue Book, in October 2013 the average new vehicle sold for about $32,000, with "new-car transaction prices increasing at such an incredible pace."

As of late 2013, we were coming off an all-time peak in used-vehicle values, said ALG's Eric Lyman. Into 2014, however, values reached some higher-yet averages. Supply constraints are still a key driver of high used-car values, though the supply of secondhand models is almost back to pre-recession levels.

When talking price with a used-car dealer or salesperson, many of us forget that those in the business function as both buyers and sellers. In order to sell a car to you, the retail customer, the dealer had to buy it from someone else (or take it in trade). He or she had to obtain it for an acceptable price, which would permit a suitable amount of profit from the subsequent resale. Therefore, for one part of the dual-section transaction, the dealer wanted the price to be as low as reasonably possible. For the other part, that dealer seeks as *high* a selling price as possible. That's how the system works.

Depreciation is the key

We all know that cars lose value as they age. Except for a handful of special models, nearly all cars depreciate rapidly during the early part of their lives. In fact, many can easily lose as much as one-third of their value in the first year. The depreciation rate then tapers off with age.

Actually, the moment a car is driven off the new-car dealer's lot, it becomes secondhand and loses a big chunk of its initial worth. After four or five years, that same car might be worth only one-fourth of its original new-car purchase price. Therefore, a one- or two-year-old car makes sense – if you can find one. You'll usually save plenty of cash compared to the new-car price, yet benefit from a vehicle that could have many years of useful life remaining.

Cars typically depreciate the most in the last quarter of each year, when most of the next year's models are on sale. Interviewed by phone early in 2014, Ricky Beggs of *Black Book* noted that average depreciation was 12.8 percent. A year earlier, the average depreciation had been a bit lower: 12.4 percent. For 2014, average depreciation is expected to be 13.5 percent. In pre-recession years, the level was around 15 percent.

To arrive at those figures, *Black Book* analysts take a group of cars on January 1 of a given year, and compare their values to those very same cars (now a year older) on January 1 of the following year.

"We're almost back to pre-recession levels" at the new-car end of the business, Beggs said, but less so with used cars. Prices have remained high, too. Depreciation over a one-year time span, from November 2012 to November 2013, amounted to only 4 percent. In pre-recession days, it would have been 15 percent or more.

During the period of limited supply of late-model vehicles, that "normal" rate of depreciation shifted quite a bit. Some models clung tightly to their original cost, selling for close to that initial figure when they were a year or so old. Eventually, the ordinary depreciation rate did kick in; but that early delay brought considerable consternation to those in the used-car business, as well as to shoppers hoping for a bargain.

Consumer demand for used vehicles was predicted to grow in 2011 for three reasons, according to Jonathan Banks, executive automotive analyst for the NADA Used Car Guide:

- Rising consumer confidence.
- Greater access to credit, with more lenders reporting a willingness to grant auto loans.
- An aging vehicle fleet: the average vehicle was already more than 10 years old.

Banks predicted that supply would "continue to be tight because of the pull-back in leasing that began in 2007." And the decline of new vehicles sold in 2008 and 2009 had resulted in fewer trade-ins.

Because of the short supply, considerable "pent-up demand" developed for replacement vehicles. AuctionNet, which studies wholesale transactions, reported a 10-percent yearly increase in the price of two- to five-year-old trucks and SUVs at that time, and an 8-percent hike for cars. Prices of those late models from the domestic automakers gained an average of 15 to 20 percent, while import-brand prices rose by about 10 percent.

Moving into 2014, consumer confidence has been sluggish, but the other two reasons remain valid. Average vehicle age has continued to grow (now 11.4 years), and credit availability has generally improved, though with fluctuations here and there.

Although there's "still a tremendous amount of pent-up demand," said Ricky Beggs, editorial director of *Black Book*, there are "more used cars coming back into the marketplace" in 2014. "Quality used is in demand," according to Beggs. And "quality means CPO."

About 60 percent of new cars sold have a trade-in, Beggs said. That's "been pretty steady" in recent times. "About 9.6 million should come into the marketplace" during 2014.

Black Book counts lease returns as part of trade-ins, Beggs advised, noting that there should be just over 3.1 million lease returns in 2014. "People stayed out of the trade cycle" during the worst of the financial turmoil, Beggs said, which helps account for the presence of so many older vehicles on the market, compared to late-models.

Certain used-vehicle prices have started to bump against new vehicle prices. This will tend to shift a portion of used-vehicle demand toward new. When you get above 60 percent of the new-car price for a used example, according to ADESA's Tom Kontos, people start to gravitate toward new. In mid-2010, the figure reached 58.5 percent. Four years later, after some fluctuation, it was down to 55.6 percent.

How the market affects consumer choices

Car dealers have to pay close attention to the wholesale market in vehicles. Their employees are active every day, seeking out and buying cars that can be resold at a profit. Therefore, those who are in the business watch the rise and fall of prices on a weekly, daily, or even hourly basis.

Anyone shopping for a personal car doesn't have to scrutinize the market nearly so closely – if at all. Still, it helps to have some idea of the ways in which prices fluctuate, and when they're likely to be at a low point, relatively.

Eric Lyman, vice-president of editorial at ALG (Automotive Lease Guide), cites several factors that affect the used-car market:

1. Population shifts.
2. Behavioral shifts (people becoming less dependent on cars).
3. Vehicle age (has been steadily increasing over the past 20 years, but will plateau).
4. Economic drivers.
5. Scrappage rates for old cars (typically 5 percent each year).

According to the January 2014 report from Manheim, a major wholesale auction group, the labor market and credit conditions continue to improve. Chief economist Tom Webb predicted declining profit margins in 2014, along with rising wholesale volumes and growing market pressures. New-vehicle sales rose for the fourth consecutive year, while franchised dealers sold a record number of certified (CPO) vehicles. Greater financing availability "balanced out inventory acquisition challenges for independent dealers," the Manheim report continued.

Because so many used-car shoppers finance their purchases, credit trends play a major role in the marketplace. Monthly payments on used cars have been relatively flat, said Joe Derkos, director of the J.D. Power Used Car Market Report: down by just $8 over the past 6 years (from $463 to $455). Meanwhile, transaction prices (what retail customers actually pay) for vehicles rose from an average of $25,500 in 2008, to $29,200 in 2013. Transaction prices continue to grow, linearly.

Longer terms won't change dramatically, Derkos believes; but if anything, they'll become longer yet, reaching the 84-month level.

Ricky Beggs credits "availability of financing" for much of the health of the used-car market. Because it's much easier to get loans these days, simple arithmetic demonstrates that more cars are going to be sold.

For prime customers, said Melinda Zabritski, senior director of automotive credit for Experian Automotive, "the rates are insanely low" at this time. In her view, "there's no good reason not to buy a car right now."

Inability to pay remains an issue for the credit-troubled, though. The volume of repossessions rose by 5 percent, with an estimated 1.37 million vehicles ready to attract the attention of the nation's "repo men." And repo women. Acquiring cars from owners who are far behind payments is one occupation that isn't likely to decline anytime soon.

Cars are getting older

Average vehicle age has seen a steady upward trend since 1996, at least, according to ALG's Eric Lyman. By late 2013, the average neared 11.5 years. As recently as 2009, the average vehicle was an even 10 years old. Experian Automotive found in mid-2012 that almost 15 percent of vehicles on the road were more than 15 years old.

According to the R.L. Polk organization, new-car buyers now keep their vehicles an average of 71.4 months (setting a record), versus just 46 months back in 2004. Used-car ownership length also has increased, but far less dramatically: from 38 months back in 2002, to 57 months today.

Impact of leasing

Lease volume dropped by 25.5 percent in 2008, and another 27 percent in 2009. By late 2010, it was rising again – up by 3.2 percent. Even so, we didn't begin seeing very many off-lease cars reaching the used-vehicle market until at least 2011-12. Not until three or four years have passed do those leased cars get returned to a dealer, ready to enter the used-car marketplace.

New lease originations totaled 1.1 million in 2009, said Manheim's chief economist Tom Webb, followed by a "substantial increase" in 2010. At the National Remarketing Conference in November 2010, Webb estimated 40-percent growth, to 1.6 million.

Leasing has a twofold impact:

- It's a way for a retail customer to obtain a new car without actually buying it (or buying a used one as an alternative).
- Lease returns are a prime source of used-vehicle inventory at dealerships.

As of late 2013, at least 23 percent of new-vehicle sales were actually lease penetration, Beggs noted. That should create 9.3 million trade-ins, when those lease terms are up. (Pre-recession sales of 16.5 million units created 9.9 million trade-ins.)

"Leasing is going up quite a bit" now, ALG's Lyman said, some five years after the 2009 low point for new-car sales and leases. New lease originations reached 3.2 million in 2013, which was the highest total since 2000.

Near-future forecast

CNW Marketing Research advised that used-vehicle retail sales in 2010 rose by 4 percent, to almost 37 million. That percentage gain was less than half that of new vehicles, but used ones had declined less during the recession. The ratio of used-vehicle sales to new-vehicle sales stayed well above 3:1 (back in 2000, it was below 2.5:1).

Franchised new-car dealers sold 9.9 million used vehicles at retail in 2013, said Joe Derkos, director of consulting & analytics for J.D. Power and Associates, during Used Car Week in November 2013. The average transaction price in 2013 was $18,800.

Derkos cites three notable recent trends:
1. Longer-term loans (over 72 months).
2. Strong residual values for new cars (which translates to high used-car prices).
3. Low interest rates.

Dealertrack's Raj Sundaram reported that according to CNW Research, used-car sales by franchised dealers totaled 14.2 million in 2012, rising to 15.1 million in 2013. For 2014, the prediction is 15.5 million.

As for overall used-vehicle sales in 2012, 37 percent were sold by franchised dealers, 35 percent by independent dealers, and 29 percent in private sales. The private-party figure has been trending downward for some time. "Franchised dealers are continuing to grow" their used-car business, Sundaram said, and credit availability continues as a major driver of sales.

"Dealers have had to develop new ways of searching for and buying used vehicles," said Stephen Wade, former chairman of the National Automobile Dealers Association. As vehicle availability grows, prices tend to ease somewhat.

Knowing the market affects consumer choices, as well as dealer decisions. If a particular vehicle is popular in your area, chances are its price will be above average. If it's popular mainly on the West Coast but you're in the Midwest, you can probably get it for a bit less.

As explained in detail in Chapter 6, covering Which Vehicle To Buy, makes, models, and body styles all make a difference. So does a car's origin, whether made in the U.S. or imported – though many import-brand vehicles are actually made in America these days.

Internet auctions for dealers

Already, most dealers are buying cars online from wholesale auctions that broadcast their bidding activities to participating dealerships. Because of reliable condition reports that are made available about the vehicles offered, they feel confident in bidding, without actually viewing the car "in person."

Retail customers have been slower to accept the notion of buying a used car without seeing it and trying it out, but it's happening. As information about specific vehicles on sale becomes more complete and accessible, most of us might soon be buying over the Internet, and having our next used car delivered to our door.

In October 2013, according to CNW Marketing, 3.2 million people shopped for used cars on the Internet – a 13 percent increase over the 2012 figure. As shoppers turn even more intently to their smartphones, concluding the transaction online is simply the next step.

"You can almost go and order a used car" now, Ricky Beggs explained. If a retail customer wants a red Chevrolet Malibu LT, the dealer can find one online, buy it at that auction (wherever it's taking place), have it shipped, and deliver that car to the customer in a couple of days. Rather than rely on what happens to be available in the dealership's local area, or what turns up in the next week or so, the participating dealer has a vast stock of possible vehicles to choose from when looking to add inventory. Therefore, they "don't have to stock as many cars."

Are those online auctions resulting in lower prices for dealers who participate? "Dealers are going to find the best bargain," Beggs said, whether they're buying cars at a regular wholesale auction or using one of the online auction services. Buying online greatly expands the dealer's reach, making it more likely that the dealership's inventory will include cars from a broad geographic area, delivered by truck after the wholesale purchase.

Gasoline prices make a difference in sales of both new and used vehicles. Rapidly-rising prices cause many shoppers to lose interest in big SUVs, for instance, and perhaps take another look at compact cars and thrifty hybrids. As soon as gas prices begin to ease, though, that newfound interest in fuel economy starts to wane.

Fuel prices have actually been quite stable lately. ADESA's Kontos observed that "we don't get the sense that it's going to keep going" up in price, as was the case when fuel prices rose sharply in the past.

Improved quality also plays a big role. Judging by the J.D. Power Quality Survey, the number of trouble spots in cars is half the rate it was a decade ago, ALG's Lyman said. People are driving fewer miles, too, so cars are bound to last longer.

The demographic shift in America matters too, ALG's Lyman added. In 2010, out of the country's population of 308 million; 246 million were of driving age. All told, the U.S. had 211 million licensed drivers (86 percent of those who were eligible to obtain a license), with 253 million vehicles in operation.

One particularly crucial factor that cannot be ignored is the "decline of the car culture," Lyman warned. Those in the car business might not like to hear it, but young people on the whole – especially those in urban areas – are simply not as interested in cars as their parents and grandparents were. Even when those in the Millennial generation purchase an automobile, they're likely to lack the enthusiasm that Baby Boomers and even Generation Xers used to exhibit.

Dealership reluctance to share invoice price with customers, along with details on the store's whole inventory, is gone, Dealertrack's Raj Sundaram explained. The big question salespeople used to ask was: "Can I qualify this customer?" If the answer was deemed to be no, he or she wasn't a serious prospect and the salesperson wouldn't bother pushing for a sale. Today's sales force has more options available, though not all of them necessarily benefit the customer in the end. Shoppers must be wary when alternatives are presented.

Way back in the 1930s, auto dealers worried about the possibility of *saturation*, meaning there might be too many used cars in the market to make selling them a viable business. Juan Flores, of AutoTrader, wonders: "Is there a saturation point" for used cars today? Because of improved quality in recent times, Flores noted, motorists have less need to return to the marketplace anytime soon.

Regardless of the trends, "you've got to keep everything transparent today," said Jack Simmons, dealer training manager at cars.com, during his presentation at Used Car Week. Auto dealers may think "we can hide things from people." They can't. Not anymore.

www.ingramcontent.com/pod-product-compliance
Lightning Source LLC
Chambersburg PA
CBHW061632040426
42446CB00010B/1374